Agamben and Radical Politics

Critical Connections

A series of edited collections forging new connections between contemporary critical theorists and a wide range of research areas, such as critical and cultural theory, gender studies, film, literature, music, philosophy and politics.

Series Editors
Ian Buchanan, University of Wollongong
James Williams, Deakin University

Editorial Advisory Board

Nick Hewlett
Gregg Lambert
Todd May
John Mullarkey
Paul Patton
Marc Rölli
Alison Ross
Kathrin Thiele
Frédéric Worms

Titles available in the series
Badiou and Philosophy, edited by Sean Bowden and Simon Duffy
Agamben and Colonialism, edited by Marcelo Svirsky and Simone Bignall
Laruelle and Non-Philosophy, edited by John Mullarkey and Anthony Paul Smith
Virilio and Visual Culture, edited by John Armitage and Ryan Bishop
Rancière and Film, edited by Paul Bowman
Stiegler and Technics, edited by Christina Howells and Gerald Moore
Badiou and the Political Condition, edited by Marios Constantinou
Nancy and the Political, edited by Sanja Dejanovic
Butler and Ethics, edited by Moya Lloyd
Latour and the Passage of Law, edited by Kyle McGee
Nancy and Visual Culture, edited by Carrie Giunta and Adrienne Janus
Rancière and Literature, edited by Grace Hellyer and Julian Murphet
Agamben and Radical Politics, edited by Daniel McLoughlin

Forthcoming titles
Balibar and the Citizen/Subject, edited by Warren Montag and Hanan Elsayed

Visit the Critical Connections website at
www.euppublishing.com/series/crcs

Agamben and Radical Politics

Edited by Daniel McLoughlin

EDINBURGH
University Press

Edinburgh University Press is one of the leading university presses in the UK. We publish academic books and journals in our selected subject areas across the humanities and social sciences, combining cutting-edge scholarship with high editorial and production values to produce academic works of lasting importance. For more information visit our website: www.edinburghuniversitypress.com

© editorial matter and organisation Daniel McLoughlin, 2016
© the chapters their several authors, 2016

Edinburgh University Press Ltd
The Tun – Holyrood Road
12(2f) Jackson's Entry
Edinburgh EH8 8PJ

Typeset in 11/13 Adobe Sabon by
Servis Filmsetting Ltd, Stockport, Cheshire

A CIP record for this book is available from the British Library

ISBN 978 1 4744 0263 7 (hardback)
ISBN 978 1 4744 0265 1 (webready PDF)
ISBN 978 1 4744 0266 8 (epub)

The right of Daniel McLoughlin to be identified as the editor of this work has been asserted in accordance with the Copyright, Designs and Patents Act 1988, and the Copyright and Related Rights Regulations 2003 (SI No. 2498).

Contents

Acknowledgements   vii

Introduction: Agamben and Radical Politics   1
Daniel McLoughlin

1. Capitalism as Religion   15
   Giorgio Agamben

2. Glory, Spectacle and Inoperativity: Agamben's Praxis of Theoria   27
   Mathew Abbott

3. On Property and the Philosophy of Poverty: Agamben and Anarchism   49
   Simone Bignall

4. 'Man Produces Universally': Praxis and Production in Agamben and Marx   71
   Jessica Whyte

5. Liturgical Labour: Agamben on the Post-Fordist Spectacle   91
   Daniel McLoughlin

6. An Alogical Space of Genetic Reintrication: Notes on an Element of Giorgio Agamben's Method   115
   Justin Clemens

7. *Zoē aiōniōs*: Giorgio Agamben and the Critique of Katechontic Time   141
   Nicholas Heron

8. Agamben, Badiou and Affirmative Biopolitics   165
   Sergei Prozorov

9. Form-of-Life and Antagonism: On *Homo Sacer* and
   Operaismo 189
   Jason E. Smith

10. What Is a Form-of-Life?: Giorgio Agamben and the
    Practice of Poverty 207
    Steven DeCaroli

11. Law and Life beyond Incorporation: Agamben,
    Highest Poverty and the Papal Legal Revolution 234
    Miguel Vatter

    Notes on Contributors 263
    Index 266

Acknowledgements

I would like to thank the participants at the 'Giorgio Agamben: Government, Radical Thought, and Political Action' Workshop at the Law School, University of New South Wales, which formed the basis for this collection. I would also like to thank all the contributors to this volume, with whom it has been a pleasure and a privilege to work. They are all experts in the field and I have learnt a great deal from their work, and from my editorial discussions with them. What is more, they always approached the editorial process in an open and generous spirit. I would like to thank Giorgio Agamben for providing a very topical chapter for the volume, and Nicholas Heron for his wonderful work in translating it. Holding together an edited collection is always a fraught task, so I am particularly grateful to those contributors – Sergei Prozorov, Steven DeCaroli, Jason Smith and Jessica Whyte – who were able to provide sterling contributions at short notice when others had fallen by the wayside. Finally, I would like to thank the team at Edinburgh University Press, and Carol Macdonald in particular, for their enthusiasm for the project, and for being so easy to work with.

A number of contributions to this volume have, in whole or in part, been published previously. Jessica Whyte's chapter first appeared as '"Man Produces Universally": Praxis and Production in Agamben and Marx', in J. Habjan and J. Whyte (eds), *(Mis)readings of Marx in Continental Philosophy* (London and New York: Palgrave Macmillan, 2014), pp. 178–94. Thanks to the author and the publisher for the permission to republish the article in this collection. The following chapters contain some material that has appeared in print previously, and I would like to acknowledge the publishers of this work. Jason E. Smith's chapter is a significantly revised version of work that originally appeared as 'Form-of-Life: From Politics to Aesthetics (and Back)', *The Nordic Journal of Aesthetics*, no. 44–5 (2012–13), pp. 50–67. Sergei Prozorov's chapter contains some material that appeared in 'Badiou's Biopolitics: The Human Animal and the Body of Truth', *Environment and Planning D: Society and Space*, vol. 32 (2014), pp. 951–67. The opening section of Steven DeCaroli's chapter reprises work from 'Political Life: Giorgio Agamben and the Idea of Authority', *Research in Phenomenology*, vol. 43, no. 2 (2013), pp. 220–42. The second section of Miguel Vatter's chapter is a revised version of work has appeared in Italian, in 'Il-limitato e s-corporato. Dalla corporazione al comune passando per il trust', *Filosofia Politica*, vol. 3 (2013), pp. 3–26.

Introduction:
Agamben and Radical Politics
Daniel McLoughlin

In an essay entitled 'In this Exile', Giorgio Agamben tells a story about his studies with Martin Heidegger, whose seminars he attended in Provence in 1966 and 1968. At some stage, Agamben asked his teacher whether he had read any Kafka, to which Heidegger replied that 'The Burrow' was the tale that had made the biggest impression upon him. 'The Burrow' is a short story about a creature that devotes their life to constructing an elaborate and impenetrable underground home. And yet despite, or perhaps because of, this zealous attention to security, the creature is haunted by the fantasy that someone could 'make his way in and utterly destroy everything ... even now when I am better off than ever before I can scarcely pass an hour in complete tranquillity'.[1] As the story develops, the burrow reveals itself 'to be a trap with no way out'[2] – and this is, Agamben suggests, an allegory for the politics of our time:

> Isn't this what has happened in the political space of Western nation-states? The homes – the 'fatherlands' – that these states endeavoured to build revealed themselves in the end to be only lethal traps for the very "peoples" that were supposed to inhabit them.[3]

This kind of scathing critique of the contemporary state has played a crucial role in Agamben's influence in critical political thought over the past decade. The *Homo Sacer* project exploded into the consciousness of the English-speaking academy following the September 11 2001 attacks on the World Trade Center, as its analysis of the sovereign power to suspend the law, and the claim that the state of emergency had 'become the rule',[4] seemed ready made to understand the security politics of the new millennium. Agamben's oft-noted 'apocalyptic tone' also seemed to suit the tenor of the times, given a media environment dominated by the spectacular violence of 9/11, the invasions of Iran and Afghanistan, 'shock and awe' tactics, and the Abu Ghraib scandal. More than a decade has passed since the moment that the sovereign exception became a central theoretical problem, and yet political events continue to confirm the relevance of Agamben's warnings about the state of emergency: many of the 'security' measures put in place as part of the War on Terror remain in place or have been extended; the Obama administration substantially expanded the War in Afghanistan and the campaign of drone strikes in Pakistan and Africa; the US government now claims the right to assassinate US citizens on foreign soil; and revelations from WikiLeaks and Edward Snowden have shown just how vast and entrenched the global security apparatus has become.[5]

The political situation has, however, also changed dramatically since the initial volumes of the *Homo Sacer* project were published. The global economy has been characterised, since the financial collapse of 2008, by a continuing crisis of capital accumulation. This has begun to undermine the political legitimacy of the neo-liberal consensus that has dominated the capitalist world system since the mid-1980s, and has also played no small role in the political crises and revolts that have flared across the globe over the past few years that go by the names Arab Spring, Syntagma Square, Indignados and Occupy. However, the current economic crisis has also given rise to a renewed assault on workers and the poor in anglophone countries and the European Union through the imposition of austerity measures, long characteristic of the structural adjustment programmes foisted on the global south. This neo-liberal prescription for the ills of the economic system has frequently been justified in the language of a budgetary emergency or debt crisis and accompanied by state repression of political dissent.

In response to these events, the coordinates of critical political theory have shifted. While the politics of emergency and the problem of state violence remain crucial within the current conjuncture, it is clearer than ever that these need to be theorised in the context of the economic and social relations of contemporary capitalism. This has important implications for the continuing relevance of Agamben's political thought. While the early volumes of the *Homo Sacer* project were influential, they were also repeatedly criticised for fetishising law and state violence at the expense of governmental and economic forms of power. For example, in a barely veiled critique of Agamben in *Commonwealth*, Hardt and Negri argue that economic and legal structures provide the horizon of intelligibility for contemporary state practices and yet the 'excessive focus' on sovereignty and state violence in contemporary critical theory tends to push these phenomena 'back into the shadows'.[6]

Agamben does, however, seem to have an uncanny knack for picking political trends as, in the years leading up to the crisis of global capitalism, his research turned from problems of state and the sovereign exception to those of government and economy. And yet Agamben's response to the 'current triumph of economy and government over every other aspect of social life'[7] does little to directly address the specifics of the current political conjuncture. Rather, his analysis of government is, like the rest of the *Homo Sacer* project, guided by two important methodological commitments. The first is the idea that to be contemporary is to be out of joint with one's moment and that, as such, the best access to the present is through the past. This leads Agamben to a conceptual strategy that reaches deep into history in order to gain access to the fundamental structures that govern our present.[8] The second impulse that guides Agamben's political thought is the sense that thought and praxis are intimately intertwined and that, as a result, political practice needs to be understood in relation both to the history of 'practical philosophy' and to the history of metaphysics as such. Agamben's response to the contemporary reign of the economy is, then, to illuminate the emergence, and subsequent historical development, of the conceptual paradigms and political practices of government and economy, with a particular focus on their development in the theology and institutional practices of the Church (an aspect of the history of government that is decisive but has remained under-studied).

The Kingdom and the Glory, published in Italian the year prior to the collapse of the US banking system, provides a genealogy of *oikonomia* from its Greek origins as the art of household management through to Trinitarian theology, which deployed the term to conceptualise the divine management of the world, up to its reactivation by modern theorists of government such as Adam Smith and Jean-Jacques Rousseau. The work also traces the development of the glorification of power in Ancient Rome and Church liturgy, which, Agamben argues, remains central to the legitimation of power in the contemporary society of the spectacle. *Opus*

Dei deepens this account of the relationship between liturgy and government through an analysis of priestly office as the root of the bureaucracy and juridification of life characteristic of modernity. *The Highest Poverty* analyses monasticism as a privileged site for the development of the practices of government that now dominate politics.

The problem of political action has also taken on greater urgency since the global financial crisis, in part due to the proliferation of revolts across the globe. It is also, I would suggest, driven by the increasing sense that new forms of political action are urgently needed in light of the basic incompatibility of neo-liberal capitalism with economic justice and environmental survival, and the increasing exposure of popular sovereignty and representative democracy as threadbare fictions. Finally, there is also a sense that, while the current crisis of the world economic system accentuates many of the worst tendencies of neo-liberal capitalism, it also opens up new possibilities for resisting, and hopefully terminating, its hegemony.

Again, this has implications for the continuing relevance of the *Homo Sacer* project. Agamben presents *Homo Sacer* as a response to the failures of the revolutionary politics of the twentieth century, arguing that this history necessitates a better understanding of the structure of sovereignty and its relation to the state, and a new and non-sovereign form of politics. The early volumes of the project do not, however, deal with this politics in any detail. Instead, they briefly suggest that it would involve a 'form-of-life' in which life is inseparable from its forms (*Homo Sacer*) and a non-instrumental form of action that would 'depose' the law by giving it a 'new use' (*State of Exception*). The dense and enigmatic nature of these claims, along with the fact that these works did not develop an account of this non-sovereign politics, combined with the withering critique of the contemporary political constellation that they do contain, led to charges that Agamben is a political pessimist whose work ignores questions of concrete praxis and instead offers us only vague and utopian gestures. Slavoj Žižek, for one, has argued that Agamben is passively waiting 'for some magical intervention'[9] in a kind of 'revolutionary version of Heidegger's "only a God can save us"'.[10]

The translation of Agamben's work on government provides an important opportunity to reflect on and reconsider the nature of his claims about political action and how they might help us conceive a response to the reign of biopolitics. In the first place, his analysis of government complicates his previous claims about the coming politics by arguing that the decisive political problem is not sovereignty per se, but its articulation with government. Perhaps more importantly, while the final instalment of the *Homo Sacer* project, *The Use of Bodies*, was yet to be translated at the time this collection was composed, Agamben had developed his account of the messianic politics of 'use' in works that were published alongside the project, such as *Profanations* and *The Time That Remains*, and had begun to integrate this into *Homo Sacer* itself in *The Highest Poverty*. This latter work argues that the particular Franciscan relation to property (a practice of use, rather than ownership) opens up the possibility of a form-of-life freed from law and government, and yet the movement was politically doomed by its incapacity to conceive and practise such a life.

The turn to questions of economy and political agency in contemporary critical theory has also been accompanied by a well-noted surge of interest in the philosophical and political legacy of Karl Marx. At first glance, this does not appear to be a promising development for the *Homo Sacer* project either, as Agamben is not exactly known for his Marxism. This is, perhaps, because the most obvious and discussed reference points for his political work are thinkers who are either avowedly anti-Marxist (Carl Schmitt) or who have a troubled relationship to Marxism (Foucault and Arendt). What is more, one of the most interesting recent developments in critical political theory has been the push to revive the 'idea of communism' as a way of framing the possibility of a different and more just world: and, while the conferences on this topic organised by Žižek and Alain Badiou attracted some of the biggest names in critical theory, Agamben was conspicuously missing from the list of speakers.

With a few notable exceptions, then, a serious analysis of Agamben's relationship to the tradition of revolutionary thought and practice has remained a largely neglected topic within the critical literature around his work.[11] Yet Agamben has long engaged with concerns and concepts central to the Marxian tradition, including labour, commodity fetishism, the classless society, the philosophy of history, the nature of political action and revolution, and the problem of the state. His work is also deeply indebted to and engages with a range of thinkers who actively identify with the Marxian tradition including Guy Debord, Walter Benjamin,

Antonio Negri, Theodor Adorno, Alain Badiou and Marx himself. Finally, *The Highest Poverty* can be seen as Agamben's own contribution to contemporary debates on the idea of communism, as it describes the monastic orders, whose practices he analyses as a way into the problem of form-of-life, in terms of common life and communism.

This volume examines the continuing contribution of Agamben's work to legal and political thought by responding to his new works on economy and government, along with his analyses of political action, which have appeared in tandem with the shift in critical theory towards these issues since the 2008 financial crisis. Agamben's genealogies raise important questions about the conceptual origins and nature of contemporary practices of administration, as well as the kind of politics that might respond to contemporary state violence and the reign of the economy. The chapters in this volume illuminate the central technical terms at play in these works, including government, glory, use, inoperativity and form-of-life. They analyse the theoretical stakes and methodological drivers of Agamben's analyses, explore their relationship to his earlier thought, and consider how they might help us to understand and resist a political situation characterised by the neo-liberal absolutisation of government and economy. Alongside this analysis of economy and political action, the volume situates Agamben as a thinker of the radical left. It shows how his work is indebted to the tradition of revolutionary thought and practice, examines his critique of Marxism and anarchism, and considers the benefits and limitations of his contribution to, and attempt to innovate upon, this tradition.

The book opens with Agamben's 'Capitalism as Religion'. In a fragment with the same title, Walter Benjamin argues that capitalism is not only a secularisation of the Protestant faith, but is itself an extreme form of religion. Agamben takes up and develops Benjamin's thesis by considering the role that money plays in the capitalist cult. The theological content of capitalism was, he argues, clarified by the end of the gold standard in 1971. From this point on, money would no longer refer to a concrete thing whose value it ostensibly represents, but rather to credit. Credit is, in turn, an act of faith. According to Agamben, then, the capitalist religion puts money in the place of God and replaces faith in God with faith in faith. He concludes by drawing out the destructive implications of this parodic form of Christian faith, considering its relationship to the contemporary hegemony of finance, the development of the spectacle, and the 'profound anarchy of the society in which we live'.

Agamben's chapter is followed by a number of contributions considering his diagnosis of contemporary capitalism and analysing his relationship to the revolutionary tradition. Chapter 2, Mathew Abbott's 'Glory, Spectacle and Inoperativity: Agamben's Praxis of Theoria', argues against the common image of Agamben as an apocalyptic thinker focused on theoretical transformation rather than political praxis. The chapter provides a concise account of the genealogies of economy and glory in *The Kingdom and the Glory* before turning to Agamben's argument that the society of the spectacle is the contemporary form of glorification. According to Abbott, the fundamental stake of Agamben's analysis is a theoretical praxis that would respond to the political conditions of spectacular capitalism. What Agamben is proposing is not, however, a matter of doing philosophy instead of acting. It is, rather, a politics that is simultaneously practical and theoretical, enacting the inoperativity at the heart of thought by jamming a political apparatus that has entered into a state of crisis.

In Chapter 3, 'On Property and the Philosophy of Poverty: Agamben and Anarchism', Simone Bignall returns to the split between the black and the red that first occurred during the First International. She notes that one of the few points at which anarchism explicitly appears in Agamben's work is *The Time That Remains* where, during a discussion of *klesis* (calling), class and the role of the proletariat in Marxist thought, he identifies in Max Stirner an 'ethical-anarchic interpretation of the Pauline *as not*'. Drawing on Marx's ridiculing of Stirner's 'ethical-anarchism' and his critique of Proudhon, Bignall argues that Agamben's recent work on poverty and use bring him closer to the communitarian anarchist tradition than to Marx's governmental communism. According to Bignall, then, Agamben's thought should be read as a restoration of anarchism to its potential for use in the present by extending anarchist critiques of property to the level of social ontology.

Jessica Whyte examines Agamben's relationship to Karl Marx in Chapter 4, entitled '"Man Produces Universally": Praxis and Production in Agamben and Marx'. Beginning with his first book, *The Man without Content*, Agamben has repeatedly ignored Louis Althusser's suggestion that 'Marx's early works do not have to be taken into account' and turned to Marx's *Economic and Philosophic Manuscripts* in the course of formulating his own accounts of praxis and history (and, more recently, inoperativity). Agamben's most substantial engagements with Marx's manuscripts are found in his earliest works, in particular, in *The Man without Content* and *Infancy and History*. The question of *praxis* has, however, become ever more central to his project, with his works on government arguing that Christianity has profoundly transformed our understanding of the relation between praxis and being. While *The Kingdom and the Glory* dismisses Marx in a mere paragraph (as a thinker who has secularised the Christian conception of the being of creatures as divine operation), Whyte argues that that a careful examination of Agamben's various readings of *The 1844 Manuscripts* sheds light on his understanding of praxis and the related concept of inoperativity.

Chapter 5 is Daniel McLoughlin's 'Liturgical Labour: Agamben on the Post-Fordist Spectacle', which responds to arguments that Agamben's work contributes little to the analysis of contemporary capitalism. It does so by reading Agamben's genealogy of government in light of the diagnosis of Post-Fordist production developed by *post-operaismo* thinkers. Agamben's analysis of glory builds upon his earlier work on sacrifice to describe an estranged practice that masks the social foundations of governmental power. While the account of liturgical glorification in *The Kingdom and the Glory* and *Opus Dei* is based on the juridical model of the Church, in *The Highest Poverty*, we find the monastic orders engaged in a 'liturgical labour' that occupies the totality of life and which simultaneously enacts and glorifies the divine order. The chapter argues that this monastic paradigm can be usefully deployed in understanding contemporary capitalism, which has integrated language into both the process of exchange (the spectacle) and the process of production (Post-Fordism). The collapse of the distinctions between labour, life, government and glory, then helps to explain the coincidence of political passivity and incessant work that characterises our time.

The collection then turns to two philosophical problems that are fundamental to understanding Agamben's contribution to contemporary political thought and practice: the question of philosophical method and the issue of temporality.

In Chapter 6, 'An Alogical Space of Genetic Reintrication: Notes on an Element of Giorgio Agamben's Method', Justin Clemens returns us to some of the most hotly contested terrain in the initial reception of Agamben's political thought: his relationship to Michel Foucault. While Agamben's work proved popular, in the first wave of its reception, for the purposes of analysing security politics, questions were soon raised about his method, and in particular, the validity of his approach to history. These criticisms often included a charge that Agamben had 'betrayed' Foucault's method by reintroducing an essentialist and teleological vision of history – an important challenge to the purchase that Agamben's thought has on political history and our contemporary moment. Clemens argues that Agamben's work involves a critical engagement with Foucault that, through a confrontation with its limits, displaces its method and problems in response to changed political conditions and a different set of philosophical reference points. In this way, Agamben proposes and practises new ways of thinking through the obscurity of an epoch in which traditional forms of political action have shown their complicity or failure. Clemens argues that Agamben's work involves a practice of profanation: this is not a substitute for 'real action', but a way of enacting, in the reading of texts, the indistinction between theory and praxis that is central to Agamben's vision of the 'coming politics'.

Agamben's approach to history is intimately related to his understanding of time, a theme that is, in turn, central to his 'messianic' approach to politics. In this light, Nicholas Heron's 'Zoē aiōnios: Giorgio Agamben and the Critique of Katechontic Time' discusses one of the central innovations in Agamben's treatment of time to emerge from *The Kingdom and the Glory*: the idea of 'eternal life'. In the final pages of his genealogy of economy, Agamben links eternal life to the messianic experience of time and the non-juridical form-of-life associated with it. This move might appear strange at first, given that that, in Christian theology, eternal life is associated with a transcendent God and is promised to the blessed only at the end of time. Heron's chapter responds to this quandary by tracing the semantic history of the term *aion* (which gives rise to the modern 'eternity') from Homeric Greek through Plotinus and Augustine, showing how its meaning gradually shifted from an immanent life force, to an unending duration associated with a transcendent and unchanging being. The chapter argues that this understanding of eternity became central to the Church, which justified its existence on the basis that the messianic event was delayed, and that this vision of the Church as *katechon* was secularised by the modern state. According to Heron, then, Agamben's account of eternal life should be read as an attempt to undermine every institutionalisation of the messianic event and restore its availability for use in the present.

The book then turns to Agamben's relationship to some of the most important contemporary thinkers that explicitly associate themselves with the communist tradition. In Chapter 8, 'Agamben, Badiou and Affirmative Biopolitics', Sergei Prozorov compares the work of two of the most important thinkers in radical theory today. He argues that the two thinkers are much closer than they, and many others, recognise, due to the ontological assumptions that they share, particularly the generic and indiscernible character of being. Indeed, Prozorov argues that there is a striking similarity between Badiou's concept of the body of truth and Agamben's notion of the form-of-life and that, despite their manifold differences, the two thinkers are united by the attempt to rethink politics on the basis of the brute facticity of being. On the basis of this proximity, Prozorov advances a more general and provocative argument about the two authors' ontopolitical stances: while Badiou has shown little interest in the problematic of biopolitics, his militant 'politics of truth' is nonetheless a version of the 'affirmative biopolitics' that Agamben has painstakingly developed.

In Chapter 9, 'Form-of-Life and Antagonism: On *Homo Sacer* and *Operaismo*', Jason E. Smith argues that one of the key concepts in Agamben's account of the 'coming politics' – form-of-life – was initially developed through a critical engagement with the post-workerist strain of Italian Marxism. Smith makes this argument through a close reading of the essay 'Form-of-Life', which appeared two years prior to the Italian publication of *Homo Sacer: Sovereign Power and Bare Life*. Here, Agamben first articulates the concept of form-of-life by appropriating and displacing three concepts central to post-workerism: general intellect, multitude and antagonism. Form-of-life – which is, Smith argues, a contribution to a revolutionary and communist tradition with which Agamben has, in his own terms, felt 'ill at ease'[12] – is a power that is irreducibly antagonistic to sovereignty and the social and is expressed in a community of singularities (or multitude). However, the chapter raises concerns that Agamben's account of antagonism does not adequately account for the fact that certain forms of social identity – namely, the categories of worker and woman – are themselves constituted through forms of antagonism that traverse the social.

The book concludes with two chapters on Agamben's recent work on form-of-life and the Franciscan practice of poverty. Steven DeCaroli examines the philosophical underpinnings and political implications of Agamben's analysis of monasticism in Chapter 10: 'What Is a Form-of-Life?: Giorgio Agamben and the Practice of Poverty'. DeCaroli argues that form-of-life should be understood as a particular form of life that is aware of the contingency of the rules that govern our existence, and does not attempt to replace them, but to patiently expose the machinery of their operation. Franciscanism was an incomplete attempt to develop such a form-of-life through a community of non-appropriative use that claimed no social or juridical foundation. The name for this way of living was poverty – which does not mean poverty in material things (although the Friars did live modestly) – but rather poverty in those less tangible things, such as possession and privilege, that profoundly shape our social reality, but of whose operation we are often only faintly aware.

The final chapter is Miguel Vatter's 'Law and Life beyond Incorporation: Agamben, Highest Poverty and the Papal Legal Revolution', which reconstructs and problematises *The Highest Poverty*'s account of form-of-life in light of the 'papal legal revolution' of the twelfth and thirteenth centuries. Vatter compares Agamben's analysis of the capture of life by law in *State of Exception* to his account of Franciscan jurisprudence and its attempt to liberate life from law. The chapter goes on to argue that Agamben's account of the conflict between the Franciscans and the Papacy fails to address the problem of incorporation – the idea that groups and associations become capable of acting collectively through a fictional legal personality whose ultimate representative is the sovereign. This absence is problematic because incorporation was the very legal *dispositif* that ultimately spelled the defeat of the Franciscan project to emancipate life from law. Vatter then reconstructs the history of the common law apparatus of the 'trust' and argues that this provides the conceptual resources for a different understanding of group action. Arguing against the antinomian tenor of the *Homo Sacer* project (and much contemporary radical political thought), Vatter suggests that the trust offers the possibility of a non-messianic rejection of corporate personality, a jurisprudence of the common that is irreducible to both political and economic theology.

Agamben has been one of the most important and influential

thinkers of the new millennium. This collection is guided by the sense that his theoretical project continues, amidst a shifting political and theoretical terrain, to make an important contribution to thinking through our political situation. It is also informed by the belief that to respond to the current conjuncture necessitates thinking it both philosophically and historically. This means, with Agamben, to understand the historical origins of the political and theoretical apparatuses that now structure our existence. For our purposes, it also means to conduct this analysis with one eye on a revolutionary tradition that has always been dedicated to ending the domination and exploitation characteristic of the capitalist mode of production and that are endemic to our neo-liberal age. It is hoped that this collection, and the meditations on Agamben's untimely thought that it offers, can thereby make some small contribution to thinking through and responding to the exigencies of the contemporary moment.

Notes

1. Franz Kafka, 'The Burrow', in *Metamorphosis and Other Stories* (Harmondsworth: Penguin, 1949), p. 127.
2. Giorgio Agamben, *Means without End: Notes on Politics*, trans. Vincenzo Binetti and Cesare Casarino (Minneapolis: University of Minnesota Press, 2000), pp. 139–40.
3. Agamben, *Means without End*, p. 139.
4. Giorgio Agamben, *Homo Sacer: Sovereign Power and Bare Life*, trans. Daniel Heller-Roazen (Stanford: Stanford University Press, 1998), p. 12.
5. For a comprehensive description of the expansion of drone strikes under the Obama administration, see Jeremy Scahill, *Dirty Wars: The World Is a Battlefield* (New York: Nation Books, 2013). One of the focal points of the book is the recent assassination, by drone strike, of two Americans on foreign soil: Anwar Awlahki and his sixteen-year-old son, Abdulrahman al-Awlahki.
6. Michael Hardt and Antonio Negri, *Commonwealth* (Cambridge, MA, and London: Harvard University Press, 2009), p. 4. For similar criticisms of Agamben's focus on sovereignty, law and state from a Marxist perspective, see Steven Colatrella, 'Nothing Exceptional: Against Agamben', *Journal for Critical Education Policy Studies*, vol. 9, no. 1 (2011), p. 97; Alberto Toscano, 'Divine Management: Critical Remarks on Giorgio Agamben's *The Kingdom and the*

Glory', *Angelaki*, vol. 16, no. 3 (2011), p. 130. For criticism of Agamben for over-emphasising the problem of sovereignty from an explicitly Foucauldian perspective, see: Andrew Neal, 'Cutting Off the King's Head: Foucault's Society Must Be Defended and the Problem of Sovereignty', *Alternatives*, vol. 29 (2004), p. 375; Thomas Lemke, '"A Zone of Indistinction" – a Critique of Giorgio Agamben's Concept of Biopolitics', *Outlines*, vol. 7, no. 1 (2005), pp. 3–13; Paul Rabinow and Nikolas Rose, 'Biopower Today', *BioSocieties*, vol. 1, no. 2 (2006), p. 202; Peter Gratton, 'A Retroversion of Power: Agamben Via Foucault on Sovereignty', *Critical Review of International Social and Political Philosophy*, vol. 9, no. 3 (2006), p. 457. For other critiques of Agamben's analysis of sovereignty for failing to account for the complexity of the contemporary operation of power, see William E. Connolly, 'The Complexities of Sovereignty', in Matthew Calarco and Steven DeCaroli (eds), *Giorgio Agamben: Sovereignty and Life* (Stanford: Stanford University Press, 2007), p. 31; Jef Huysmans, 'The Jargon of Exception – on Schmitt, Agamben and the Absence of Political Society', *International Political Sociology*, vol. 2 (2008), pp. 165–83; Anthony Burke, *Beyond Security, Ethics and Violence: War against the Other* (London: Routledge, 2007), p. 10.
7. Giorgio Agamben, *The Kingdom and the Glory: For a Theological Genealogy of Economy and Government*, trans. Lorenzo Chiesa with Matteo Mandarini (Stanford: Stanford University Press, 2011), p. 1.
8. Giorgio Agamben, 'What Is the Contemporary?', in *What Is an Apparatus? and Other Essays*, trans. David Kishik and Stefan Pedatella (Stanford: Stanford University Press, 2009), p. 50.
9. Slavoj Žižek, 'Divine Violence and Liberated Spaces: Soft Targets Talks with Slavoj Žižek', available at <http://www.softtargetsjournal.com/web/zizek.php> (last accessed 13 May 2007).
10. Slavoj Žižek, *In Defence of Lost Causes* (London: Verso, 2007), p. 338. For further criticism of the poverty of Agamben's account of political action, see Nina Power 'Potentiality or Capacity – Agamben's Missing Subjects', *Theory & Event*, vol. 13, no. 1 (2010). For criticism of the absence of resistance in Agamben's work, see Simon Behrman, 'Giorgio Agamben in Perspective', *International Socialism: A Journal of Socialist Theory* 140 (2013), available at <http://xtest2.swp.org.uk/giorgio-agamben-in-perspective/> (last accessed 14 December 2013). For criticism of Agamben's response to contemporary politics for being too abstract and removed from concrete

politics, see Robert Sinnerbrink, 'From Machenschaft to Biopolitics: A Genealogical Critique of Biopower', *Critical Horizons*, vol. 6 (2005), p. 259; Richard Bailey, 'Up against the Wall: Bare Life and Resistance in Australian Immigration Detention', *Law and Critique*, vol. 20, no. 2 (2009), p. 116; Matthew Sharpe, '"Thinking of the Extreme Situation . . ." on the New Anti-Terrorism Laws, or against a Recent (Theoretical and Legal) Return to Carl Schmitt', *Australian Feminist Law Journal*, vol. 24 (2005), p. 17. There has, however, been a recent shift in the literature, in particular with the publication of two books that rebut the charge that Agamben is a political pessimist: see Sergei Prozorov, *Agamben and Politics* (Edinburgh: Edinburgh University Press, 2014); Jessica Whyte, *Catastrophe and Redemption: The Political Thought of Giorgio Agamben* (Albany: State University of New York Press, 2013).

11. The exceptions are Jessica Whyte, *Catastrophe and Redemption*; Lorenzo Fabbri, 'From Inoperativeness to Action: On Giorgio Agamben's Anarchism', *Radical Philosophy Review*, vol. 14, no. 1 (2011), pp. 85–100; Brett Nielson, 'Politics without Action, Economy without Labour', *Theory & Event*, vol. 13, no. 1 (2010); Arne de Boever, 'Agamben and Marx: Sovereignty, Governmentality, Economy', *Law and Critique*, vol. 20, no. 3 (2009), pp. 259–70; Miguel Vatter, 'In Odradek's World: Bare Life and Historical Materialism in Agamben and Benjamin', *diacritics*, vol. 38, no. 3 (2008), pp. 45–70.

12. Giorgio Agamben with Adriano Sofri, 'Un'idea di Giorgio Agamben', *Reporter* (9–10 November 1985), pp. 32–3.

I

Capitalism as Religion
Giorgio Agamben
Translated by Nicholas Heron

I

There are signs of the times (Mt. 16: 2–4), which, despite their obviousness, those who examine the signs in the heavens do not succeed in perceiving. They are crystallised in events that herald and define the coming epoch, events that can pass unobserved and almost in no way alter the reality to which they are added; yet which, precisely because of this, count as signs, as historical indices, *sēmeia ton kairōn*. One of these events took place on 15 August 1971, when the American government, under the presidency of Richard Nixon, declared that the convertibility of the dollar into gold had been suspended. Although this declaration signalled the end of a system that had always bound monetary value to the gold standard, the news, which arrived at the height of the summer holidays, elicited far less discussion than one would have expected. Yet, from that moment on, the inscription that we still read on many banknotes (for example, on the pound sterling and the rupiah, but not on the euro) – 'I promise to pay the bearer the sum of . . .', countersigned by the governor of the central bank – had definitively lost its meaning. This sentence now meant that, in exchange for the note, the central bank could have provided to whomever requested it (conceding that someone would have been so foolish as to do so), not a particular amount of gold (for the dollar, a thirty-fifth of an ounce), but a note exactly the same. Money was emptied of every value that was not purely self-referential. This makes the ease with which the American sovereign's gesture was accepted, which amounted to liquidating the gold assets of money owners all the more stupefying. And if, as has been suggested, the exercise of monetary sovereignty on the part of a state consists in its capacity to lead market actors to spend its debts like money, even that debt had now lost any real consistency: it had become pure paper.

The process of dematerialisation of money had begun many centuries earlier when market demands led to the issuing of letters of exchange, banknotes, juros, goldsmiths' notes and so on, alongside the necessarily scarce and cumbersome metal currency. All these paper currencies are actually instruments of credit, which is why they are called finance currencies. Metal currency, by contrast, was worth (or could have been worth) its content of precious metal; a content that, moreover, as is well known, was uncertain (the limit case being that of the silver money minted by Frederick II, which, as soon as used, allowed the red of copper to be made out below). Nonetheless, Joseph Schumpeter – who, it is true, lived in an epoch in which paper currency had not yet prevailed over metal currency – could with good reason assert that in the final analysis all money is only credit. After 15 August 1971, one would have to add that money is a form of credit which is grounded on itself alone and which corresponds to nothing other than itself.

2

'Capitalism as Religion' is the title of one of the most penetrating posthumous fragments of Walter Benjamin. That socialism might be something like a religion has been observed many times (among others, by Carl Schmitt: 'Socialism purports to create a new modern religion, which would have the same meaning for the people of the 19th and 20th centuries as Christianity did for the people of two millennia ago'[1]). According to Benjamin, capitalism represents not only a secularisation of the Protestant faith (as it does in Weber), but is itself an essentially religious phenomenon, which develops parasitically off Christianity. As such, as the religion of modernity, it is defined by three characteristics:

1. It is a cultic religion, perhaps the most extreme and absolute that has ever existed. In it, everything acquires meaning only in reference to the consummation of a cult, and not in relation to a dogma or an idea.
2. This cult is permanent; it is 'the celebration of a cult *sans trêve et sans merci*'.[2] In it, it is impossible to distinguish between workdays and holidays; rather, there is a single, uninterrupted

holy workday, in which work coincides with the celebration of the cult.
3. The capitalist cult is directed not toward redemption or the expiation of guilt, but toward guilt itself:

> Capitalism is perhaps the only instance of a cult that is not expiatory but guilt-inducing [...] A monstrous guilty conscience that is unable to find relief seizes on the cult, not in order to expiate its guilt in it, but in order to make it universal [...] and ultimately to include God himself in the system of guilt [...] God is not dead; he has been incorporated into human destiny.[3]

Precisely because it strives with all its might not toward redemption but toward guilt, not toward hope but toward despair, capitalism as religion aims not at the transformation of the world but at its destruction. And its dominion in our time is so complete that, according to Benjamin, even the three great prophets of modernity (Nietzsche, Marx and Freud) conspire with it; even they are somehow in solidarity with this religion of despair.

> This passage of the planet 'man' through the house of despair in the absolute loneliness of his trajectory is the ethos that Nietzsche defined. This man is the superman, the first to recognise the capitalist religion and bring it to fulfilment.[4]

But Freudian theory, too, belongs to the priesthood of the capitalist cult: 'what has been repressed, the idea of sin, is capital itself, which pays interest on the hell of the unconscious'.[5] And in Marx, capitalism 'becomes socialism by means of the simple and compound interest that are functions of guilt'.[6]

3

Let us take Benjamin's hypothesis seriously and attempt to develop it. If capitalism is a religion, how can we define it in terms of faith? In what does capitalism believe? And what does Nixon's decision entail with respect to this faith?

David Flusser, a great scholar of the science of religions (there even exists a discipline with this strange name), was working on the word *pistis*, which is the Greek term that Jesus and the apostles used for 'faith'. One day he was by chance in an Athenian square and, at a certain point, he raised his eyes and saw written in large letters before him: *trapeza tēs pisteos*. Surprised by the coincidence, he looked more closely and after a few seconds realised that he was simply outside a bank: in Greek, *trapeza tēs pisteos* means 'credit bank'. This was the sense of the word *pistis*, which he had been seeking for months to understand: *pistis*, 'faith', is simply the credit that we enjoy with God and that the word of God enjoys with us – once we believe. This is why, in a famous definition, Paul can say that 'faith is the substance of things hoped for' (Heb. 11: 1): it is what gives reality and credit to what does not yet exist, but in which we believe and have faith, in which we stake our credit and our word. *Creditum* is the past participle of the Latin verb *credere*: it is that in which we believe, in which we place our faith, at the moment we establish a fiduciary relationship with someone by taking them under our protection or by lending them money, by entrusting ourselves to their protection or by borrowing money from them. In the Pauline *pistis*, that is to say, the ancient Indo-European institution of 'personal loyalty' (*fides*) that Émile Benveniste has reconstructed is revived:

> he who holds the *fides* placed in him by a man holds this man at his mercy. [...] In its primitive form this relation implied a certain reciprocity, placing one's *fides* in somebody in turn secured in return his guarantee and his support.[7]

If this is true, then Benjamin's hypothesis of a close relationship between capitalism and Christianity receives a further confirmation: capitalism is a religion founded entirely on faith; it is a religion whose adepts live *sola fide*. And just as, according to Benjamin, capitalism is a religion in which the cult is liberated from any object and guilt from any sin (and thus from any redemption), so capitalism, from the perspective of faith, has no object: it believes in the pure fact of believing, in pure credit, that is, in money. Capitalism is thus a religion in which faith – credit – is substituted for God. In other words, since the pure form of credit is money, it is a religion in which God is money.

This means that the bank, which is nothing other than a machine for producing and administering money, has taken the place of the Church; and that, by governing credit, it manipulates and manages the faith – the scarce, uncertain trust – which our time still has in itself.

4

What does the decision to suspend the convertibility into gold mean for this religion? Certainly something like a clarification of its own theological content, which is comparable to the mosaic destruction of the golden calf or the establishment of a conciliar dogma; in any case, a decisive step toward the purification and crystallisation of its own faith. In the form of money and credit, the latter now liberates itself from any external referent, revokes its idolatrous nexus with gold and asserts itself in its absoluteness. Credit is a purely immaterial being, the most perfect parody of that *pistis* which is but the 'substance of things hoped for'. Faith – so runs the celebrated definition from the Letter to the Hebrews – is the substance (*ousia*, the technical term par excellence of Greek ontology) of things hoped for. What Paul means is that the one who has faith, who has placed their *pistis* in Christ, takes Christ's word as if it were the being, the substance. But it is precisely this 'as if' that the parody of the capitalist religion repeals. Money, the new *pistis*, is now immediately and without remainder substance. The destructive character of the capitalist religion of which Benjamin spoke appears here on full display. The 'thing hoped for' is no longer there; it has been nullified, and necessarily so, because money is the very essence of the thing, its *ousia* in the technical sense. And in this way, the final obstacle to the creation of the money market, to the integral transformation of money into a commodity, is removed.

5

A society whose religion is credit, which believes only in credit, is condemned to live on credit. Robert Kurz has illustrated the transformation of nineteenth-century capitalism, which was still grounded on solvency and on mistrust regarding credit, into contemporary finance capitalism:

> For nineteenth-century private capital, with its personal proprietors and its family clans, the principles of respectability and solvency still held, in the light of which the increasing recourse to credit appeared almost as obscene, as the beginning of the end. The feuilletons of the epoch are full of stories in which great families go to ruin on account of their dependence on credit: in certain passages of *Buddenbrooks*,

> Thomas Mann even made it a subject for the Nobel Prize. The productive capital of interests was of course from the very beginning indispensable for the system that was then forming, but it did not yet play a decisive role in the total capitalist reproduction. The affairs of 'fictitious' capital were considered typical of a milieu of swindlers and dishonest people at the margins of genuine capitalism. Even Henry Ford for quite some time refused recourse to bank credit, stubbornly wanting to finance his investments only with his own capital.[8]

In the course of the twentieth century, this patriarchal conception has completely dissolved and business capital today increasingly appeals to monetary capital borrowed from the banking system. This means that in order to be able to continue to produce, businesses must basically mortgage in advance increasing quantities of future labour and production. Commodity-producing capital fictitiously feeds on its own future. Consistent with Benjamin's theses, the capitalist religion lives on a continuous borrowing, which neither can nor should be extinguished.

But it is not only businesses that live, in this sense, *sola fide*, on credit (or debt). Individuals and families, who increasingly appeal to it, are equally religiously engaged in this continuous and generalised act of faith regarding the future. And the Bank is the high priest that administers to the faithful the only sacrament of the capitalist religion: credit-debt.

Sometimes I ask myself how it is possible that people so tenaciously maintain their faith in the capitalist religion. For it is clear that were they to cease having faith in credit and stop living on it, capitalism would immediately collapse. This seems, however, to presage the signs of an incipient atheism with respect to the credit God.

6

Four years prior to Nixon's declaration, Guy Debord published *The Society of the Spectacle*. The book's central thesis was that capitalism, in its extreme phase, appears as an immense accumulation of images, in which everything that was once directly used and experienced is distanced in a representation. At the point in which commodification reaches its apex, not only does all use-value disappear, but the very nature of money is transformed. It is no longer simply 'the abstract general equivalent of all commodities' themselves still endowed with some use-value: 'the spectacle is money *for contemplation only*, for here the totality of use has already been bartered for the totality of abstract representation'.⁹ It is clear, even though Debord does not say it, that such money is an absolute commodity, which cannot refer to a concrete quantity of metal. In this sense, the society of the spectacle is a prophecy of what the American government's decision would realise four years later.

According to Debord, there is a corresponding transformation of human communication, which no longer has anything to communicate and which thus appears as a 'communication of the incommunicable'.¹⁰ To money as pure commodity there corresponds a language whose nexus with the world has been broken. Language and culture, separated in the media and in advertising, become 'the star commodity of the society of the spectacle',¹¹ and they begin to hoard an increasing share of the national product for themselves. It is the linguistic and communicative nature of human beings which is thus expropriated in the spectacle: what prevents communication is its absolutisation in a separate sphere, in which there is no longer anything to communicate except communication itself. In spectacular society, human beings are separated by what should unite them.

That there might be a resemblance between language and money, that (according to the Goethean adage) '*verba valent sicut nummi*', is a legacy of common sense. If, however, we attempt to take the relation implicit in the adage seriously, it reveals itself to be something more than an analogy. Just as money refers to things by establishing them as commodities, by making them commercial, so language refers to things by making them sayable and communicable. And just as what for centuries enabled money to perform its function as the universal equivalent of all commodities was its relation with gold, so what guarantees the communicative capacity of language is the intention to signify, its actual reference to the thing. The denotative nexus with things, actually present in the mind of every speaking being, is what in language corresponds to the gold standard of money. This is the meaning of the medieval principle according to which it is not the thing that is subjected to the discourse, but the discourse to the thing ('*non sermoni res, sed rei est sermo subiectus*'). And it is significant that a great canonist of the thirteenth century, Godfrey of Trani, expressed this connection in juridical terms, by speaking of a *lingua rea*, to which one could, that is to say, impute a relation with the thing: 'only the mind's real connection with the thing actually makes the tongue imputable (that is, signifying) [*ream linguam non facit nisi rea mens*]'. If this signifying nexus collapses, language literally says nothing ('*nihil dicit*'). The signified – the reference to reality – guarantees the communicative function of language, just as the reference to gold secures money's capacity to be exchanged with all things. And logic keeps watch over the connection between language and the world, just as the 'gold-exchange standard' kept watch over money's connection with the gold standard.

It is against the nullification of these guarantees implicit, on the one hand, in money's detachment from gold, and on the other, in the rupture of the nexus between language and the world, that critical analyses of finance capitalism and the society of the spectacle have with good reason been directed. The medium that makes exchange possible cannot itself be exchanged: money, which measures commodities, cannot itself become a commodity. Likewise the language that makes things communicable cannot become itself a thing, the object in turn of appropriation and exchange: the medium of communication cannot itself be communicated. Separated from things, language communicates nothing and in this way celebrates its ephemeral triumph over the world; detached from gold, money reveals its own nullity as the absolute measure, and at the same time, as the absolute commodity. Language is the supreme spectacular value, because it reveals the nothingness of all things; money is the supreme commodity, in the final analysis because it shows the nullity of all commodities.

But it is in every sphere of experience that capitalism attests both to its religious character and its parasitic relationship with Christianity. In the first instance, with respect to time and history: capitalism has no *telos*; it is essentially in-finite. And yet, precisely because of this, it is incessantly in the grip of a crisis, is always in the act of ending. Yet even here it attests to its parasitic relationship with Christianity. In response to David Cayley, who had asked him if ours is a post-Christian world, Ivan Illich observed that it is not a post-Christian world but the most Christian world that has ever existed, that is to say an apocalyptic world.[12] Indeed, the Christian philosophy of history (but every philosophy of history is necessarily Christian) is grounded on the assumption that the history of humanity and the world is essentially finite: it runs from creation to the end of time, which coincides with the Last Judgement, with salvation or damnation. But in this chronological historical time, the messianic event inscribes another kairological time, in which each and every instant is kept in direct relation with the end, experiences a 'time of the end', which is nonetheless also a new beginning. If the Church appears to have closed its eschatological office, today it is above all scientists, transformed into apocalyptic prophets, who announce the imminent end of life on earth. And in every sphere, in economics as in politics, the capitalist religion proclaims a state of permanent crisis (*crisis* etymologically means 'definitive judgement'), which is at the same time a state of exception become normal, whose only possible outcome appears, exactly as in the Book of Revelation, as 'a new earth' (Rev. 21: 1). But the eschatology of the capitalist religion is a blank eschatology, with neither redemption nor judgement.

Indeed, just as it cannot have a real end and because of this is always in the act of finishing, so capitalism knows no beginning, is intimately an-archic. Yet, precisely because of this, it is always in the act of recommencing. Hence the consubstantiality between capitalism and innovation, which Schumpeter had put at the basis of his definition of capitalism. The anarchy of capital coincides with its own incessant need for innovation. Nonetheless, once again capitalism reveals its intimate and parodic connection with Christian dogma. For what is the Trinity if not the device that enables the reconciliation of the absence of any *archē* in God with the simultaneously eternal and historical birth of Christ, divine anarchy with the government of the world and the economy of salvation?

7

I would like to add something regarding the relation between capitalism and anarchy. There is a line, pronounced by one of the four villains of Pasolini's *Salò*, which runs: 'The only true anarchy is the anarchy of power.' In the same sense, Benjamin had written many years earlier: 'Nothing is as anarchic as the bourgeois order.' Once again, I believe that their suggestions should be taken seriously. Here Benjamin and Pasolini grasp an essential characteristic of capitalism, which is perhaps the most anarchic power that has ever existed, in the literal sense that it can have no *archē*, neither beginning nor foundation. But even in this case, the capitalist religion shows its parasitic dependence on Christian theology.

Here it is Christology that functions as the paradigm of capitalist anarchy. Between the fourth and the sixth centuries, the Church was deeply divided by the controversy over Arianism, which violently embroiled, together with the Emperor, the entirety of Eastern Christianity. The problem concerned precisely the *archē* of the Son. Indeed, both Arius and his adversaries concurred in declaring that the Son was generated by the Father, and that this generation took place 'before eternal times' ('*pro chronōn aiōniōn*' in Arius; '*pro pantōn tōn aiōnōn*' in Eusebius of Caesarea). Arius is even careful to specify that the Son was generated '*achronōs*', atemporally. What is at issue here is not so much a chronological precedence (time did not yet exist), nor merely a problem of rank (that the Father is 'better' than the Son is an opinion shared by many of the anti-Arians); rather, it is a question of determining whether the Son – which is to say, the word and the praxis of God – is grounded in the Father, or whether he is, like the Father, without principle, *anarchos*, that is, ungrounded.

A textual analysis of the letters of Arius and the writings of his adversaries shows that the decisive term in the controversy was precisely *anarchos* (without *archē*, in the double sense that the term has in Greek: foundation and principle). Arius asserts that while the Father is absolutely anarchic, the Son is in the beginning (*en archē*), but is not 'anarchic', because he has his foundation in the Father. Against this heretical thesis, which gives the Logos a solid foundation in the Father, the bishops assembled by Emperor Constantius at Serdica (343) clearly affirmed that the Son is also 'anarchic', and that, as such, he 'reigns absolutely, anarchically and infinitely [*pantote, anarchōs kai ateleutētōs*] together with the Father'.

Why does this controversy, beyond its Byzantine subtleties, appear so important to me? Because, since the Son is nothing other than the word and action of the Father – indeed, more precisely, the principal actor in the 'economy' of salvation (which is to say, in the divine government of the world) – what is at issue here is the problem of the anarchic (that is, ungrounded) character of language, action and government. Capitalism inherits, secularises and carries to an extreme the anarchic character of Christology. If we do not understand this originary anarchic vocation of Christology, it is impossible to grasp either the successive historical development of Christian theology, with its latent atheological drift, or the history of Western philosophy and politics, with its caesura between ontology and praxis, being and acting, and its consequent emphasis on the will and freedom. That Christ is anarchic means, in the last instance, that in the modern West language, practice and economy have no foundation in being.

We now better understand why the capitalist religion and the philosophies subordinate to it have such a great need of the will and freedom. Freedom and will simply mean that being and acting, ontology and praxis, which in the classical world were strictly conjoined, now go their separate ways. Human action is no longer grounded in being: this is why it is free, which is to say, condemned to chance and randomness.

I would like to interrupt my brief archaeology of the capitalist religion here. There will be no conclusion. Indeed, I believe that in philosophy, as in art, we cannot conclude a work: we can only abandon it, as Giacometti once said of his paintings. But if there is something that I would like to leave to your reflection, it is precisely the problem of anarchy. Against the anarchy of power, I do not mean to invoke a return to a solid foundation in being: even if we had possessed such a foundation, we have surely lost it or have forgotten the way to it. I nonetheless believe that a lucid comprehension of the profound anarchy of the society in which we live is the only way to correctly pose the problem of power, and at the same time, that of true anarchy. Anarchy becomes possible only at the point in which we grasp the anarchy of power. Construction and destruction coincide here without remainder. But, to cite the words of Michel Foucault, what we thereby obtain 'is nothing more, and nothing less, than the unfolding of a space in which it is once more possible to think'.[13]

Notes

1. Carl Schmitt, 'A Pan-European Interpretation of Donoso Cortés', trans. Mark Grzeskowiak, *Telos*, vol. 122 (2002), p. 107 (trans. modified).
2. Walter Benjamin, 'Capitalism as Religion', trans. Rodney Livingstone, in *Selected Writings, Volume 1: 1913–1926*, ed. Marcus Bullock and Michael W. Jennings (Cambridge, MA: The Belknap Press of Harvard University Press, 1996), p. 288.
3. Benjamin, 'Capitalism as Religion', pp. 288–9 (trans. modified).
4. Benjamin, 'Capitalism as Religion', p. 289.
5. Benjamin, 'Capitalism as Religion', p. 289.

6. Benjamin, 'Capitalism as Religion', p. 289.
7. Émile Benveniste, *Indo-European Language and Society*, trans. Elizabeth Palmer (London: Faber and Faber, 1973), p. 97.
8. Robert Kurz, 'Die Himmelfahrt des Geldes', *Krisis*, no. 16/17 (1995), available at <http://www.exit-online.org/textanz1.php?tabelle=schwerpunkte&index=6&posnr=71&backtext1=text1.php> (last accessed 1 October 2015).
9. Guy Debord, *The Society of the Spectacle*, trans. Donald Nicholson-Smith (New York: Zone Books, 1995), pp. 32–3.
10. Debord, *The Society of the Spectacle*, p. 136.
11. Debord, *The Society of the Spectacle*, p. 137.
12. Ivan Illich and David Cayley, *The Rivers North of the Future: The Testament of Ivan Illich* (Toronto: House of Anasi Press, 2005), pp. 169–70.
13. Michel Foucault, *The Order of Things: An Archaeology of the Human Sciences* (New York: Random House, 1970), p. 342.

2

Glory, Spectacle and Inoperativity: Agamben's Praxis of Theoria
Mathew Abbott

Agamben concludes his essay on Deleuze with a prediction that is also a demand. He writes: '*Theôria* and the contemplative life, which the philosophical tradition has identified as its highest goal for centuries, will have to be dislocated onto a new plane of immanence.'[1] He goes on to say that the dislocation of theoria – the root of which is the Greek *theoros*, meaning 'spectator', but which is often translated as 'contemplation' – will require us to rethink the status of political philosophy and its difference from ontology. Of course, such a rethinking is exactly what he was pursuing at the time of writing his essay, with the *Homo Sacer* series then in its early stages: a revision of the traditional distinction between politics and ontology that, as I have argued elsewhere, should be understood as post-Heideggerian political ontology.[2] In these works, the difference and relation between theory and practice – which goes back at least as far as Aristotle's *Nicomachean Ethics*, with its distinction between practical life and the life of contemplation – is called into question, and thereby reaches a new level of sophistication and difficulty.

In this chapter, I work to show how Agamben has extended and complicated his account of this differential relation in *The Kingdom and the Glory*. Connecting theoria with spectatorship, he intertwines a quasi-Marxist critique of spectacle with a Heideggerian thesis regarding the history of being as nihilism. The resultant political ontology has at its centre a dialectical notion of theoria as a form of praxis. Contra some of Agamben's critics, this is not an attempt at erasing the distinction between philosophy and politics, such that 'doing ontology' is taken as an immediately political act, or to provide a substitute for material political change.[3] Rather, dislocating theoria onto a plane of immanence is to render it a practical problem. For this we need a politics capable of rousing the human inoperativity that has lain dormant in theoria, and which the 'blinding light'[4] of glory has been obscuring from us. As a form of fundamental ontology, Agamben's thinking cannot lay down a prescriptive blueprint for political action, but it can help us rethink the very concept, founding new strategies for anti-work politics. The task for Agamben is not to unify theory and practice but to find a praxis of theoria: a politics that follows up on the consequences of the worklessness at the heart of human life, and the empty centre of the 'double machine'[5] of Kingdom and Government, theology and economy, being and acting. The problem of theory and practice thus takes on a fascinating reflexivity in *The Kingdom and the Glory*. It is a theoretical text concerned with finding a praxis adequate to the schism of theoria and praxis.

As I indicate below, part of the significance of *The Kingdom and the Glory* consists in how it develops some fascinating yet elliptical – and in some respects, unsatisfactory – claims regarding spectacle first made in *The Coming Community*. Agamben argued there that the society of the spectacle, in alienating human beings from language, raises a rather paradoxical political opportunity: 'a positive possibility that can be used against it'.[6] This is the case not in spite but because the spectacle represents the apotheosis of nihilism and the destruction of human experience. For the Agamben of *The Coming Community*, the spectacle has raised the possibility of our owning up to our groundlessness, the fact that 'there is no essence, no historical or spiritual vocation, no biological destiny that humans must enact or realise'.[7] This is quite a fascinating synthesis of ontological and ontic arguments: the political task is not to resist the spectacle but to 'carry it to completion'[8] in such a way that its own destructive power is turned against it; further, this would be equivalent to arriving at the 'other beginning'[9] Heidegger sought (if in a fashion that would have horrified him).

But just what kind of practical political engagement is Agamben recommending here? In an important recent contribution to the literature on Agamben, Jessica Whyte has linked his work with 'accelerationist' tendencies of Marxism and Deleuzianism ably critiqued by Benjamin Noys,[10] for which 'the only way out of capitalism is to take it further, to follow its lines of flight or deterritorialization to the absolute end [...]'.[11] As Noys's work indicates, such recommendations probably tell us more about current impasses of Leftist praxis than about the potential for capital to transform itself if pushed to – or through – its limit. And one can see how the Agamben of *The Coming Community* might be read in these terms, especially with his vulgar Hegelian-sounding remark about carrying the spectacle to completion. As I want to show, however, in *The Kingdom and the Glory* Agamben fleshes out his argument regarding spectacle such that its fundamental differences from accelerationist strategy come to light. The book makes clear that, unlike accelerationism – for which 'a kind of radical or quasi-Marxist "cunning of reason [. . .]"' will see 'the very worst [. . .] produce the "good"'[12] – Agamben's thought should be understood as resolutely anti-teleological and non-'apocalyptic'.[13] Indeed the argument he nuances in *The Kingdom and the Glory* has profound affinities with the counter-accelerationist strategies proposed by Noys, which he crystallises via Walter Benjamin's image of revolution as an 'emergency brake' on the runaway train of history[14] (think of the images recurring in Agamben of machines that must be stopped, jammed, rendered inoperative).

My argument in this chapter moves in three parts. First, I present an account of Agamben's genealogy of economy, clarifying the paradox he claims is constitutive of the economic paradigm: that it functions both as the foundation of the theological paradigm and as a supplement to it. This grounds my analysis of the function of glory for Agamben, which is to cover over this aporia at the heart of power – this essential disarticulation between its axes – and which has reached a crisis in the society of the spectacle. I conclude by demonstrating the anti-teleological underpinnings of his concept of inoperativity.

Locating itself 'in the wake'[15] of Michel Foucault's analysis of governmentality, *The Kingdom and the Glory* presents a genealogy of 'economic theology'.[16] This paradigm is the hidden double of political theology: though it has been working alongside it from the start, it has been 'left in the shadows'[17] by historians and philosophers – which is no doubt part of why, for Agamben, it has taken on such astonishing power in late modernity. At first glance, the two paradigms seem to be opposed to one another: if political theology 'founds the transcendence of sovereign power on the single God', then economic theology 'replaces this transcendence with the idea of an *oikonomia*, conceived as an immanent ordering – domestic and not political in a strict sense – of both divine and human life'.[18] Agamben also seems to make a rather blunt sweeping claim about their respective spheres of influence when he writes that '[p]olitical philosophy and the modern theory of sovereignty derive from the first paradigm; modern biopolitics up to the current triumph of economy and government over every other aspect of social life derive from the second paradigm.'[19] Here as elsewhere, however, we should bear in mind that one of the conclusions of *Homo Sacer* was that there is a 'hidden point of intersection between the juridico-institutional and the biopolitical models of power [. . .] that the two analyses cannot be separated'.[20] And indeed, in *The Kingdom and the Glory* Agamben claims that the governmental, biopolitical paradigm of economic theology and the sovereign, juridico-institutional paradigm of political theology are 'functionally related',[21] tracking how they have worked with and against one another throughout the philosophical, theological and political histories of the West. In fact it is precisely the ambiguous and aporetic nature of their interplay – the sense that the two paradigms are resolutely opposed to each other yet in some sense co-dependent – that interests him most. This is the source of one of the work's main surprises: the economic paradigm, insofar as it is where the tension between government and sovereignty is managed, appears to take a certain precedence over the political theological paradigm in *The Kingdom and the Glory*. As the book develops, however, it becomes clear that the aporia of the economic paradigm consists in the fact that it must somehow be both primary *and* secondary, simultaneously functioning as a supplement to the theological paradigm and as its condition of possibility. Agamben exploits this paradox when in the book's conclusion he presents his outline of the potentials for political transformation concealed within the present.

Beginning with the Aristotelian demarcation of the sphere of the house [*oikos*] from the sphere of the polis, Agamben traces the nascence of the economic paradigm through Paul's figuring of the messianic community in terms of an *oikonomia* – or 'the fulfilment of a task of domestic administration'[22] – to early Christian discussions of divine tasks, the 'arrangement' [*oikonomian*] of men who keep the law, and the organisation [*oikonomias*] of the human body. Agamben argues that these deployments of *oikonomia* and related words are theologically innocuous: they are not employed in any technical sense, but simply used to signify the idea of an ordered arrangement, activity, or assignment, as per common usage at the time. Thanks to lexical developments evolving out of

Iranaeus's confrontation with Gnostic ditheism, Hippolytus and Tertullian use *oikonomia* as a rhetorical metaphor for the Trinity in the second and third centuries – but even here there is no attempt at expounding a new, specifically theological definition.[23] As they defend the Trinity from the Monarchian claim that it was 'in danger of relapsing into polytheism',[24] however, it nevertheless starts to acquire a 'particular poignancy':[25] when Hippolytus reverses Paul's phrase 'economy of the mystery' in an attempt at explaining the paradox of a God that takes flesh and lives among men, he unwittingly confers a new meaning on it that renders divine praxis *as such* mysterious;[26] similarly, when Tertullian 'tries to come to terms with the impossibility of a philosophical formulation of the Trinitarian articulation' he transforms Paul's syntagma into *oikonomias sacramentum* and 'confers on economy all the semantic richness and ambiguity of a term that means, at the same time, oath, consecration, and mystery'.[27] Through these contingent tactical decisions – which are, of course, partly just a function of the philosophical bizarreness of the concept of the Trinity – *oikonomia* is made to bear serious theological weight. The ground was thus prepared for a transformation of the very notion of economy.

For as Agamben shows, over subsequent centuries *oikonomia* sheds its theological innocuousness and turns into a crucial technical term, coming to signify the only means by which a transcendent God can act immanently in the world, founding a praxis of government. Taking on all the metaphysical tensions of the contradictory requirement of having to reconcile 'noninvolvement in the world and government of the world; unity of being and plurality of actions; ontology and history',[28] the term thus also becomes highly aporetic, charging not just the technical debates of the Church Fathers but also 'the development and the global arrangement of Western society'[29] with its bipolar energy. By inserting 'the Gnostic antinomy within the divinity', *oikonomia* is meant to reconcile the divinity's transcendence of the world with its governing of it – yet of course, this is more of a displacement of the problem than a resolution of it. And so it returns in various guises over the development of Christian theology, the unity of which therefore 'always runs the risk of collapsing and must be acquired again at each turn'.[30] Agamben reads accounts of the division between Kingdom and Government – including Augustine's figuring of the relation between God and order, the distinction between primary and secondary causes in Aquinas, the doctrine of the two swords, the notion of divine impotence, and the relation between decision and act in Ockham – and of providence – including Chrysippus's treatment of the link between the origin of evil and divine government, Alexander's early attempt at reuniting general and special providence with his concept of providential action, the medieval notion of *pronoia*, Aquinas's account of government, and the notion of vicarious power – in terms of this originary fracture. Along the way, he jumps forward in time to find its modern exemplars, including the ambiguous status of economy in Carl Schmitt and Erik Peterson's esoteric debates on political theology, the notion of the separation of powers, the concept of collateral damage, and the scientific image of the world.

In the book's sixth chapter, Agamben introduces a concept that will become crucial for the link he wants to establish between economic theology and the problem of spectacle: glory. He turns to Peterson's 'Monotheism as a Political Problem', which seems to give a rather profane twist to the Augustinian celestial city: it figures its angels as 'the guarantors of the originary relation between the Church and the political sphere',[31] establishing the public character of worship. According to Peterson, the angels guarantee the relation between the Church and the political with something that, on the face of it at least, appears to be highly insubstantial: their 'ceaseless praise'[32] of God. For Peterson, 'the song of praise and glory is not merely one characteristic of the angels among others, but defines their essence and therefore their "politicality"'.[33] Perhaps surprisingly, it is actually Peterson's rejection of Schmitt's political theology that leads him to insist on 'the politico-religious character of the Church';[34] his strategy is to demonstrate that political theology is impossible because Christian politics only consists in the relation, guaranteed by glorifying angels, between the Church and the celestial city. Christian liturgy was always already directly political, and so the Church does not need to have politicality conferred on it by the state. The glorious 'anthem of the Church' – ceaselessly sung by the angels – 'transcends all national anthems'.[35]

However, in keeping with an earlier claim that Peterson consciously represses the economic paradigm in his genealogy of political theology, Agamben argues that the theologian must have deliberately ignored the other essential function of angels: administration. He invokes Aquinas:

Angels are represented as being present and as administering by analogy with those who attend [*famulantur*] upon a king. Some remain always present to the king and hear his commands directly. And there are others (for example, those in charge of the provincial administration) to whom the royal commands are announced by those present to the king. These latter are said to be ministers but not to be present.[36]

Angels are divided into two broad types, here described via analogy (which for Agamben must be more than an analogy) with the division between a king's attendants and his administrators, those who attend on the monarch directly, and those who are not granted audience with him, but who are nevertheless tasked by intermediaries with fulfilling his royal commands. It is a perfect – and as Agamben intimates, perfectly Kafkaesque – image of the paradoxical nature of the economic paradigm and its relation to political theology, which it must both supplement and found.

After all, questions naturally arise for Thomas's analogy: if the attendants are always in the presence of the king, then how can they pass on his commands to the administrators, who may not hold court with him? And if they cannot pass on his commands, then who will execute them? And if his commands cannot be executed, then will this not render the monarch impotent? The aporia becomes clearer as Aquinas goes on:

[A]ll angels see the divine essence directly, and in this respect all those who minister are also said to be 'present to God' [. . .] [n]evertheless, not all the angels are capable of apprehending the hidden secrets of the divine mysteries [. . .] but only the higher angels through whom these secrets are made known to the lower ones.[37]

Seeming to qualify his claim that administering angels cannot be granted audience with the divine, Aquinas acknowledges that all angels are present to God; yet to retain his hierarchy of angelic orders he must nevertheless insist that only some can understand divine secrets.

The paradox is illustrated in Kafka's 'An Imperial Message'. An emperor sends a message from his deathbed, but the messenger tasked with delivering it finds himself unable to make his way out of the interior of the imperial palace – and even if he could get out, he knows he cannot make it down the stairs – and even if he could make it down, he would then have to cross the courtyard, then of course the second enclosing outer palace, then further stairways and courtyards, all of which would be impossible.[38] After all, Kafka seems to be asking, just how *can* one deliver a message from the emperor? As soon one takes the job, one would be overcome with a kind of vertigo, as an infinite regress yawns at one's feet. To put this back in terms of Thomas's analogy: to have a command executed, a monarch has to employ an intermediary, because the king cannot hold an audience with just anyone; yet will not this intermediary need his own intermediary if he is to pass his message down the hierarchy? Perhaps this explains why angels and angelic orders (and indeed, managers) have a tendency to proliferate, as if this problem of intermediaries could somehow be solved with more intermediaries.

This is why Agamben writes that '[t]he caesura between assistants and administrators [. . .] cuts through each angel.'[39] The only way to resolve the paradoxes caused by the division between angels is to reintroduce that division into the heart of each angel. Grafting an exclusive disjunction onto a logical conjunction, Aquinas will try to have it both ways: angels either attend or administer; yet attending angels also administer. This aporetic logic is familiar by now, pertaining as it does to the double structure of *oikonomia*, with the connective contradiction between Kingdom and Government now appearing in the doubling of angelic tasks. This is how Agamben tries to show that Peterson, despite his best efforts at staving off political theology, ends up being drawn back into it, as the dual function of angels means he can no longer lean on his distinction between liturgical participation in the celestial city and state power. If angels do not only glorify but also administrate, then angelology loses the political innocuousness he wanted to bestow upon it, as it can no longer be maintained in a sphere separate from earthly power. His angelology represses administration because it connects glorification back to profane politics.

Agamben argues that Peterson must have been aware of this, at least on some level, for nine years earlier he had published a dissertation on the ceremonial aspects of power which trades in the kind of political theological speculation that his 1935 work on monotheism would attempt to head off. Linking the expression *heis theos* with the acclamatory practices associated with magistrates, emperors and bishops – and emphasising both their legal and liturgical aspects – Peterson argues that it is wrong to understand acclamations as professions of faith and, at the same time, traces their origins to pre-Christian cults and post-Christian heresies, to pagan, Greek, Mithraic, Gnostic and Manichean festivals. As such Peterson effectively makes way for Schmitt's 1927 thesis that 'acclamation is an eternal phenomenon of all political communities',[40] which the jurist uses to bolster his anti-liberal argument against Weimar representative democracy (which, Schmitt claimed, was reneging on its political status by employing secret ballots). Only six years later, of course, the public character of glorification would be demonstrated very clearly in Schmitt's Germany, when the *Hitlergruß* officially became the required greeting of all government employees.[41] Peterson's attempt 'to exclude the very possibility of a Christian "political theology", so as to found in glory the only legitimate political dimension of Christianity, comes dangerously close to the totalitarian liturgy'.[42] Against Peterson, Agamben wants to deactivate political theology not by repressing the economic paradigm that secretly founds it, but by exploiting the paradoxes it instils in it. Agamben's account of the aporetic structure of *oikonomia*, in other words, leads him to a theory of glory as that which not only supplements but also – through the same paradoxical logic – constitutes sovereign power:

> The economy glorifies being, as being glorifies the economy. And only in the mirror of glory do the two trinities appear to reflect into one another; only in its splendor do being and economy, Kingdom and Government appear to coincide for an instant.[43]

In the political sphere and in the celestial, glory has 'the function of a cover',[44] serving to conceal the inoperativity at the heart of power, the caesura between its axes. For all its emphasis on the subtle and painstaking ways in which theologians and political theorists have tried to bring being and acting, Kingdom and Government, theology and economy into functional relation, the key discovery of *The Kingdom and the Glory* – and this is what separates it from the tracts it analyses – is that there is *no* articulation between the two axes of power. The function of glory, then, is not really to establish a relationship between the poles as much as to hide the fact that no such relationship exists. Glory, Agamben writes, 'is nothing but the splendor that emanates from this emptiness, this inexhaustible *kabhod* that at once reveals and veils the central vacuity of the machine'.[45] This is how Agamben answers the question that opens the book and to which he returns in his final chapter: power needs glory – insignias, crowns, flags, acclamations, coronations, robes, sceptres, pageants, hymns, thrones, salutes, etc. – in order to obscure its unthinkable emptiness.

Now we can begin to understand one of the book's most important and provocative claims: contemporary liberal democracies – which in many ways appear to be abandoning Kingdom altogether, allowing economy to take precedence – have not actually renounced glory but have instead transposed it. Connecting Guy Debord's theory of spectacle to Schmitt's claim that 'public opinion is the modern form of acclamation',[46] Agamben argues that contemporary capitalist societies have achieved a historically unprecedented level of glorification: 'What was confined to the spheres of liturgy and ceremonials has become concentrated in the media and, at the same time, through them it spreads and penetrates at each moment into every area of society, both public and private.'[47]

So Agamben's genealogy of economy ends up chiming with the Western Marxist critique of reification, the Lukácsian idea that under capitalism human beings become 'less and less active and more and more *contemplative*'.[48] As their labour-power is commodified and the 'traditional amalgam of the empirical experiences of work'[49] is annihilated through rationalisation, Lukács claims the worker experiences a subjective fragmentation: her 'idiosyncrasies' are ironed out of the work process, where they can only appear as errors; processes that were once organic and self-directed start to appear to operate according to 'fixed laws' separate from her; she effectively becomes a 'mechanical part incorporated into a mechanical system'.[50] Inheriting and transforming this critique in response to a new phase in the development of capital – in which commodification had extended its reach more deeply into daily life as commodity consumption became integral to the subject's ordinary experience, and the development of mass communication technologies undergirded a multinational culture industry – Debord argued that reification had become the basic form in which we experience the world. '[R]eality unfolds in a new generality as a pseudo-world apart', Debord says, 'solely as an object of contemplation.'[51] This is why Agamben's genealogy of economy and archaeology of glory concludes with a fascinating analysis of the spectacular function of media, opinion and consensus in contemporary liberal democracies. These are forms of glorification in the particular sense he has outlined: simultaneously functioning as its supplement and foundation, they work to consecrate and thus legitimate power. As Agamben writes:

> If we link Debord's analysis with Schmitt's thesis [...] the entire problem of the contemporary spectacle of media domination over all areas of social life assumes a new guise. What is in question is nothing less than a new and unheard of concentration, multiplication, and dissemination of the function of glory as the center of the political system.[52]

As in the earlier instalments of the *Homo Sacer* series, Agamben posits a secret solidarity between democratic and totalitarian forms of government: glorification is 'mediatic and objective' in the former, and 'immediate and subjective'[53] in the latter – but it is central to legitimation in both.

This is not all, however, for the problem of spectacle also appears in a more oblique but no less significant fashion in the final chapter's various accounts of contemplation. Here is what is perhaps the crucial moment in these accounts:

> Contemplation and inoperativity are [...] the metaphysical operators of an anthropogenesis, which, by liberating the living man from his biological or social destiny, assigns him to that indefinable dimension we are accustomed to calling 'politics.' Opposing the contemplative life to the political as 'two *bioi*,' Aristotle deflected politics and philosophy from their trajectory and, at the same time, delineated the paradigm on which the economy-glory apparatus would model itself. The political is neither a *bios* nor a *zoē*, but the dimension that the inoperativity of contemplation, by deactivating linguistic and corporeal, material and immaterial praxes, ceaselessly opens and assigns to the living.[54]

I will return to this passage; here I want to underline how Agamben locates the early stages of the paradigm of glory and economy in the Aristotelian distinction between theoria and praxis. As we should expect given Agamben's commitment to Heidegger, the machine that will reach its crisis in the spectacular society of late capitalism can be traced back to the Ancient Greeks. Yet of course, this is not a simple negative critique: he is working to find at the heart of spectacular life a certain radical political potential – a potential that could be exploited in order to render inoperative the very machine of glory that has produced it. This is what the later

Heidegger, with his insistence that epochal change could never depend on any kind of human action, misses – and why, in a move that demonstrates a small but crucial Benjaminian distance from him, Agamben goes on to try to correct Heidegger's philosophy of technology by restoring it to its 'political locus'.[55] After all, the problem of theoria is not simply a problem of mass media or even mediation, but also – and more primarily – a problem of action. This is particularly clear in *Opus Dei* and *The Highest Poverty*, two other recent instalments of the *Homo Sacer* series: the former performs an archaeology of duty centred on the figure of the priest, setting up a problematic of being versus action, ontology versus command, which – with its emphasis on how the category of action has been mystified – echoes Lukács's critique of capital; the latter traces a (failed) response to this distinction in the Franciscan variant of the monastic phenomenon. In both the figure of the priest and the figure of the monk we find failed attempts at resolving the split between theoria and praxis. If the latter provides a more useful and interesting exemplar for Agamben, however, that may because the life in question is precisely a contemplative one. But what radical potential is there in theoria?

Before answering this question, it is worth pausing to raise a few caveats, which pertain to issues running deeper than the commonly made point – which is probably correct enough – that philosophy should not be expected to address our political problems by prescribing particular actions. If Agamben's thought is, as I have argued, a form of political ontology, then he cannot coherently provide even a general prescription for concrete action (in the way that, for example, someone like Marx clearly can). This is because its primary concern is our metaphysical inheritance – an inheritance that, by its nature, cannot simply be 'opposed' (in the way one opposes fascism, the undermining of the welfare state, barbarous immigration policies, or a neo-liberal political party). At the same time, however, unlike that of Heidegger, Agamben's thought does identify points of apparent contact between the ontic and the ontological. This is perhaps at its clearest in Agamben's notion of a paradigm, which is one of the methodological underpinnings of the *Homo Sacer* series (and which plays a particularly important role in *The Kingdom and the Glory*). A paradigm is 'a form of knowledge'[56] in which 'there is no duality' between the singular phenomenon and the whole it exemplifies insofar as the whole 'only results from the paradigmatic exposition of particular cases'.[57] This is to say that a paradigm does not relate universal to particular, or particular to universal; it is not a principle of set membership. Rather, a paradigm 'moves from singularity to singularity'.[58] Agamben goes on:

> *Homo sacer* and the concentration camp, the *Muselmann* and the state of exception, and, more recently, the Trinitarian *oikonomia* and acclamations are not hypotheses through which I intended to explain modernity by tracing it back to something like a cause or historical origin. On the contrary, as their very multiplicity might have signaled, each time it was a matter of paradigms whose aim was to make intelligible a series of phenomena whose kinship had eluded or could elude the historian's gaze.[59]

The economic paradigm is not a historical hypothesis designed to explain modernity (in the way that Marx, at least on a certain reading of him, traces the historical origins of capitalism to the mercantile system) – rather, it is a way of illuminating the (singular)[60] history of being with a series of singular ontic figures that exemplify its trajectory. Though Agamben's analyses in *The Kingdom and the Glory* are historically meticulous, he is not doing history. As he writes: 'The intelligibility in question in the paradigm has an ontological character. It refers not to the cognitive relation between subject and object but to being.'[61] Like the *Homo sacer*, *oikonomia* is not the origin of modernity (or any kind of explanation for it) but a paradigm of how its constitutive fissures have been managed (and, in being managed, brought to light). Agamben's concrete historical examples – for instance, the debates regarding the Trinity between Tertullian and the Monarchians – are contingent events, emerging out of a highly complex confluence of aleatory ontic causes, yet through their participation in a paradigm they give us a glimpse of an overarching logic.

Agamben thus makes an advance on the later Heidegger. It is not simply that he wants to link philosophically the ontological and the ontic – Heidegger tries to do this too, for example with his concept of *Ereignis* – but that, unlike Heidegger,[62] he is able to grant decisiveness to particular ontic events. For it is not only that Tertullian's debate with the Monarchians exemplifies the economic paradigm – it also played a role in its development. Tertullian did not intend to put serious theological weight on *oikonomia*, and could never have predicted how later Church Fathers and medieval theologians would take up – and struggle with – the concept; he just invoked the term because it was tactically useful for clarifying his Trinitarian arguments. In doing so, though, he cleared the way for the concept's transformation, and so for the bequeathal to us of the aporias of economy. Franciscanism must be understood in similar (though opposing) terms, as a direct attempt at escaping liturgy: 'Use and form of life', Agamben writes, 'are the two apparatuses through which the Franciscans tried, certainly in an insufficient way, to break this mold and confront that paradigm.'[63] The radical potential of Franciscanism was nullified by the Church, but it need not have been: if things had been handled differently, perhaps more strategically, the outcome could have been different. What happens 'on the ground', in other words, is more than an epiphenomenon; paradigmatic historical events are more than mere *effects*. At the same time, it would also be wrong to call such events *causes* of the paradigms in which they participate. As Agamben often employs metaphors of energy – and in particular bipolar energy – in describing the tensions generated by the aporias of the economic and theological paradigms, it may be useful to imagine a lightning rod. The rod is not the *cause* of the lightning strike, which comes about because two regions (whether they be different clouds, or a cloud and the ground) have been charged at opposite polarities; yet the rod helps direct the strike, which would not have occurred at the same time, in the same place, with the same intensity, or in the same shape without it. Similarly, Tertullian's deployment of *oikonomia* did not bring the economic paradigm into being, but provided a particular ontic, historical point at which a tension could be discharged. It was not the cause of the strike, but it was nevertheless decisive for it.

This is part of the subtle means by which Agamben is able to connect fundamental ontology with ontic political struggle. Though his thinking cannot prescribe any particular action, it *can* help us experiment with the kinds of apparatuses – or counter-apparatuses – we might deploy for overcoming the impasses of contemporary politics. What does Agamben's genealogy of the economic paradigm tell us in this respect? That perhaps above all it is around questions of work – and its refusal – that we need to strategise. This is more than the (obviously true) claim that the category of labour must be central to any anti-capitalist politics: it is about finding a political potential in the human inoperativity capital has revealed, and setting it against the force that revealed it. This is a piece of strategic advice: Agamben's genealogy of economy, just like his critique of the paradoxical structure of sovereignty, is meant to highlight sites of disavowal, tension and pressure – sites that, if exploited in the right way, could become political flashpoints. In *The Kingdom and the Glory*, Agamben identifies inoperativity as something like the secret of the economic paradigm: it is what charges it with energy, but also – and for that reason – what it must work to conceal. As the machine of glorification reaches its apotheosis in the society of the spectacle, it is as though its powers of concealment have started to falter, and it has inadvertently begun to reveal something about human life: that we have no historical tasks to carry out; that we have no natural productive capacity to liberate from the alienating imposts of capital; that we have no *ergon* proper to us; that there is nothing we must do or be. An inoperative life is a life not dedicated to any particular way of life, any particular vocation or office. It would be a form-of-life: a life for which the fact of living is always at stake in living.[64] Living the grace and gratuity of life in and as one's way of life: this is the ethical task of inoperativity. The political task is to live it in common, disconnecting it from those who seek to privatise it, or set it to work.[65]

This is why Agamben claims in the passage I invoked earlier that Aristotle's life of theoria relieves the human being from its destiny: a theoretical life is a life in which humans revel in their own lack of purpose, contemplating their own gratuity as an eternal perfection. It is a life in which human beings find a collective happiness in their release from fate, like the inhabitants of limbo in *The Coming Community*, on whose unsavability 'the powerful theological machine of Christian *oiconomia* runs aground'.[66] *And life in spectacular society is theoretical life.* Aristotle opposed the life of theoria to political life; but now, as the economic paradigm founded on the separation of the two *bioi* reaches its crisis, theoria has collapsed back into politics, as both a problem and a potential. It is a potential not because of where it may take us if carried to completion, but because it is showing up the inoperativity of human life. There is nothing teleological or necessitarian about this claim regarding the historical development of capital: this disclosure need not have taken place, and if capital had not made the human contemplative by reifying its labour and then its very experience of the world, then it would not have taken place, and inoperativity would have remained largely hidden, appearing only for brief moments at historical flashpoints, only to be covered again in glory. '[F]ar from realizing philosophy' – as an accelerationist reading of Karl Korsch might have it[67] – the spectacle actually 'philosophizes reality'[68] – separating it out from us as a glorious object to be contemplated theoretically. The political task is not to push the spectacle further (whatever that would mean), but to seize the inoperativity spectacle has brought to light.

We may be able to derive a notion of absolute equality from this inoperativity: if there is nothing a human being must do or be, then there is no means of ranking (or acclaiming) human forms of life according to their abilities, talents or achievements. We may find in it strategic resources for a renewed anti-work politics: one that rejects productivist forms of Marxism[69] as it challenges 'the imposition and organization of work'[70] in the form of a wage system.[71] Because of how it reveals human beings as existing without purpose, this thought of inoperativity contains an implicit critique of the idea of the moral necessity of labour, chiming with the critique of work articulated by the situationists. It could help ground demands for an unconditional basic income or, in a more radical register, for a society no longer structured around the exploitation of abstract labour for commodity production. Inoperativity is more than just a lack of operativity – it is something we might actualise.[72] As Kathi Weeks writes:

> [T]he refusal of work, as both activism and analysis, does not simply pose itself against the present organization of work; it should also be understood as a creative practice, one that seeks to reappropriate and reconfigure existing forms of production and reproduction.[73]

A practice of inoperativity – or what I want to call a praxis of theoria – would be an inglorious practice that seeks the means to sabotage the apparatuses deployed by power in its endless attempts to resolve its constitutive aporias, revealing the lack of articulation between sovereignty and government. One such counter-apparatus (if it has not already reached obsolescence) may be the *general strike*, which can turn the refusal of work into something more than a temporary means to a particular political end (which is to say, something more than another type of operativity). Another may be the *occupation*, which uses the clearest figure of inoperativity – human existence itself, the common fact of being-there: *Dasein* – as a weapon.

One might ask: how can Agamben, with his Heideggerian commitment to a thesis regarding the singular history of being, coherently claim that human life is without essence and without destiny, that political happiness must be found in purposelessness? Because for him that history is not running according to any kind of plan or scheme but on a central emptiness that we have continually failed to recognise. This is all the so-called 'sending' of being consists in. Perhaps that is something Heidegger was unable (or unwilling) to properly face. It would explain his resorting to pseudo-poetic, indeed glorifying language in describing being (as though he was trying to cover something up). This is the paradox at the heart of *The Kingdom and the Glory*: while it may seem as though Agamben is establishing conceptual and historical connections between being and acting, the theological and the economic paradigms – and indeed, the ontological and the ontic – he is really tracing the paradoxical effects of their connective *contradiction*, the simultaneous necessity and impossibility of their ever coinciding. This is why the language of a 'completion' of spectacle deployed in *The Coming Community* had to be modified: the task is not to complete a historical progression, but to disrupt a historical progression by showing the hiatus that was always already at its heart. Agamben's anti-teleological philosophy of history is founded on the wager that the machine can be stopped if we learn to see its emptiness for what it is, and live it as such.

Notes

1. Giorgio Agamben, 'Absolute Immanence', in *Potentialities: Collected Essays in Philosophy*, trans. Daniel Heller-Roazen (Stanford: Stanford University Press, 1999), p. 239.
2. See Mathew Abbott, *The Figure of This World: Agamben and the Question of Political Ontology* (Edinburgh: Edinburgh University Press, 2014), where I connect Agamben's project in the *Homo Sacer* series with his earlier texts on poetry, language and aesthetics, and show the crucial influence of Heidegger on his work. I argue that, as a form of political ontology, Agamben's thought is concerned with studying the political stakes of the question of being. His thinking thus centres on the political metaphysics of modernity, and does not primarily work in a sociological or critical theoretical register, at least in the usual senses of these terms. As well as providing a further defence of Agamben and an account of some of his newer concepts,

part of my goal in this chapter is to follow up on some problems that arose in the final chapter of that book, particularly regarding the relation between the ontic and the ontological.
3. For example, see Matthew Sharpe, 'Only Agamben Can Save Us?', *The Bible and Critical Theory*, vol. 5, no. 3 (2009), p. 10.
4. Giorgio Agamben, *The Kingdom and the Glory: For a Theological Genealogy of Economy and Government*, trans. Lorenzo Chiesa with Matteo Mandarini (Stanford: Stanford University Press, 2011), p. 242.
5. Agamben, *The Kingdom and the Glory*, p. 99.
6. Giorgio Agamben, *The Coming Community*, trans. Michael Hardt (Minneapolis: University of Minnesota Press, 1993), p. 42.
7. Agamben, *The Coming Community*, p. 42.
8. Agamben, *The Coming Community*, p. 83.
9. Martin Heidegger, *Contributions to Philosophy (Of the Event)*, trans. Richard Rojcewicz and Daniela Vallega-Neu (Bloomington: Indiana University Press, 2012), p. 47.
10. Whyte writes: 'Agamben is too prone to see the intensification of catastrophe as the precondition of redemption [. . .] instead of reassuring ourselves that the dangers of the present are the birth pangs of a new redeemed form of life, it is necessary to invent new political forms that are capable both of forestalling the dangers of the present and contributing to a world in which we are able to make free use of our own capacities. This will require not the intensification of the dangers of the present (a strategy Benjamin Noys has aptly dubbed "accelerationism"), but a rupture with the truly catastrophic dominance of capital' (Jessica Whyte, *Catastrophe and Redemption: The Political Thought of Giorgio Agamben* (Albany: State University of New York Press, 2013), pp. 7–8).
11. Benjamin Noys, *Malign Velocities: Accelerationism and Capitalism* (Winchester: Zero Books, 2014), p. x. See also Benjamin Noys, *The Persistence of the Negative: A Critique of Contemporary Continental Theory* (Edinburgh: Edinburgh University Press, 2010), pp. 4–13.
12. Noys, *Malign Velocities*, p. 64.
13. Agamben's account of the 'coming politics', at least prior to his turn to government, has been repeatedly interpreted as apocalyptic: as an example of the latter see Mitchell Dean, 'Governmentality Meets Theology: "The King Reigns, but he Does not Govern"', *Theory, Culture & Society*, vol. 29, no. 3 (2013), p. 146.
14. See Noys, *Malign Velocities*, pp. 83–92.
15. Agamben, *The Kingdom and the Glory*, p. xi.

16. Agamben, *The Kingdom and the Glory*, p. 1.
17. Agamben, *The Kingdom and the Glory*, p. xi.
18. Agamben, *The Kingdom and the Glory*, p. 1.
19. Agamben, *The Kingdom and the Glory*, p. 1.
20. Giorgio Agamben, *Homo Sacer: Sovereign Power and Bare Life*, trans. Daniel Heller-Roazen (Stanford: Stanford University Press, 1998), p. 6.
21. Agamben, *The Kingdom and the Glory*, p. 1.
22. Agamben, *The Kingdom and the Glory*, p. 23.
23. Agamben, *The Kingdom and the Glory*, p. 35.
24. Agamben, *The Kingdom and the Glory*, p. 36.
25. Agamben, *The Kingdom and the Glory*, p. 37.
26. Agamben, *The Kingdom and the Glory*, p. 39. Suddenly, as Agamben argues, there is 'no economy of the mystery, that is, an activity aimed at fulfilling and revealing the divine mystery; it is the very "*pragmateia*," the very divine praxis, that is mysterious'.
27. Agamben, *The Kingdom and the Glory*, p. 40.
28. Agamben, *The Kingdom and the Glory*, p. 51.
29. Agamben, *The Kingdom and the Glory*, p. 1.
30. Agamben, *The Kingdom and the Glory*, p. 62.
31. Agamben, *The Kingdom and the Glory*, p. 146.
32. Erik Peterson, *Ausgewählte Schriften*, vol. 1, *Theological Traktate* (Würzburg: Echter, 1994), p. 215, quoted in Agamben, *The Kingdom and the Glory*, p. 147.
33. Agamben, *The Kingdom and the Glory*, p. 147.
34. Agamben, *The Kingdom and the Glory*, p. 145.
35. Peterson, *Ausgewählte Schriften*, p. 206, quoted in Agamben, *The Kingdom and the Glory*, p. 146.
36. Thomas Aquinas, *Summa Theologiae*, trans. Thomas Gilby et al. (London: Blackfriars, 1964–81), I, q.112, a.3, p. 43, quoted in Agamben, *The Kingdom and the Glory*, p. 151.
37. Thomas Aquinas, *Summa Theologiae*, trans. Thomas Gilby et al. (London: Blackfriars, 1964–81), I, q.112, a.3, p. 43, quoted in Agamben, *The Kingdom and the Glory*, p. 151.
38. Franz Kafka, *Parables and Paradoxes* (New York: Schocken Books, 1961), pp. 12–15.
39. Agamben, *The Kingdom and the Glory*, p. 151.
40. Carl Schmitt, *Volksentscheid und Volksbegehren: Ein Beitrag zur Auslegung der Weimarer Verfassung und zur Lehre von der unmittelbaren Demokratie* (Berlin: Walter de Gruyter, 1927), p. 34, quoted in Agamben, *The Kingdom and the Glory*, p. 172.

41. Ian Kershaw, *The 'Hitler Myth': Image and Reality in the Third Reich* (Oxford: Oxford University Press, 1987), p. 60.
42. Agamben, *The Kingdom and the Glory*, p. 193.
43. Agamben, *The Kingdom and the Glory*, p. 209.
44. Agamben, *The Kingdom and the Glory*, p. 155.
45. Agamben, *The Kingdom and the Glory*, p. 211.
46. Agamben, *The Kingdom and the Glory*, p. 256.
47. Agamben, *The Kingdom and the Glory*, p. 256.
48. György Lukács, 'Reification and the Consciousness of the Proletariat', in *History and Class Consciousness*, trans. Rodney Livingstone (London: Merlin Press, 1971), p. 89.
49. Lukács, 'Reification and the Consciousness of the Proletariat', p. 88.
50. Lukács, 'Reification and the Consciousness of the Proletariat', p. 89.
51. Guy Debord, *The Society of the Spectacle*, trans. Donald Nicholson-Smith (New York: Zone Books, 1995), p. 12.
52. Agamben, *The Kingdom and the Glory*, p. 256.
53. Agamben, *The Kingdom and the Glory*, p. 258.
54. Agamben, *The Kingdom and the Glory*, p. 251.
55. Agamben, *The Kingdom and the Glory*, p. 253.
56. Giorgio Agamben, 'What Is a Paradigm?', in *The Signature of All Things: On Method*, trans. Luca D'Isanto with Kevin Attell (New York: Zone Books, 2009), p. 31.
57. Agamben, 'What Is a Paradigm?', p. 27.
58. Agamben, 'What Is a Paradigm?', p. 31.
59. Agamben, 'What Is a Paradigm?', p. 31.
60. That the history of being is singular is Agamben's most problematic claim. It is also one of his most interesting. I will not try to defend this Heideggerian idea here, except to say that we should perhaps regard it as of the same order as Kant's synthetic a priori, Hegel's speculative identity of subject and object, or Badiou's more recent thesis that mathematics is ontology: something not fully defendable within the relevant philosophical system, which nevertheless must constantly seek to establish it, despite and because of the fact that it founds it.
61. Agamben, 'What Is a Paradigm?', p. 32.
62. At least on standard readings of him. In this context, another way of framing what Agamben is doing would be to say that he is performing a strategic rereading of Heidegger.
63. Agamben, *The Highest Poverty*, p. 145.
64. For an extended treatment of what it would mean for the fact of living to be put at stake in one's way of living, see chapter 7 of Abbott, *The Figure of This World* (especially pp. 158–9).

65. Jean-Luc Nancy's essay 'The Inoperative Community', in *The Inoperative Community*, trans. Peter Connor (Minneapolis: University of Minnesota Press, 1991) – to which Agamben's *The Coming Community* is often read as a response – provides a brilliant account of these two aspects of community, arguing that it is always more than a conglomerate of private individuals, and that it can never come about as the result of work.
66. Agamben, *The Coming Community*, p. 6.
67. Karl Korsch develops a dialectical notion of communism as the simultaneous completion and abolition of philosophy, and concludes with a quotation from the young Marx: 'Philosophy cannot be abolished without being realized' (Karl Korsch, *Marxism and Philosophy*, trans. Fred Halliday (London: New Left Books, 1970), p. 85).
68. Debord, *The Society of the Spectacle*, p. 17.
69. Weeks mounts a persuasive critique of 'productivist Marxism' for relying on a 'vision of unalienated and unexploited work in the guise of living labor, one that could live up to the work ethic's ideals about labor's necessity and virtues . . .' (Kathi Weeks, *The Problem with Work: Feminism, Marxism, Antiwork Politics, and Postwork Imaginaries* (Durham, NC: Duke University Press, 2011), p. 15). When Agamben critiques Marx in *The Kingdom and the Glory* for 'secularizing the theological idea of the being of creatures as divine operation', it is worth acknowledging that it is really the productivist Marx he has in mind. And as Weeks argues, it is possible to find the resources for a critique of productivism in Marx himself. For a powerful anti-productivist reading of Marx, see Moishe Postone, *Time, Labor, and Social Domination: A Reinterpretation of Marx's Critical Theory* (Cambridge: Cambridge University Press, 1996).
70. Weeks, *The Problem with Work*, p. 96.
71. As Postone writes: '"[F]reeing" the forces of production from the "fetters" of the relations of production requires the abolition of both value and the specific character of labor in capitalism' (Postone, *Time, Labor, and Social Domination*, p. 35).
72. Earlier works from the series, such as *State of Exception* and *Homo Sacer*, can provide similar sorts of strategic insights, though regarding different fields of tensions. Consider the intense anxieties associated with the figure of the refugee, which pertain to more than racism, bringing to light fractures in our notions of citizenship; think of how states and sovereigns must, to establish and police the extra-judicial zones on which they are increasingly dependent, flirt with renouncing their traditional claims to legitimacy. Agamben's political thinking

does not demand we push these contradictions further for the sake of the new political possibilities this may engender. It simply indicates that, strategically speaking, these sites could become flashpoints if exploited in the right way. It should go without saying that this is not necessarily to recommend exploiting them (that is a tactical decision, and will depend on myriad ontic conditions).

73. Weeks, *The Problem with Work*, p. 99. As Weeks makes clear, this is not ultra-left utopianism (though it is indeed left-communist): one of the upshots of framing political struggle around the refusal of work is that the question of reform vs revolution should become moot (see pp. 228–9). In that sense, this account of Agamben sits very happily with Whyte's commitment to 'conceptualizing the fight for reforms in the present as co-extensive with a revolutionary position' (Whyte, *Catastrophe and Redemption*, p. 15).

3

On Property and the Philosophy of Poverty: Agamben and Anarchism
Simone Bignall

Despite his interest in a non-sovereign and anomial politics, Agamben makes scant reference to thinkers in the anarchist tradition.[1] However, particularly with the turn to questions of government and economy in his latest works, he delves increasingly into themes at the heart of anarchist philosophy: the renunciation of property and the practice of poverty as a means of living outside of determination by law and state; the negative and positive moments of transformation variously associated with revolt or revolution; the 'idea of communism' and the figure of 'the Ungovernable'. It is noteworthy how, at the point in *The Time That Remains* where he first explicitly references anarchist theory, Agamben identifies in Max Stirner an 'ethical-anarchic interpretation of the Pauline *as not*'.[2] While this reference to anarchist theory is brief, it nonetheless suggests that anarchism is important to understanding Agamben's account of the 'coming politics'. That he refers to the anarchist tradition in the wider context of a discussion of Marxist thought concerning the 'messianic' vocation of the proletariat class and Marx's 'ridiculing' of the anarchic egoism of Stirner, invites reflection on Agamben's relation to anarchism and to Marxism. In this chapter I explore these connections in the context of the ideological conflict that strained relations between Marx and the anarchists, and ultimately resulted in the collapse of the First International Workingmen's Association in 1872.[3]

For Agamben, 'philosophical archaeology' returns thought to an unstable moment, manifestly past, in order to apply its methodological pressure: recovering the productive potential of the uncertainty that was lost when the crisis passed resolutely into history; reinvesting this potential with a redemptive power to transform radical thought and practice in its current responses to contemporary configurations of power and economy.[4] In an 'archaeology' of radical thought in the Western political tradition, the First International stands as a flashpoint where internal conflicts gave rise to selectively victorious strategies with significant historical effects. These include the dominance within the Left of the Marxist paradigm of historical materialism; the perceived failure of communism with the eventual collapse of the Soviet Union; and, hence, the spectacular hegemony of late capitalism that has become our inheritance. Uncovering the philosophical ground of the fractures compromising the First International reveals what was at stake for radical politics of the time, exposing in the harsh light of history the opportunities lost for the world that was then yet to come. At the same time, it posits the question of the continuing relevance of those same stakes, and so makes them accessible for politics in the time of the now. The conflicts that scarred the First International and resulted in its demise revolved around three core questions: the source of revolutionary causation and the nature of its process; the issue of authority in the revolutionary government; and the divide between the *being* of the classless society and revolutionary social *praxis* that continues to assume the legitimacy of property in a collective form. As we know, these are some of the very same themes and concerns that animate Agamben's recent works. If we look at each of these more closely, we may observe with improved vision what Agamben's arguments imply for radical thought and politics today.

The sections of this chapter examine how Agamben responds to these questions in his recent work on redemptive transformation, government, poverty and use. I begin by explaining how Agamben supports a theory of transformation that is critical of the Marxist theory of class-based revolution, and instead approximates and develops anarchist practices of dissolution. I then consider how anarchism provides the only possible solution to the 'archist' aporias that reside in the ontopolitical division Agamben identifies between being and practice; between the rule of sovereignty and the economy of government. Finally, I explain how Agamben's recent attention to a politics of common 'use' of things, opposed to the appropriation and possession of things, revives a constructive practice of anarchism as an anomial technique of social organisation. In making these claims about Agamben's anarchism, I consider his work in relation to anarchist ideas on property and social justice presented, for example, by Proudhon in *What Is Property?* and *The Philosophy of Poverty*, and in other classic work by anarchists such as Godwin, Kropotkin, Tolstoy and Stirner. In light of Marx's critical assessments of Stirner in *The German Ideology*, and of Proudhon in the *The Poverty of Philosophy*, I argue that Agamben's recent ideas bring him closer to the socialist anarchist tradition than to Marx's governmental communism. I also suggest that Agamben's most recent work on the positive constitution of community in terms of shared practices of 'use' represents a significant shift from his preoccupation with the negative paradigm of inoperativity and, consequently, signals his distancing from, or his complication of, the political egoism of Stirner's 'ethical-anarchism'. By reconstructing Agamben's approach to key problems in revolutionary political philosophy, I argue that what is at stake in his work is a rethinking of the paradigm of anarchy in the contemporary light of political ontology, restoring the potential of that tradition for use in the present.

Revolutionary causation and process, or the time that remains

In *The Coming Community*, Agamben outlines a theory of transformative sociality independent of a normative politics of identification. This paradigm is developed further in *The Time That Remains* when Agamben discovers in Saint Paul's epistles the idea of 'messianic time as a paradigm of historical time'.[5] He argues that the internal structure of messianic time reveals an immanent cause of historical transformation, contracted between the two simultaneous moments Paul describes as *ho nyn kairos* – the 'time of the now' – and *hōs mē* – the moment of revocation or redemption, in which everything that is, becomes 'as not'. The messianic vocation does not require identification with a worldly profession (of Christianity) and an associated status of being (a Christian). It is, rather, '*the revocation of every vocation*'[6] produced by the radically equalising experience of grace and exigency felt in the presence of the Messiah. The messianic vocation thus 'calls for nothing and to no place':[7] it does not substitute a 'less authentic' state of being with a 'truer' one, but rather involves the emptying out of the content of every factical form, 'nullifying' everything that is, by 'setting it against itself in the form of the "as not"'.[8]

Agamben emphasises that 'the messianic vocation is a movement of immanence, or, if one prefers, a zone of absolute indiscernibility between this world and the future world'.[9] The messianic event of redemption will not happen in a time to come, but always already abides with us here, in the time of the now, in the ability for things as they are to be deactivated and rendered 'as not'. The capacity for the negation of existing states of affairs – which Agamben terms their 'impotentiality' – is not purely destructive: rather, it reveals in reserve the possible existence of alternative 'uses' and constructions of the infinitely divine world, whose providence is never 'used up' in the course of its development in a contingently finite and human form. This impotential quality of things thus coincides perfectly with their existential potentiality; their 'destituent power' resides permanently within them as a power of exigency, which makes discernible an excessive and 'unused' potential of worldly conditions to 'not be' such as they are, thereby opening up the possibility of alternative formations.[10] Messianic redemption therefore does not involve the institution of a new order, but rather involves an internal shifting of existing content in a movement which radically transforms the significance of the world as it is presently experienced. Indeed, it is not through the institution of a new world, but through a new use of *this* world that salvation will arrive, via a redeeming praxis with a deactivating consequence in its rendering inoperative of present operations.

Agamben's conception of a cause or a 'movement' that is immanent to history and manifest in practices of deactivation brings his understanding of social transformation quite close to the classical anarchism of William Godwin, whose *Political Justice* concerns a deconstructive notion of 'perpetual revisal' that 'places the subject in process and unfixes thinking from institution'.[11] It also approximates the theory of insurrection described by the libertarian anarchist thinker Max Stirner, for whom social change is best conceived as 'a rising of individuals, a getting up, without regard to the arrangements that spring from it'. For Stirner, revolt or insurrection differs from revolution in that it is not 'a fight against the established', culminating in the institution of 'a new arrangement', but is 'only a working forth of me out of the established. If I leave the established, it is dead and passes into decay.'[12] Indeed, Agamben affirms that Stirner's theses represent an 'ethical-anarchic interpretation of the Pauline *as not*'.[13] The salient feature of this interpretation is that, like Godwin and Paul, Stirner resists the politics of identification – that is, a politics of property or law, or of class – that conventionally attaches to the idea of 'vocation', or 'calling'. To have a vocation is, implicitly, to profess an identity on the basis of one's occupation: either individually in accordance with a set of defining properties or rules of inclusion; or collectively in concert with others, with whom one thereby forms an occupational class. Stirner revolts against any established form that makes a claim upon him and requires his identification.

For Marx in *The German Ideology*, Stirner's egoism presumes too much efficacy on the part of the individual who revolts, and so fails to understand the ways in which individuals are themselves nourished and sustained by social structures. However, Stirner's avoidance of a politics of identification, Agamben points out, is something Marxian thought has been unable to achieve, since for Marx the revolution as a practical activity that calls for the 'complete loss of man', produces a redemptive emancipation that 'can win itself only through the complete rewinning of man'.[14] Marxian philosophy prioritises social revolution over private revolt and insists that individual liberty can arise in conditions of equality only as the consequence of a suitable social organisation and revolutionary praxis in a moment of social action. This makes it susceptible to the problem of dogma: revolutionary change presumes a righteous 'class consciousness' capable of identifying and organising the moment of revolution. Even if the egalitarian, *classless* society projected by Marx and Engels can be interpreted as a secularisation of the Pauline paradigm of redemption, it remains the case that class identification is a prerequisite condition subtending the moment of social action that *then* gives birth to the universal nature of the 'classless society', within which individual liberty and equality may *then* become possible. As Proudhon and Bakunin had already perceived in the young Marx, this requirement of class identification as a preliminary step to the classless society troubles Marxist revolutionary thought with the (perhaps infinite) deferral of the 'complete loss of man'.

Thus, even if Agamben agrees with Marx that Stirner's lonely egoism is finally 'ridiculous', he nonetheless does not interpret the classless society as a secularisation of the Pauline paradigm of redemption, since this interpretation is deflected by Marx's theory of class-based revolution as a definitive step between capitalism and communism, between 'this world and the future world'. In fact, Agamben perceives a 'third interpretation', latent in the work of Taubes, Benjamin and Heidegger, which he calls 'anarchic-nihilistic'.[15] Unlike Stirner, who prioritises private revolt as an efficient cause of transformation – and unlike Marx, who prioritises the action of a revolutionary class in a public event of revolution – this interpretation 'plays on the absolute indiscernibility between revolt and revolution'.[16] Here, what is essential in the notion of transformative causation is not identification with a set of properties defining a class or a calling, but instead 'factical experience' and 'comportment' in 'the way worldly relations are lived'.[17] According to Agamben, this 'third interpretation' of the messianic movement finds a partial expression in Heidegger's dialectic of the proper and the improper, in which Being ceaselessly appropriates experiences and affects that bring it into relation with that which it is not, and simultaneously finds its given properties rendered inessential – or 'improper' – in its fundamental exposure to non-Being. This conceptual structure accordingly is taken up in Agamben's subsequent works, where Heidegger's emphasis on the role of appropriation undergoes an anarchic transvaluation in relation to the concept of 'use', which Agamben has already defined in *The Time That Remains* as 'the definition Paul gives to messianic life in the form of the *as not*'.[18] Revolutionary consciousness is something to use, and not to possess. Agamben eventually elaborates his account of the 'nihilistic' social practice of use in *The Highest Poverty*, providing a 'fourth interpretation' of the radical transformation signalled by Paul as an anarchic technique of redemption employed in and by a community. However, he must first explain why anarchy is at once the source of the states of exception that he has previously identified in the *Homo Sacer* volumes as characterising the operation of government, *and* anarchism is the promise of redemption or release from this powerful snare of exclusive-inclusion. This is the task to which he turns in *The Kingdom and the Glory*.

Government and glory

The Kingdom and the Glory sets out to understand why 'power in the West has assumed the form of an *oikonomia*: that is, a government of men'.[19] If secular power has its paradigm in divine rule and providence, then Agamben locates the structural operation of political authority in the original theological fracture that divides the transcendently divine *being* of power from the immanent *exercise* of that power in the management of worldly affairs. In Christian theology, this is the necessary fissure that separates the absolute and essential unity of the divine Being from his practical manifestation in the Holy Trinity.[20] Thus, power has an ontology and an economy, a being and a practice. Power is sovereign at the level of ontology; but divided in its managerial economy, or in practical administration. However, just as the sovereign divinity and the Holy Trinity are distinct and yet at the same time only refer to different aspects of the same entity, these two aspects of power are never really independent and self-sufficient. They always already rely upon each other for their efficacy, and must be combined in a 'governmental machine' that encompasses sovereignty as the rule of law, and government as the practice that puts law into effect: in fact, 'they are correlated and become fully intelligible only in their functional relation'.[21]

Agamben's anarchism crucially concerns the nature of this 'functional relation' between the powers of sovereignty and government, which causes them perpetually to 'refer back to each other for the solution of their aporias'.[22] They are aporetic because the governmental machine that articulates them as a functional unity expresses the working of an economic power that has no substantial foundation, but rather circulates between the various registers 'according to an essentially vicarious paradigm':[23] 'no figure of being is, as such, in the position of the *archē*'.[24] The governmental machine is void at its heart: a power without foundation; an empty throne. This is why, according to Agamben, it relies upon popular approval encouraged by techniques of glorification. The free consent of the people, who acclaim (as self-evident) the power they affirm and uphold, works to found political legitimacy by concealing power's anarchic basis or centre, making government appear natural and legitimate. All types of governmental machine – despotic, proletarian, democratic, liberal contractarian, corporate, and so forth – must contain and conceal the anarchy that resides constitutively at their heart. However, simultaneously, because the anarchy at their core is constitutive of their political operation, governments must also continually create the states of exception that sit at their anomial heart.[25] Governmental power does not simply oppose anarchy as an external condition of liberty, but rather relies upon anarchy for its being as such, and on freedom as its internal condition of legitimacy. This, then, is the complex double operation of consent and exception – glory and violence – that defines the governmental form, and which ultimately produces *homo sacer* as the paradigmatic subject of sovereign state power.

Agamben follows the classical anarchists in asserting that anarchy is the natural state of sociality – as the basis and horizon of the political – but he also warns about the 'problem of anarchy' inherent in the intimate nexus between anarchy and government. Nonetheless, for Agamben, this intimate relationship between anarchy and government 'does not mean that, beyond government and anarchy, it is not possible to think an Ungovernable, that is, something that could never assume the form of an *oikonomia*'.[26] The thought of 'the Ungovernable', the 'rethinking of the problem of anarchy', is precisely what Agamben returns to in the 'final paragraphs of Chapter 8', which he has already (wittily) identified in the preface as the 'hidden centre' of the book.[27] In these concluding remarks, he asks: 'is it possible to think inoperativity outside the apparatus of glory?', and he seeks an answer in the concept of 'eternal life',[28] referring us finally to the Spinozan notion of life considered '*sub species aeternite*' in Book V of *The Ethics*. For Agamben, the emphasis in this syntagm falls strictly on 'life' rather than on 'eternal'.[29] Thus, he explains, 'eternal' here 'does not have a merely temporal significance but designates a special quality of life',[30] which, as he has already explained in *The Time That Remains*, is the quality of a life lived 'as not'. Redemption 'means precisely to revoke and render inoperative at each instant every aspect of the life that we live, and to make the life for which we live [. . .] appear within it'.[31] This eternal 'life for which we live' is characterised by its 'ek-stasis', its potentiality or its essential freedom. It is life contemplated outside the constraints of the existing properties that define any particular factical form of life.[32] Accordingly, 'properly human praxis' is revealed as an inoperativity that, 'by rendering the specific functions of the living inoperative, opens them to possibility',[33] that is, to their potential for being 'as not' and, thus, for becoming otherwise. The special quality of eternal *life*, then, is its being 'marked by a special indicator of inoperativity', which renders it forever potential, indeterminate and renewable. The *operation* of exception and capture defining the governmental machine is thus contrasted with *inoperativity* 'as a properly human and political praxis';[34] and eternal life is 'the name of this inoperative centre of the human [. . .] that the machine of economy and glory ceaselessly attempts to capture within itself'.[35]

We can now see that Agamben's 'rethinking of the problem of anarchy' refers us back to that which he has previously named in *The Time That Remains* as the 'mystery of anomia',[36] and throughout *The Kingdom and the Glory* as the 'mystery of the *oikonomia*'. This mystery results from the essential ambiguity of free praxis: how, in the time of the now, will we use the constitutive groundlessness of our legal system – the essential anarchy of social forms? On the one hand, this fundamental indetermination may be appropriated 'Satanically', used for the glory and naturalisation of power.[37] On the other, it can be lived 'messianically', as a permanent praxis of inoperativity, towards the glorious beatitude of an eternally 'improper' life. These twin possibilities constitute the hidden mystery of free praxis: what will we make of the freedom that resides at the heart of every political machine, in the anarchic 'subjectivity'[38] of the lives it orders and governs? Will we use it to consent to government and its power of legislation, implicitly sanctioning 'the law of violence' that expresses the fundamental operation of 'exception' characteristic of the governmental machine? What reasons do we have for thinking societies can use their fundamental anomia constructively as 'anthropogenesis', to organise collective life outside of law and its associated identifications and assignments of property? Is it possible to organise social life such that *zoē* and *bios* may coincide perfectly according to a human capacity for acting freely in an ethical manner of 'mutual aid', or, if you like, in alignment with the divine providence of a world ordered by love, charity and grace? In these questions, we can perceive in Agamben a parallel with classical anarchist thinkers such as Kropotkin and Tolstoy, and the compelling questions they pose to humanity in anti-government works such as *Mutual Aid*, *The Kingdom of God Is Within You* and *The Law of Love and The Law of Violence*. In general, these parallels concern the crucial anarchist issue of the relationship between 'social regulation' and 'free praxis' in the self-organisation of an anomial political community. This issue, which is signalled at the end of *The Kingdom and the Glory*, is taken up as the focus of Agamben's subsequent work on the Franciscan fraternity as he investigates its 'regular life' of poverty used as a technology of salvation.

Property and poverty

The central concept of *The Highest Poverty* is *form-of-life*, which Agamben defines as 'a life that is linked so closely to its form that it proves to be inseparable from it'.[39] Everything hinges on the nature of this link: a life may be connected to its form – its organisational structure or rule – in terms of the set of properties it embodies and which thereby define it formally; but, alternatively, its form may result from the living practices it engages through its patterns of conduct, in the regular *uses* life establishes in relation to itself and the world. In the first case, the interpretive emphasis falls on the *form* that contains and rules life as a consequence of its properties; in the second conceptualisation, *life* is privileged as a practical *force* that establishes emergent formal orders by shaping habits. Thus, for Agamben, when it comes to understanding the nature of a form-of-life, 'it is first of all a matter of understanding the dialectic that [. . .] comes to be established between the two terms *rule* and *life*'.[40] His focus on the monastery as a microcosm for examining this dialectic is a consequence of his aim to conceptualise the directive force of a freely practised way of life and its potential to disrupt existing orders and produce new ones. This, for him, is the 'most precious legacy of Franciscanism':

> how to think a form-of-life, a human life entirely removed from the grasp of the law and a use of bodies and of the world that would never be substantiated into an appropriation [. . .] to think life as that which is never given as property but only as a common use.[41]

Agamben's thinking here is remarkably close to the ideas and arguments put forward by Proudhon in his work on property and on the philosophy of poverty. This affiliation is important in view of the longstanding antipathy that marked the relationship between Proudhon and Marx, since it offers a way of understanding Agamben's political thought as departing from the Marxist tradition in significant respects and not simply participating in it. Understanding Agamben's fidelity to key anarchist principles can shed light upon his original contribution to radical political philosophy and to the theories of social transformation emerging from the contemporary Left.

Proudhon was, like Marx, deeply repulsed by the effects of the 'bourgeois revolution' of July 1830 and by the hypocrisy he saw in a society ostensibly founded on ideals of liberty, equality and fraternity, which nonetheless entrenched the economic slavery of the working poor by its concentration, in the hands of the ruling rich, of the institution of private property and by its associated profiteering from the alienating extraction of wage labour. Tension between Marx and the anarchists was suppressed at first by the considerable agreement that united the socialist factions: although Marx always disputed aspects of Proudhon's economic philosophy, there is no doubt that Marx initially regarded Proudhon as a collaborator. The short review 'On Proudhon' in *The Holy Family*[42] clearly values Proudhon's ideas; here and in *The German Ideology*, Marx defends Proudhon against the attack of the Young Hegelians, principally Bruno and Edgar Bauer. Marx's early celebration of Proudhon's *What Is Property?* as 'the first resolute, pitiless and scientific examination' of 'private property taken in its entirety'[43] was redoubled by his subsequent request to Proudhon in 1846 that they might enter fruitfully into correspondence. This epistolary appeal, however, was met with a very guarded response: Proudhon's reply urges resistance to their becoming 'leaders of a new intolerance' by means of a revolutionary 'moment of action' aimed at installing a new political order.[44] Marx never replied in turn, and the relationship was irrevocably damaged when in 1847 Marx published *The Poverty of Philosophy*, which was a scathing and frequently misrepresentative critique of Proudhon's 1846 work, *The Philosophy of Poverty*.

Proudhon's *What Is Property?* famously insists that 'property is theft!' because it has no founding legitimacy. He demonstrates that it cannot be considered as a natural right;[45] or as arising from occupation;[46] or as founded in or justly sanctioned by civil law.[47] Neither, he argues, can labour act as 'the efficient cause of the domain of property'.[48] However, when Proudhon asks: 'When property is abolished, what will be the form of society? Will it be communism?',[49] his answer is firmly *no*. This is because he believes 'systematic communism', although ostensibly 'the deliberate negation of property, is conceived under the direct influence of the prejudice of property, and it is property that is to be found at the root of all communistic theories'. He elaborates: 'The members of a community, it is true, have no private property, but the community is proprietor, and proprietor not only of goods but of persons and wills.'[50] Communism expands the principle of private property to the public realm, and its result is the total capture of life under the rule of the collective property form. Proudhon's own 'dialectic' of social transformation does not oppose private property and equality to find their resolution in a higher (communist) form; instead, the social forms of both private property *and* communal ownership are negated by the idea of liberty.[51]

Proudhon investigates and develops this form of negation in his later work on the *Philosophy of Poverty* (which is firstly titled 'System of Economic Contradictions'). This work describes a dialectic of expropriation which proceeds not as a relation of tension between two actualities – two classes defined against each other in mutual opposition – but between an actual and its virtuality; between an actual social life defined by the institution of property, and the potential for its being made 'as not'. We see here, not a resolution or reconciliation of terms, but the absolute revocation of one economy – one form of life – by another.

Proudhon's scheme of social redemption thus contrasts strongly with Marx's revolutionary model, in which class conflict stemming from exploitation and private property is ultimately resolved in a condition of communism and collectivised property. According to Proudhon, anti-capitalist revolution necessarily involves the restoration of sociability by the abolition of property in all its forms, in favour of mobile practices of occupation or use (and for Proudhon as for the Franciscans, 'possession' for the purpose of use can 'never be substantiated into an appropriation'). Just as Agamben finds in monasticism and its practices of poverty a situation where 'both rule and life lose their familiar meaning in order to point in the direction of a third thing', which he seeks to 'bring to light',[52] Proudhon finds in anarchism a 'third form of society', in which both rule and life become transformed by their link with 'liberty'.[53] The force of liberty is, for Proudhon, an 'organising principle' of the coming sociability; in the *Philosophy of Poverty* we are led to understand how its effect is not the dialectical *synthesis* of property and equality in a new communal form, but is rather the absolute negation of *all* social forms 'prejudiced by property', clearing the way for a new economy of common use.

Although he found much to celebrate in Proudhon's early work Marx finds even more to fault in Proudhon's last work, *The Philosophy of Poverty*, going so far as to dismiss Proudhon's thinking as 'foggy'.[54] This is not only a criticism of Proudhon's admittedly opaque style of expression; nor is it simply a consequence of the problems he perceives in Proudhon's economic theory, or because he believes Proudhon is subscribing to an idealism of the worst sort when his work proceeds from the 'idea of liberty' as an organising principle of an imagined anarchist society (and thus, by failing to turn him on his head, Proudhon is uncritically adopting Hegel's worst traits). More crushingly, it is because he thinks Proudhon has misunderstood the very method of the dialectic, or has failed to articulate this movement successfully (and thus has neglected to retain from Hegel the conceptualisation of history as a process of oppositional struggle and the synthetic resolution of conflict in a higher form, a model Marx himself holds is essential for conceiving revolutionary politics).[55]

While Marx makes fun of Proudhon, perhaps the real joke here is actually on Marx, for he entirely fails to see that Proudhon is dancing to a different 'dialectical' choreography. As Proudhon disclosed in his letter to Marx, he himself 'put the problem this way: *to bring about the return to society, by an economic combination, of the wealth which was withdrawn from society by another economic combination*'.[56] Here we see Proudhon analysing social formations in a Spinozan way, in terms of their composing forces and their contrasting styles of 'economic combination'. As Paul Thomas explains, Proudhon regarded 'contradiction' as 'an opposition inherent in some of the forces constituting society, which will tear it apart unless we understand them'.[57] The dialectic employed by Proudhon in the *Philosophy of Poverty* proceeds by the critical revocation of certain problematic forces within a social economy (those bolstering the institution of property, in all its forms). These, he considers, are the source of its internal contradictions; and they cause the social structure as a whole to be unjust and unsustainable. This total revocation of property – that is, not of the social structure in its entirety but of a set of problematic elements within a social composition – opens up a potential for the partial and incremental renewal of the social structure itself: the abolition of all constitutive elements related to the economy of property frees stymied productive forces for the anarchic emergence of new and more socially harmonious combinations, while at the same time maintaining those aspects of the composition that already contribute positively to an egalitarian society. This, then, is a 'dialectical' process of sorts, but it is not Hegelian in its movement and it does not rely upon a revolutionary 'moment of action'. Transformation is propelled by the contradictions inherent to a formation and it proceeds as the perpetual decomposition and recomposition of forms: this is an ongoing collective activity justly guided by the social ideals of equality and harmony (and for Proudhon, such ideals cannot coexist with the institution of private property). For Proudhon, this endless destructive–creative process of free social organisation *is* anarchist society, and 'liberty' is its condition. In his critical demolition of *The Philosophy of Poverty*, Marx assumes that the only dialectic of note is Hegel's, or more precisely, the dialectical model he (Marx) has adopted from Hegel and transformed to conceive a historical materialism. Thus, Marx unwittingly repeats the same spurious criticism of Proudhon that, many years earlier, Hegel himself had expressed in his 'formidable misreading' of Spinoza.[58]

An implicit Spinozan spirit likewise infuses Agamben's *The Highest Poverty*.[59] This Spinozan influence is observable especially in his attention to the Franciscan notion that (God's) natural law is separate from (human) civil law, and indeed is primordial to it and alone constitutes an adequate idea of 'right' (according to necessity). This separation of natural and civil right, and the privileging of natural law, presupposes an idea of commonality in the 'doctrine of the originary communion of goods'.[60] For Spinoza, 'under nature everything belongs to all'.[61] According to the natural law perspective we find in Spinoza, all things in nature are available for *everyone* to *use* as a matter of necessity, as they strive to persevere in their being. It is only according to the legislative principles of civil society that the primordial common substance of nature is considered divisible and takes the form of private property. Thus, the ownership and the use of things are understood as really separate practices: natural law 'prescribes that everyone has the use of things necessary to their conservation, but does not obligate them in any way to ownership'.[62] What is genuinely common, then, is not ownership, but *use*, and 'the common use of things also genealogically precedes common or divided ownership of things, which derives only from human law'.[63] In their conscientious renunciation of the right to property, the Franciscans make a technical '*usus*' of poverty as a practice 'extraneous to the law',[64] meaning that they reject the determinations and divisions of the civil law of human society, and they live decisively according to that which Spinoza describes as the universal law of 'God, Substance or Nature'. In this way, 'they have renounced all property and every faculty of appropriating but not the natural right of use, which is, insofar as it is a natural right, unrenounceable'.[65] Their shared practice of 'poverty' as a religious renunciation of the right to property does not *identify* the community according to a rule of liturgical duty and observance,[66] but instead *organises* the community according to its way of living; its living practices. Thus, Agamben explains that, for the first time, what was in question in the movement was not the *rule* but the *life*, not the ability to profess this or that article of faith, but the ability to live in a certain way, to practice joyfully and openly a certain form of life.[67]

Accordingly, 'it is not a matter so much of applying a form (or norm) to life, but of *living* according to that form, that is of a life that, in its sequence, makes itself that very form, coincides with it'.[68] From this perspective, walking barefoot does not observe a rule, so much as it materialises 'a spiritual attitude' in a deliberate way of life.[69]

Two significant practical consequences emerge from Agamben's description of the separation of ownership and use in the practices of the Franciscan brotherhood. The first is a negative effect, associated with the renunciation of ownership. This is the praxis through which civil law is rendered inoperative, ineffectual in the light of willed poverty. The second is a positive effect, which emerges in the way shared practices of use can give consistency to a community. Agamben emphasises: '*usus* here no longer means the pure and simple renunciation of the law, but that which establishes this renunciation as a form and as a way of life'.[70] Thus, 'use' may be understood as a 'third term' 'with respect to law and life, potential and act, and could therefore have defined – not only negatively – the monk's vital practice itself, their form-of-life'.[71] In this case, the individual life lived messianically in the condition of being 'as not' is taken up in a community, which is then characterised by the non-appropriative use of things as a strategy of living-together. Resonating with classical anarchist thinking about the relationship between personal revolt and non-dogmatic social revolution, this strategy of socialist organisation combines individual and communal forms of praxis and thereby renders them indiscernible in transformative processes of social construction.

Threshold

Agamben's achievement, at the level of political thought, is to extend the anarchist critique of law and property to the germinal level of social ontology, characterised as 'a field of forces run through by two intensities that are opposed and, at the same time, intertwined'.[72] These two intensities of life and power intertwine where property first becomes 'political' in the form it provides to life. When, at the close of *The Highest Poverty*, Agamben asks: 'what is a life outside of the law, if it is defined as that form of life which makes use of things without ever appropriating them?',[73] the answer that emerges from analysis of his recent texts is that this life is, essentially, the *being of anarchy*. And when Agamben asks: 'And what is use, if one ceases to define it solely negatively with regard to ownership?',[74] the answer appears as the *practice of anarchism*. This anarchist 'form-of-life' is a social praxis in which *zoē* and *bios* – life and norm – are rendered indiscernible through conduct that negates powerful forms of property and propriety. This points to a way of thinking a political being that is void of juridical properties but is not a bare life subjected to sovereign power. Truly anomic being, life lived in the '"real" state of exception'[75] experiences the 'sweetness' of anarchic liberty.[76] However, Agamben's anarchism is not, as it is for Stirner, a practice of self-interest in a condition of lawlessness, but rather a strategy of expropriation and impropriety that is at once individual and collective, and renders the governmentality of law ineffectual or inoperative.

Agamben's reinterpretation of anarchist principles insulates them from the attacks directed by Marx against Stirner and Proudhon, restoring to anarchism its potential for use in the present, in the contemporary 'time of the now'. This differentiates Agamben from Marxist analyses of political transformation, which emphasise a revolutionary 'moment of action' that seizes upon the anomic crises produced by capitalism to usher in a redeemed form of society.[77] I have instead suggested that Agamben starts, not with the catastrophe of capitalism or with the state of legal exception that increasingly has become the norm in Western political formations, but rather with that basic anarchic potentiality which Benjamin refers to as the 'real state of exception'. This anomic void or fundamental indetermination provokes two alternative and perfectly coexisting possibilities. One is the catastrophic use of law and sovereignty to conceal the anarchic basis of political society. This, so far, is overwhelmingly the use we have made of our political potentiality, as is evidenced by the prevalence of legal states of exception and the alarming instances of lives rendered *homo sacer*. But the other, absolutely simultaneous possibility is anarchist liberty of the kind Proudhon celebrates, and which Agamben suggests we may find in 'the coming community' and in the mode of subjectivity he terms 'whatever'. Our redemption in this case lies precisely in a 'new use' we may make of the constitutive groundlessness of our political systems, such that political action no longer works to conceal and constrain this indetermination, but instead acknowledges it as the source of a constructive common politics of permanent renewal and reform. I wager that Agamben's writing is guided by an unframed or hidden question, which constitutes the secret heart of his political thought: 'what is anarchic potentiality today?' And in response, he provides answers that articulate innovative anarchist concepts: whatever being, the coming community, and form-of-life.

Notes

1. I owe very sincere thanks to Daniel McLoughlin and to James Martel. This chapter is dedicated in fond memory of Paul Nursey-Bray.
2. Giorgio Agamben, *The Time That Remains: A Commentary on the Letter to the Romans*, trans. Patricia Dailey (Stanford: Stanford University Press, 2005), p. 32.
3. Proudhon's influence led to the creation in 1864 of the First International Workingmen's Association as a broad-based group of socialist anarchists, whose constitution disavowed the need for an entrenched order of rules. Following the death of Proudhon in 1865, the First International rapidly became the scene of increasing factional conflict. Eventually, Marx drafted a set of rules and gained virtual control of the General Council established in London. At the Basel Congress of 1872, the Marxists expelled Bakunin and transferred the General Council to New York, beyond the reach of the anarchist factions, where it survived only two years until dissolving in 1874. The anarchists responded by creating a rival International, which likewise collapsed in 1877. See Paul Thomas, *Karl Marx and the Anarchists* (London: Routledge and Kegan Paul, 1980); George Woodcock, *The Anarchist Reader* (London: Fontana, 1977), pp. 40–2.
4. Giorgio Agamben, *The Signature of All Things: On Method*, trans. Luca D'Isanto with Kevin Attell (New York: Zone Books, 2009); Giorgio Agamben, 'What Is the Contemporary?', in *What Is an Apparatus? and Other Essays*, trans. David Kishik and Stefan Pedatella (Stanford: Stanford University Press, 2009), pp. 39–54.
5. Agamben, *The Time That Remains*, p. 3.
6. Agamben, *The Time That Remains*, p. 23 (original emphasis).
7. Agamben, *The Time That Remains*, p. 23.

8. Agamben, *The Time That Remains*, p. 24.
9. Agamben, *The Time That Remains*, p. 25.
10. Giorgio Agamben, 'What Is a Destituent Power?', trans. Stephanie Wakefield, *Environment and Planning D: Society and Space*, vol. 32 (2014), pp. 65–74.
11. Jared McGeough, '"So Variable and Inconsistent a System": Rereading the Anarchism of William Godwin's Political Justice', *Studies in Romanticism*, vol. 52, no. 2 (2013), p. 281; William Godwin, *An Enquiry Concerning Political Justice* (London: Robinson, 1793). See also George Crowder, *Classical Anarchism: The Political Thought of Godwin, Proudhon, Bakunin and Kropotkin* (Oxford: Oxford University Press, 1991).
12. Max Stirner, *The Ego and Its Own*, trans. Steven Byington (Cambridge: Cambridge University Press, 1995 [1907]), pp. 279–80.
13. Agamben, *The Time That Remains*, p. 32.
14. Karl Marx and Friedrich Engels, *Collected Works* (London: Lawrence & Wishart, 1975–), vol. 3, p. 186, quoted in Agamben, *The Time That Remains*, p. 30.
15. Agamben, *The Time That Remains*, p. 33.
16. Agamben, *The Time That Remains*, p. 33.
17. Agamben, *The Time That Remains*, p. 33.
18. Agamben, *The Time That Remains*, p. 26.
19. Giorgio Agamben, *The Kingdom and the Glory: For a Theological Genealogy of Economy and Government*, trans. Lorenzo Chiesa with Matteo Mandarini (Stanford: Stanford University Press, 2011), p. xi.
20. Agamben, *The Kingdom and the Glory*, p. 45.
21. Agamben, *The Kingdom and the Glory*, p. 51.
22. Agamben, *The Kingdom and the Glory*, p. 51.
23. Agamben, *The Kingdom and the Glory*, p. 138.
24. Agamben, *The Kingdom and the Glory*, p. 139.
25. Agamben, *The Kingdom and the Glory*, pp. 64–5. *State of Exception* tended to present the legal anomy as wilfully manufactured by the state apparatus, and so at this point in Agamben's thinking it appears that the state enjoys primacy over anarchy, and thus exercises supreme control over the lawlessness it creates and contains. However, in *The Kingdom and the Glory*, we are led to understand that the 'governmental machine' is fundamentally anarchic – indeed, that anarchy precedes the governmental form – and so the existence and operation of power in fact *depends* upon the anomy that is the consequence of the fracture between being and praxis, between sov-

ereignty and government. The manufactured state of exception now appears less as a deliberate exercise of power than it is a compulsive response to recreate the anarchic conditions of power's constitution. However, at the same time, the state of exception is manifestly an exercise in sovereign control, as an attempt by a state to assert its power in the face of anarchic chaos that threatens its order. While the constructed state of exception is the way in which states manage anarchy by capturing it within the legal apparatus as a radical exterior of sovereign law, other potential uses can be made of the fundamental anarchy that lies at the constitutive heart of social formations; it is to these alternative non-Statist and antinomian uses that Agamben turns in his works on the coming politics.

26. Agamben, *The Kingdom and the Glory*, p. 65.
27. Agamben, *The Kingdom and the Glory*, p. xiii.
28. Agamben, *The Kingdom and the Glory*, p. 247.
29. For an alternative reading of 'eternal life' according to Agamben, see Miguel Vatter, 'Eternal Life and Biopower', *New Centennial Review*, vol. 10, no. 3 (2011), pp. 217–47.
30. Agamben, *The Kingdom and the Glory*, p. 247.
31. Agamben, *The Kingdom and the Glory*, p. 248.
32. Agamben, *The Kingdom and the Glory*, p. 253. Giorgio Agamben, *The Coming Community*, trans. Michael Hardt (Minneapolis: University of Minnesota Press, 1993), p. 68, *passim*.
33. Agamben, *The Kingdom and the Glory*, p. 251.
34. Agamben, *The Kingdom and the Glory*, p. xiii.
35. Agamben, *The Kingdom and the Glory*, p. 251.
36. Agamben, *The Time That Remains*, p. 108.
37. Agamben, *The Time That Remains*, pp. 108ff.
38. Agamben, *The Kingdom and the Glory*, p. 251.
39. Giorgio Agamben, *The Highest Poverty: Monastic Rules and Form-of-Life*, trans. Adam Kotsko (Stanford: Stanford University Press, 2013), p. xi.
40. Agamben, *The Highest* Poverty, p. xi.
41. Agamben, *The Highest* Poverty, p. xiii.
42. Karl Marx and Friedrich Engels, *The Holy Family*, trans. Richard Dixon (Moscow: Foreign Languages Publishing House, 1956 [1845]).
43. Marx and Engels, *The Holy Family*, pp. 45–6.
44. George Woodcock, *Anarchism: A History of Libertarian Ideas and Movements* (London: Pelican, 1986), pp. 100–1.
45. Pierre-Joseph Proudhon, *What Is Property?*, trans. D. Kelly and

B. Smith (Cambridge: Cambridge University Press, 1994 [1840]), pp. 35ff.
46. Proudhon, *What Is Property?*, pp. 43ff.
47. Proudhon, *What Is Property?*, pp. 46ff.
48. Proudhon, *What Is Property?*, pp. 67ff.
49. Proudhon, *What Is Property?*, p. 189.
50. Proudhon, *What Is Property?*, p. 196.
51. Proudhon, *What Is Property?*, pp. 211–13.
52. Agamben, *The Highest Poverty*, p. xii.
53. Proudhon, *What Is Property?*, p. 212.
54. Karl Marx, *The Poverty of Philosophy* (New York: International Publishers, 1963 [1848]), p. 76.
55. In one of Marx's more grating attempts to discredit Proudhon and to treat him as an intellectual inferior, he claims that Proudhon had failed to learn adequately from his (Marx's) early efforts at tutelage: 'During my stay in Paris in 1844 I came into personal contact with Proudhon. I mention this here because to a certain extent I am also to blame for his "SOPHISTICATION": as the English call the adulteration of commercial goods. In the course of lengthy debates often lasting all night, I infected him very much to his detriment with Hegelianism, which, owing to his lack of German, he could not study properly.' This extraordinary obituary review, written around the time of Proudhon's death, continues on to diminish and infantilise Proudhon: 'For an estimate of his book [*The Philosophy of Poverty*], which is in two fat volumes, I must refer you to the refutation I wrote [*The Poverty of Philosophy*]. There I have shown, among other things, how little he had penetrated into the secret of scientific dialectics. [. . .] I show furthermore how extremely deficient and at times even schoolboyish is his knowledge of the "political economy" which he undertook to criticise [. . .] Proudhon had a natural inclination for dialectics. But as he never grasped really scientific dialectics he never got further than sophistry [. . .]' (Karl Marx, 'Letter to Johann Baptiste von Schweitzer', *Der Social Demokrat*, no. 16–18 (1 February 1865), available at <http://www.marxists.org/archive/marx/works/1865/letters/65_01_24.htm> (last accessed 1 May 2014).
56. Woodcock, *Anarchism*, p. 101 (original emphasis).
57. Thomas, *Karl Marx and the Anarchists*, p. 214.
58. Pierre Macherey, *Hegel or Spinoza*, trans. Susan Ruddick (Minneapolis: University of Minnesota Press, 2011), p. 11, *passim*. In this classic work, Macherey writes: '[I]t would be absurd to dis-

cover in Spinoza a rough draft or promise of a dialectic that is manifestly absent in his work. Nevertheless, this does not prevent us from beginning with Spinoza ourselves to be able to think of the dialectic anew [. . .] According to Hegel, Spinoza's thought is not yet dialectical enough. And what if it were too much – or at least, if it were so in a way that was unacceptable to Hegel?' (Macherey, *Hegel or Spinoza*, p. 12).

59. I am not suggesting that Agamben is untouched by Hegel or by dialectical materialism. I believe Agamben is indebted both to Spinoza and to Hegel, and his political complexion is ambivalently Marxist-anarchist. This accounts for his apparent oscillation, eloquently described by Jessica Whyte (*Catastrophe and Redemption: The Political Thought of Giorgio Agamben* (Albany: State University of New York Press, 2013)), between a Marxist accelerationism born of a deepening sense of catastrophe, and his tendency towards a more prudent anarchic vision of redemption in the tradition of Benjaminian messianism.
60. Agamben, *The Highest Poverty*, p. 112.
61. Baruch Spinoza, *Political Treatise*, trans. Samuel Shirley (Indianapolis: Hackett, 2000), pp. 299–300.
62. Agamben, *The Highest Poverty*, p. 123.
63. Agamben, *The Highest Poverty*, p. 133.
64. Agamben, *The Highest Poverty*, p. 122.
65. Agamben, *The Highest Poverty*, p. 115.
66. Giorgio Agamben, *Opus Dei: An Archaeology of Duty*, trans. Adam Kotsko (Stanford: Stanford University Press, 2013).
67. Agamben, *The Highest Poverty*, p. 93.
68. Agamben, *The Highest Poverty*, p. 99.
69. Agamben, *The Highest Poverty*, pp. 108, 118.
70. Agamben, *The Highest Poverty*, p. 142.
71. Agamben, *The Highest Poverty*, p. 142.
72. Agamben, *The Highest Poverty*, pp. xi–xii. See Mathew Abbott, *The Figure of this World: Agamben and the Question of Political Ontology* (Edinburgh: Edinburgh University Press, 2014).
73. Agamben, *The Highest Poverty*, p. 144.
74. Agamben, *The Highest Poverty*, p. 144.
75. Giorgio Agamben, *Homo Sacer: Sovereign Power and Bare Life*, trans. Daniel Heller-Roazen (Stanford: Stanford University Press, 1998), p. 55.
76. Agamben, *Homo Sacer*, p. 11. Agamben's thinking here is indebted to Walter Benjamin's notion of 'divine violence', as a non-sovereign

force of justice that relies upon a 'real state of emergency'. See especially Walter Benjamin, 'Theses on the Philosophy of History', in *Illuminations*, ed. Hannah Arendt (London: Pimlico, 1999), p. 248; Agamben, *State of Exception*, p. 58; and the discussion by Daniel McLoughlin, 'The Fiction of Sovereignty and the Real State of Exception: Giorgio Agamben's Critique of Carl Schmitt', *Law, Culture and the Humanities* (2013), pp. 1–20.
77. Cf. Whyte, *Catastrophe and Redemption*.

4

'Man Produces Universally': Praxis and Production in Agamben and Marx
Jessica Whyte

In *The Kingdom of the Glory*, in the midst of outlining what he sees as a specifically Christian account of governing as constant praxis, Giorgio Agamben turns his attention to a text that has preoccupied him for several decades: the *Economic and Philosophic Manuscripts* of Karl Marx. Beginning with his first book, *The Man without Content*, Agamben has repeatedly ignored Louis Althusser's suggestion that 'Marx's early works do not have to be taken into account'[1] and turned to the *Paris Manuscripts* in the course of formulating his own accounts of praxis and of history.[2] Indeed, references to Marx in Agamben's texts can be found as early as his first published essay, 'On the Limits of Violence',[3] in which he defends Marx from the charge that his radical transformation (or *Aufhebung*) of man and nature relies on a form of historical Darwinism 'which configures History as a linear progression of necessary laws, similar to the laws governing the natural world'.[4] These themes – non-linear history and 'human nature' – are ones to which Agamben returns repeatedly in subsequent decades. And, again and again, he is drawn to the *1844 Manuscripts*, in which he finds an account of praxis as that which 'founds the unity of man with nature, of man as natural being and man as *human* natural being'.[5]

When Agamben returns to Marx in *The Kingdom and the Glory*, however, he dismisses him in a mere paragraph as a thinker who has secularised the Christian conception of the being of creatures as divine praxis. As the theologian Augustine articulated this, the being of creatures utterly depends on the continuous praxis of God, to the point of being indistinguishable from it.[6] Referring to the *Economic and Philosophic Manuscripts*, in which the young Marx pronounced the 'rich, living, sensuous, concrete activity of self-objectification' to be the true essence of man,[7] Agamben writes:

After having conceived of being as praxis, if we take God away and put man in his place, we will consequently obtain the result that the essence of man is nothing other than the praxis through which he incessantly produces himself.[8]

Here, Marx stands accused of secularising a theological account of praxis: in conceiving the 'being of man as praxis and praxis as the self-creation of man',[9] Marx places man in the empty space of the creator God. More seriously, Agamben implicitly suggests that the early Marx secularises a Christian paradigm of the permanent government of the world: just as, for Augustine, creatures are dependent for their being on the constant operation of God, Agamben sees in Marx's account of praxis the secularisation of a paradigm marked by the constant activity of government.

How are we to understand this charge of secularisation? Hans Blumenberg[10] has distinguished a descriptive sense of the term 'secularisation' (associated with Max Weber) that refers simply to the view that the world has been stripped of transcendence and become more 'worldly', and a second sense, which makes a more specific claim, apparent in propositions like 'B is a secularised A' (revolutionary politics is a secularised eschatology, for instance). The view that Marx's thought is a secularisation of Jewish or Christian messianism, in this latter sense of the term, is hardly original. From Walter Benjamin's[11] positive assessment of Marx's classless society as a secularisation of messianic time to Leszek Kolakowski's[12] attack on Marxism as a caricature of religion which 'presents its temporal eschatology as a scientific system', these secularisation theses have tended to converge on the claim that the Marxist theory of history is a secularisation of an eschatological salvation history.

For Agamben, things are otherwise: the eschatology of salvation, he argues, is only one aspect of a far larger theological paradigm of the divine *oikonomia*. Thus, while Carl Schmitt infamously declared that 'all significant concepts of the modern state are secularised theological concepts',[13] Agamben suggests that this account of secularisation should be extended to economic concepts. And yet, 'this thesis according to which the economy could be a secularized theological paradigm acts retroactively on theology'[14] by showing that Christian theology itself conceived the history of humanity as an *oikonomia*, or a task of household administration, and was thus *originally* economic. It was this quotidian economic meaning, he argues, that was transferred into early Christianity, which made of the *oikonomia* 'an activity or task performed according to God's will'.[15] Rather than conceiving secular concepts as deriving from theological ones, Agamben's suggestion is that Christianity takes up the secular vocabulary of the Aristotelian household, and the *oikonomia* of early Christianity should therefore be conceived not as a divine plan, but as 'the fulfillment of a task of domestic administration'.[16]

Although Agamben identifies Adam Smith's account of the 'invisible hand' as the moment the Christian *oikonomia* was transferred to modern economics, the *economy* with which he is principally concerned is the 'economy of salvation' of Christian theology. This raises questions about the specificity of 'the economy' whose genealogy Agamben seeks to provide, especially as he situates his account of economic theology in the context of what he terms the 'current triumph of economy and government over every other aspect of social life'.[17] As Ellen Meiksins Wood has noted, it was the classical political economists who 'discovered the "economy" in the abstract and began emptying capitalism of its social and political content'.[18] In contrast, in his late works, Marx sought to analyse not 'the economy', but the specificity of *capitalist* social relations. In this chapter, I examine Agamben's argument that Marx secularised a Christian account of the Being of creatures as divine praxis, and highlight the extent to which this is bound up with a larger critique of the metaphysics of the will. This focus on the will as a central category of the economy, I argue, reveals the limitations of Agamben's account of secularisation for understanding the current 'triumph of the economy'.[19] The form of compulsion that typifies a *capitalist* economy differs significantly from that which characterised the 'despotic' relations between master and slave in the Aristotelian *oikos*. To grasp the 'silent compulsion of economic relations' under capitalism, Marx therefore had to leave the terrain of Feuerbach's secularised Christianity, on which the *1844 Manuscripts* unfold, and develop a critique of political economy.

Early Agamben on early Marx

In his first book, *The Man without Content*, Agamben provides the most succinct formulation of the position that is central to all of his later critiques of Marx: 'Marx thinks of man's being as production.'[20] *The Man without Content* contains what remains Agamben's most sustained engagement with Marx's thought. This is perhaps surprising, given that this work is devoted to a theme that is far from Marx's central preoccupations: the nihilism of modern aesthetics. The importance of Marx becomes clearer, however, when Agamben situates his work in the context of a broader argument that, in modernity, the border between three distinct forms of human activity (praxis, *poiesis* and labour) has been lost, and all human doing has been reinterpreted simply as an expression of *the will*. Here, Agamben draws heavily on Hannah Arendt's account of the modern valorisation of labour, which the Greeks had considered a 'curse' because it tied the labourer to necessity and the biological life process.[21] Marx, Agamben writes, is the thinker for whom labour becomes the 'expression of man's very humanity'.[22] Yet Marx, on this account, is not only the thinker who defines man's being as production – he is also the thinker for whom '[p]roduction means praxis, "sensuous human activity"'.[23] From Hegel's *Phenomenology of Spirit* onwards, Agamben argues, post-Hegelian thinkers have been faced with the problem of mediating between the universal concept of man and particular, sensuous men. *Gattungwesen*, or species being, he suggests, is the concept through which this mediation has been attempted. Although the term 'Gattungwesen' appeared in Hegel's *Encyclopedia*, it referred there 'to the "natural" component of human life, in particular its sexual and reproductive aspects'.[24] In the hands of Ludwig Feuerbach, however, this term became central to formulating a principle of collective essence that broke with the atomised individual of the Christian personalism of his time.[25] On Agamben's reading, when Marx takes up the idea of a generic or species-being, he conceives it not as 'a common naturalistic character inertly underpinning individual differences' but as praxis – 'free and conscious activity'.[26] Thus, as Agamben writes, the 'middle term, which constitutes man's genus [. . .] is for Marx, praxis, productive human activity'.[27] Turning to Marx's account of the specificity of *human* praxis, Agamben notes that while the animal is at one with its vital activity, the human, for Marx, makes of it a means to its existence. 'He produces not unilaterally but universally.'[28]

Here, once more, Agamben follows Arendt, who writes: 'For Marx labor is the uniting link between matter and man, between nature and history.'[29] Consequently, Agamben writes – prefiguring his later critique of Marx's secularisation of Christian *oikonomia*

– man frees himself of the creator God and of nature and 'posits himself in the productive act, as the origin and nature of man'.[30] In this context, Agamben is more positive about this originary praxis, which he frames as the foundation of history, through which the human essence becomes nature and nature becomes human. This is important given Agamben's own (very un-Arendtian) concern with overcoming the split between human and animal, *oikos* and *polis*, nature and history. On this account, Marx appears as a thinker who overcomes the constitutive divisions that have resulted in what Agamben sees as the abandonment of bare life.[31] Ultimately, however, Agamben's judgement is that Marx provides an account of the human that remains metaphysical: 'although he locates praxis in man's original dimension,' Agamben writes, 'Marx does not think the essence of production beyond the horizon of modern metaphysics'.[32] For, if we ask what distinguishes human praxis from the vital activity of animals, Marx's answer in the *1844 Manuscripts*, Agamben suggests, refers back to a metaphysics of will: 'Man makes of his vital activity itself the object of his *will* and his *consciousness*.'[33] Thus, if we accept, with Nietzsche, that a 'person who *wills* – commands something inside himself that obeys',[34] then Marx, according to this reading, re-establishes the cleavage between inert life and commanding will within each individual.

Given this critique of Marx's productivism and metaphysics of will, it is surprising that when Agamben returns to the question of Marx's theory of praxis in *Infancy and History*, less than ten years later, he echoes Martin Heidegger's remark that 'the Marxist concept of history is superior to any other historiography'.[35] In this book, devoted to reconceptualising history and temporality, Agamben stresses that, for Marx, praxis is man's original historical dimension – it is that which makes him a *Gattungswesen*. Having previously charged Marx with remaining trapped within metaphysics, Agamben now seeks to clear him of such charges. In opposition to Theodor Adorno's insistence on dialectical mediation between base and superstructure, Agamben argues that this relies on a causal understanding of their relation, which presupposes the sundering of reality into two different levels. Pre-empting his later critique of economic theology, he writes:

> A materialism which conceived of economic factors as *causa sui* and first principle of everything, in the same way in which the God of

metaphysics is *causa sui* and first principle of everything, would only be the obverse of metaphysics, not its rout.[36]

Far from attributing such a position to Marx, Agamben argues 'an interpretation of this relationship in a causal sense is not even conceivable in Marxist terms'. Against every vulgar interpretation of cause and effect, he suggests, we should set Marx's account of praxis as 'a concrete and unitary source reality'.[37]

This account of Marx's praxis is worth quoting at some length:

> If man finds his humanity in praxis, this is not because, in addition to carrying out productive work, he also transposes and develops these activities within a superstructure (by thinking, writing poetry, etc.); if man is human – if he is a *Gattungswesen*, a being whose essence is generic – his humanity and his species-being must be integrally present within the way in which he produces his material life – that is within his praxis.[38]

Here, in contrast to his earlier indictment of Marx's metaphysical splitting of praxis and will, Marx appears as the thinker who 'abolishes the metaphysical distinction between *animal* and *ratio*, between nature and culture, between matter and form'[39] through a theory of praxis for which man's humanity is immediately present in the way he produces his conditions of life.

In Agamben's earliest engagements with Marx, we find the earliest elaborations of his critiques of productivism (or what he will later call *operativity*), the will and historicism. It is, at least in part, by working through Marx's early thought that Agamben develops the specificity of his own account of politics. In these early readings, however (readings that pre-date Agamben's explicitly political *Homo Sacer* series by decades), we find him oscillating between an Arendtian critique of the valorisation of biological life in philosophies of labour and an enthusiasm for a model of praxis in which life would be inseparable from its form. On the one hand, Marx is portrayed as a biopolitical thinker who sunders biological life from consciousness and makes of man's vital activity the object of his will. On the other, he is celebrated for overcoming the metaphysical separation of animality and humanity through a conception of praxis that 'from the beginning possesses wholeness and concreteness'[40] and so resists ontological splitting. In the following section, I turn to Agamben's more recent theorisations of praxis and will. In doing so, however, I seek to show that Marx's thought poses challenges to the way in which Agamben seeks to resolve the problems of operativity and the compulsion to labour, and that these problems cannot be resolved on the terrain of the *1844 Manuscripts*. Because he inadequately theorises the problem of capitalism, I argue, Agamben is unable to bring to fruition his critique of operativity and will.

Quia voluit: because he willed it

Although Agamben's most substantial engagements with Marx's *1844 Manuscripts* are found in his own earliest works, the question of praxis has become ever more central to his project. Indeed, as Agamben has turned his attention from sovereignty to government, he has also focused on what he views as a decisive ontological transformation Christianity has brought in our understanding of the relation between praxis and being. In brief, Agamben's contention is that two distinct paradigms emerge from Christian theology and continue to shape both the theory and the practice of politics. The first, 'political theology', gives rise to political philosophy and the theory of sovereignty. The second, to which his recent works are devoted, is what he terms 'economic theology': an economic or governmental strand of Christianity in which he finds a crucial precursor to contemporary non-juridical governmental practices. While the former is a paradigm of transcendence (the transcendent God or sovereign), the latter is a paradigm of the immanent ordering, or government, of life. The central concern of *The Kingdom and the Glory* is to discover why power, in the West, 'has taken the form of an *oikonomia*, that is, a government of men'.[41] In answering this question, Agamben is drawn not to the Christian pastorate, in which Michel Foucault[42] had located the emergence of a specifically governmental form of power, but to the debates between the early Church Fathers that led to the construction of the doctrine of the Trinity.

The problem that faced early Christianity, Agamben suggests, was how to reconcile a transcendent God with the immanent government of the world. In attempting such a reconciliation, it was necessary to steer carefully between two heretical reefs: the Gnostic gulf between transcendence and immanence, which manifested in the belief in both an absent creator God and an evil demiurge, and the pantheistic collapse of transcendence into immanence. The administrative paradigm of the *oikonomia*, Agamben suggests, becomes central to the formulation of the Trinity, as the Church Fathers attempt to steer this course. In distinguishing between the three hypostases of God, they overcame the threat of polytheism by situating this distinction at the level of praxis rather than being. In the words of the early father Tertullian: 'The Father and the Son are two, and this not as a result of separation of substance, but as a result of an economic disposition.'[43] In locating the separation between the Father and the Son (who governs the world on the Father's behalf) at the level of praxis, not being, Agamben argues, the Fathers succeeded in preserving the unity of the divine being; '[t]he caesura that had to be averted at all costs on the level of being re-emerges, however, as a fracture between God and his action, between ontology and praxis.'[44] In contrast to the Aristotelian God, or prime mover, who moves the celestial spheres simply because it is his nature to do so, the Christian *oikonomia* is 'a praxis unanchored to any ontological necessity'.[45] Economic theology, as Agamben sees it, is therefore a form of governmental praxis lacking a foundation in being.

If we now return to Agamben's claim that 'in thinking the being of man as praxis, and praxis as the self-production of man' Marx secularised the theological idea of the being of creatures as divine operation, it may at first seem that this simply reiterates the earlier critique of Marx's alleged productivism in a theological key.[46] However, those earlier critiques of Marx were framed in the terms of *classical ontology* and pursued using Aristotelian categories. As late as the essay 'The Work of Man', Agamben could argue that 'the thought of Marx, which seeks the realization of man as a generic being (*Gattungswesen*), represents a renewal and radicalization of the Aristotelian project'.[47] In contrast, Agamben's more recent critique situates Marx in the context of what he sees as the *new ontology* of praxis bequeathed by Christianity. Thus, in commenting that, in Marx's *Paris Manuscripts*, 'the essence of man is nothing other than the praxis through which he incessantly produces himself',[48] Agamben connects Marx to a Christian theological belief in God as a being of ceaseless operation – a being who is not only substance but the praxis of governing the world.

We get a sense of what Agamben sees as these two distinct ontologies (one Greek and one Christian) in a work by Thomas Aquinas, whose title *Of God and his Creatures*[49] bears directly on Agamben's critique of Marx. In a chapter devoted to demonstrating that God is 'the origin of creatures', Aquinas distinguishes the perspective of the philosopher from that of the Christian by noting that, in contrast to the philosopher's concern with 'what attaches to them in their proper nature' (the question of being), the Christian 'considers about creatures only what attaches to them in their relation to God, as that they are created by God, subject to God, and the like'.[50] Directly relating his account of the second ontology to political sovereignty, Aquinas argues that the order of effects must be proportionate to the order of causes; thus, just as 'the king is the universal cause of government in his kingdom, over the officials of the kingdom, and also over the officials of individual cities', there must be some cause of that being which is common to all creatures.[51] As pure being, Aquinas responds, God is the *cause* of the being of all creatures, who are, in turn, His effects, or the result of His operation. As Agamben stresses, in Augustine's account, not only does the being of creatures entirely depend on a governmental praxis – 'it is, in its essence, praxis and government'.[52]

For the ancients, who naturalise potentiality by deriving praxis directly from being, 'there is no need to presuppose the existence of a special will or a specific activity aimed at the care of the self or the world'.[53] In contrast, in treating God as the cause and creatures as effects, Aquinas stresses that God acts not by physical necessity but by free will: 'whoever does some and leaves out others of the things that he can do, acts by choice of will and not by physical necessity', he writes.[54] God creates not as an expression of his being but gratuitously. Once God's praxis was separated from his being, Agamben argued, this led to the heretical question of *why* he created the world, if it was not simply in his nature to do so: '*quia voluit*', was the answer provided by Augustine: because he willed it.[55] Once praxis is conceived as free, rather than as a necessary expression of one's nature, the will, Agamben argues, is the apparatus that is necessary to link praxis and being together again. The 'primacy of the will' in contemporary thought 'has its roots in the fracture between being and acting in God and is, therefore, from the beginning in agreement with the theological *oikonomia*'.[56] The will of God is the attempt to find a foundation for anarchic divine praxis: God created the world because He willed it, and thus all creation is conceived instrumentally as material to be manipulated by a sovereign will.[57]

This can help us to understand more fully the stakes in Agamben's critique of Marx for turning man's vital activity into the object of his will. In retaining the split between activity and will, Marx, according to this critique, replicates this command structure within each individual. The consequences of this become clearer in Aquinas's commentary on the text of Aristotle, *De Anima* (On the Soul),[58] which Agamben views as marking the 'decisive moment' in which 'bare life as such' was identified in the history of Western philosophy.[59] In that text, Aristotle sets out to determine what it means to say that something – whether a plant, an animal or a human – is alive; 'For living beings', he writes, 'Being is life.'[60] To this end, Aristotle establishes a series of divisions, in the continuum of life, between what he terms nutritive, sensitive, appetitive, locomotive and intellectual life. For Aquinas, it is a short step from this to conceiving the will as the only properly human function, which rules over the body just as God subjects his creatures to his will. '[I]n every mere man', Aquinas writes, 'the operations of the elemental body and of the vegetative soul are distinct from the will's operation, which is properly human [. . .] The operations of the sensitive and nutritive parts are not strictly human.'[61] At stake in this is the transformation of human potentiality into brute vital power, subjected to the command of a transcendent will.

Bringing our essence back to earth: on Feuerbach

For Agamben to suggest that Marx of the *1844 Manuscripts* secularises a theological conception of praxis may at first seem surprising, given the extent to which the *Manuscripts* were written under the influence of the materialism of Ludwig Feuerbach, for whom man projects his own essence onto an exterior power that he calls God, which then subjects him to its government and command. 'The Divine Being', as Feuerbach famously wrote, 'is nothing other than the being of man himself.'[62] In the will of God, Feuerbach saw a projection of our own moral nature, which we then treat as an external obligation to which we are obedient and enthralled. As Warren Breckman[63] has noted, like his Young Hegelian contemporaries, Feuerbach was deeply engaged in a struggle against Christian personalism and its affirmation of the link between God, monarch and egoistic atomised property owner. For Feuerbach, then, the omnipotent God was not only a projection of the human essence – it was the projection of an *egoistic* conception of the human that reflected the decline of ancient political life.

In an early text, Feuerbach noted that while the Greeks and the Romans had sought immortality in the posterity of their actions in the public sphere, the collapse of the Greek *polis* and the Roman Republic led newly atomised individuals to project themselves *out* of the world.[64] These individuals were unsatisfied with a worldly personhood in which their supposedly unique individuality was, in Feuerbach's words, 'restricted on all sides, determined, oppressed, depressed and bothered by all kinds of conditions and painful qualities that contaminate and tarnish it'.[65] Thus, these atomised individuals established a second, unrestricted life, 'a life that is lived out in an element as bright and transparent as the purest crystal water'.[66] Although this direct political context is absent from *The Essence of Christianity*, Feuerbach continues to argue that God's will is not a projection of the real, restricted human will, but a fantasy: 'the will of the imagination – the absolute subjective, unlimited will'.[67] Thus, while Feuerbach sees the creator God as a projection of our own productive natures, in the doctrine of creation *ex nihilo* he sees a projection of a human subjectivity that makes Nature 'merely the servant of his will and needs, and hence in thought also degrades it to a mere machine, a product of the will'.[68] Notably Feuerbach overcomes this egoism by complementing the will with love and reason, to provide a Trinitarian account of the human essence. The 'divine trinity in man, above the individual man', he writes, 'is the unity of reason, love, and will'.[69] Here the Christian *oikonomia* comes down to earth, where it is revealed as the very essence of man.

Agamben's charge that, in the *1844 Manuscripts*, Marx secularises a theological conception of the human was prefigured more than a century and a half earlier in Max Stirner's critique of Feuerbach's 'thoroughly theological'[70] liberation of humanity from religion. In Feuerbach's account of God as a projection of the human essence, Stirner sees simply a redesignation, whereby what was formerly called 'God' is now 'our essence'. Feuerbach, Stirner charges, 'clutches at the total substance of Christianity, not to throw it away, no, to drag it to himself, to draw it, the long-yearned-for, ever-distant, out of its heaven with a last effort, and keep it by him forever'.[71] As Althusser puts it, Stirner's charge is that Feuerbach does not get beyond the limits of religion, but simply 'replaces God with himself in calling Him Man'.[72] At the hands of Stirner, Althusser argues, 'Man' was 'dealt a mortal blow'. No longer would 'Man' and 'Humanism' appear as the real, the concrete; rather, 'Man and Humanism were the stuff of priests' tales, a moral ideology of an essentially religious nature, preached by a petty-bourgeois in laymen's dress.'[73]

It was on the basis of his own reading of Feuerbach's rational theology that Marx developed his early insights into the alienation and instrumentalisation of human potentiality. In the *1844 Manuscripts*, Marx analysed the way in which, under capitalism, our own activity takes on objective form (as capital) and becomes an independent power hovering over us. 'Capital', or stored-up past labour, as Marx puts it, 'is thus the *governing power* over labour and its products.'[74] Thus while Feuerbach argues that '[i]n order to enrich God, man must become poor',[75] Marx locates this poverty in the structure of alienated labour: 'The worker becomes all the poorer the more wealth he produces, the more his product increases its power and range.'[76] Under capitalism, human praxis creates a powerful, alien, objective world that lurks over the individual worker. In Marx's words, 'the life which he has conferred on the object confronts him as something hostile and alien'.[77] What is alienated, according to the *1844 Manuscripts*, is no longer simply a product of the human mind but the products that are the result of a labour process. Yet, as Althusser stresses, what Marx retains of the Feuerbachian schema is the view that the 'human essence' can be disclosed in its object, and that there remains a privileged object 'that constitutes a compendium of the human essence'.[78]

In the *1844 Manuscripts*, Marx tends to portray the alienation that is inherent to capitalist labour as *analogous* to the religious alienation identified by Feuerbach. Thus, after describing the impoverishment of the worker's inner world as he creates an objective world outside himself, Marx writes: it is 'the same in religion. The more man puts into God, the less he retains in himself.'[79] If Agamben is able to situate his own thought within what he terms 'an integrated Marxian analysis',[80] this is in no small part because of the extent to which he takes up the early Marx's analogy between religious and worldly separation. Not only does Agamben define *sacrifice* as an apparatus of separation, but he depicts law, politics, praxis and even capitalism as marked by a form of separation whose model is religious: 'capitalism, in pushing to the extreme a tendency already present in Christianity', he writes, 'generalizes in every domain the structure of separation that defines religion'.[81] By modelling worldly separations on religious ones, Agamben takes up a Marxian inheritance that remains Feuerbachian.

Within a year of the *1844 Manuscripts*, however, Marx brought the critique of heaven down to earth and replaced this analogical account of religious and productive alienation with the argument that the separation of the secular and the theological world can only be understood on the basis of 'the inner strife and intrinsic contradictoriness of this secular basis'.[82] It was only by overcoming the alienation and instrumentalisation of human capacities in the labour process, he now argued, that these powers could be returned to human beings. This means that Marx ultimately criticised Feuerbach's attempt to resolve the religious essence into the human essence, both because his focus on overcoming false ideas was insufficient for overcoming the real alienation of capitalist society, and because it presupposes an overly abstract and ahistorical account of the human essence. The 'essence of man is no abstraction inherent in each single individual',[83] Marx writes in his sixth thesis on Feuerbach. 'In reality it is the ensemble of social relations.'

Here, he criticises Feuerbach for abstracting from the historical process and inadequately breaking with the presupposition of the atomised individual. On the basis of such abstraction from history, and from society, Feuerbach, Marx argues, can regard man's essence 'only as "species", as an inner, mute, general character which unites the many individuals *in a natural way*'.[84] For Marx, there is no essence innate in each individual. He thus criticises Feuerbach for failing to see that both the religious sentiment and the isolated individual are social products, and for his insufficiently critical attitude to *this* world. The Young Hegelians, Marx and Engels argued in *The German Ideology*, see in history only spectacular events, and religious and theoretical struggles. They forget that the root of religious 'fancies' lies in real material conditions, and ultimately, for them, 'the *theatrum mundi* is confined to the Leipzig book fair'.[85] To Feuerbach's 'contemplative materialism' Marx famously opposes a 'practical materialism', which, in the words of the famous thesis eleven, seeks to *change* the world rather than merely interpret it.[86]

A 'major epistemological blockage': on the concept of labour

Agamben's analytical reliance on an account of separation modelled on the relation of heaven to earth can help us to understand why, while he criticises the early Marx's account of praxis, he repeatedly returns to the *1844 Manuscripts*, to the exclusion of Marx's later works, and explicitly rejects Althusser's suggestion that the works of the early Marx should be abandoned. Nonetheless, there are aspects of Althusser's critique of the early Marx that not only prefigure much of the critique that Agamben will later direct at the *Paris Manuscripts*, but also break with the lingering reliance on secularised Christianity that informs that work's account of praxis. Of all the concepts that Althusser sees as evidence of 'idealist blackmail' and 'unbearable, if not criminal demagoguery',[87] he singles out a concept that has been taken to be central to Marxist thought: labour. The 'concept of labour', he writes, '*is not a Marxist concept*'.[88] Althusser goes further than Agamben in rejecting 'all the ideologies of labour' whether they take their starting point from the *1844 Manuscripts* or set out to produce a 'phenomenology of "praxis"'.[89] The language of project, praxis and creation, Althusser argues, is a form of spiritualist idealism – 'the most reactionary form of idealism because it is craven enough to model itself on religion'.[90]

Marx's theoretical innovation in the *1844 Manuscripts*, Althusser argues, was to introduce the concepts of labour and history into Feuerbach's conceptual schema – the former from Smith; the latter from Hegel. The ultimate consequence of this union of classical political economy, the Hegelian dialectic and a humanist theory of history as the alienation and disalienation of man was, in Althusser's view, a great theoretical impasse; moreover, the concept of labour was 'a major epistemological blockage'.[91] As is well known, Althusser's view is that Marx would not overcome this impasse until 'the break' in 1845. 'Marx's whole critique of classical Political Economy', he writes, 'consisted in exploding the concept of *labour* accepted by the Economists' in order to replace it with a new set of concepts, including 'labour process', 'labour power (not labour)', 'abstract labour', etc.[92]

Here, I do not wish to enter into the voluminous debate about this supposed break, except to suggest that Althusser is right to note that the Marx of *Capital* had become critical of abstractions such as 'labour' and 'production' because they obscure and naturalise the specificity of capitalist labour and the capitalist mode of production. Indeed, such a position was central to Marx's critique of the classical political economists, who presented a historically specific figure of the human as 'the Natural Individual appropriate to their notion of human nature, not arising historically but posited by nature'.[93] By the time of the *Grundrisse* (1857–8), Marx had isolated the object of his investigation, which he defined as *'material production'*[94] – that is, individuals producing in a specific form of society. The point Marx stresses is that '[a]ll production is appropriation of nature on the part of an individual within and through a specific form of society.'[95] The labour of the slave is not the labour of the serf or the labour of the proletarian, and none can be viewed as the essence of man. Although 'labour' appears to be a simple category, Marx notes in the introduction to the *Grundrisse*, the abstract category 'labour' presupposes a developed totality of real kinds of labour, and a form of society in which individuals are not bonded to a single form of labour but 'can with ease transfer from one labour to another', making the specific kind of labour a matter of chance, or indifference.[96]

Seen from this perspective, Marx's early account of labour in the *1844 Manuscripts* can be seen to obscure the specificity of labour under capitalism. What is definitive of labour under capitalism is *not* that the labourer is subjected to the will of another, but that he or she is subjected to the impersonal domination of capital: 'the rule of past, dead labour over the living'.[97] As Marx put it, '[t]he silent compulsion of economic relations sets the seal on the domination of the capitalist over the worker'.[98] This does not mean that direct force becomes unnecessary, or that relations of coercion – slavery, for instance – disappear. And yet, as Wood notes, under capitalism, 'it is the "autonomous" laws of the economy and capitalism "in the abstract" that exercise power, not the capitalist willfully imposing his personal authority upon labour'.[99] Agamben's deconstruction of the metaphysics of will inherited from Christianity tends to conflate the paradigmatic figure of the slave of the Aristotelian *oikos*, who is subjected directly to the master's will, with the contemporary labourer in a capitalist economy. Thus, it leaves untouched the specifically economic compulsion of capitalism that the late Marx sought not only to understand but also to overthrow.

Agamben seemed to recognise this several years before *The*

Kingdom and the Glory, when he turned to analyse the specificity of *capitalist* labour, in *The Time That Remains*, and singled out what 'Marx presents as the redemptive function of the proletariat'.[100] Not only does the proletariat incarnate the contingency of every specific vocation, or form of labour, he wrote there, but the proletariat is 'only able to liberate itself through autosuppression'.[101] Agamben's development of Marx's account of this revolutionary self-negating proletarian subject as the model for the subject that could break with the homogenous time and deferred redemption of the Christian *oikonomia* is a topic for a further investigation.

Notes

 1. Louis Althusser, 'Lenin and Philosophy', in *Lenin and Philosophy and Other Essays*, trans. Ben Brewster (London: NLB, 1971), p. 35.
 2. According to Louis Althusser, 'The Humanist Controversy', in *The Humanist Controversy and Other Writings*, ed. François Matheron, trans. G. M. Goshgarian (London: Verso, 2003), p. 258, 'the *1844 Manuscripts* is, theoretically speaking, one of the most extraordinary examples of a total theoretical *impasse* that we have'.
 3. This essay was originally published in Italian in 1970 in the literary journal *Nuovi argomenti*.
 4. Giorgio Agamben, 'On the Limits of Violence', trans. Lorenzo Fabbri, *diacritics*, vol. 29, no. 4 (2009), p. 106.
 5. Giorgio Agamben, *The Man without Content*, trans. Georgia Albert (Stanford: Stanford University Press, 1999).
 6. Giorgio Agamben, *The Kingdom and the Glory: For a Theological Genealogy of Economy and Government*, trans. Lorenzo Chiesa with Matteo Mandarini (Stanford: Stanford University Press, 2011), p. 90.
 7. Karl Marx, *Economic and Philosophic Manuscripts of 1844*, trans. Martin Milligan (Amherst: Prometheus Books, 1988), p. 163.
 8. Agamben, *The Kingdom and the Glory*, p. 91.
 9. Agamben, *The Kingdom and the Glory*, p. 91.
10. Hans Blumenberg, *The Legitimacy of the Modern Age*, trans. Robert Wallace (Cambridge, MA: The MIT Press, 1999), pp. 1–4.
11. Walter Benjamin, 'Paralipomena to "On the Concept of History"', in *Selected Writings, Volume 4: 1938–1940*, trans. Howard Eiland et al., ed. Howard Eiland and Michael W. Jennings (Cambridge,

MA: Harvard University Press, 2003), p. 401.
12. Leszek Kolakowski, *Main Currents of Marxism: Its Origin, Growth and Dissolution, Vol. 3: The Breakdown*, trans. P. S. Falla (Oxford: Clarendon Press, 1978), p. 526.
13. Carl Schmitt, *Political Theology: Four Chapters on the Concept of Sovereignty*, trans. George Schwab (Cambridge, MA: The MIT Press, 1988), p. 36.
14. Agamben, *The Kingdom and the Glory*, p. 3.
15. Agamben, *The Kingdom and the Glory*, p. 17.
16. Agamben, *The Kingdom and the Glory*, p. 23.
17. Agamben, *The Kingdom and the Glory*, p. 1.
18. Ellen Meiksins Wood, *Democracy against Capitalism* (Cambridge: Cambridge University Press, 1995), p. 19.
19. Agamben, *The Kingdom and the Glory*, p. 1.
20. Agamben, *The Man without Content*, p. 3.
21. Hannah Arendt, 'Karl Marx and the Tradition of Western Political Thought', *Social Research*, vol. 69, no. 2 (2002), p. 285.
22. Agamben, *The Man without Content*, p. 70.
23. As an aside, in this chapter, I refer, on numerous occasions to 'man' and 'men'. I have retained these terms not because I think they are adequate terms to designate a universal humanity, but in order to signal the extent to which these thinkers are, to a large extent, preoccupied with men – in the sense of the male of the human species. Obscuring this by referring to 'men and women' or 'humanity' may bring them into line with contemporary sensibilities, but it would also obscure the extent to which what is at stake in many of the debates on 'the nature of man' is a form of thought for which women, along with slaves, foreigners and children, were relegated from the *polis* to the *oikos*, and, consequently, excluded from what the Greeks saw as the properly human activities of the *zoon politikon*.
24. Warren Breckman, *Marx, the Young Hegelians, and the Origins of Radical Social Theory* (Cambridge: Cambridge University Press, 1999), p. 206.
25. Breckman, *Marx, the Young Hegelians, and the Origins of Radical Social Theory*, p. 206.
26. Agamben, *The Man without Content*, p. 81.
27. Agamben, *The Man without Content*, p. 79.
28. Agamben, *The Man without Content*, p. 79.
29. Arendt, 'Karl Marx and the Tradition of Western Political Thought', p. 309.

30. Agamben, *The Man without Content*, p. 83.
31. Giorgio Agamben, *Homo Sacer: Sovereign Power and Bare Life*, trans. Daniel Heller-Roazen (Stanford: Stanford University Press, 1998).
32. Agamben, *The Man without Content*, p. 83.
33. Agamben, *The Man without Content*, p. 84.
34. Frederich Nietzsche, *Beyond Good and Evil*, trans. Judith Norman (Cambridge: Cambridge University Press, 2002), p. 19.
35. Giorgio Agamben, *Infancy and History: The Destruction of Experience*, trans. Liz Heron (London: Verso, 1993), p. 103.
36. Agamben, *Infancy and History*, p. 119.
37. Agamben, *Infancy and History*, p. 119.
38. Agamben, *Infancy and History*, p. 119.
39. Agamben, *Infancy and History*, p. 119.
40. Agamben, *Infancy and History*, p. 119.
41. Agamben, *The Kingdom and the Glory*, p. 3.
42. Michel Foucault, *Security, Territory, Population: Lectures at the Collège de France, 1977–1978*, ed. Michel Senellart, trans. Graham Burchell (New York: Palgrave Macmillan, 2007).
43. Agamben, *The Kingdom and the Glory*, p. 41.
44. Agamben, *The Kingdom and the Glory*, p. 53.
45. Agamben, *The Kingdom and the Glory*, p. 66.
46. Agamben, *The Kingdom and the Glory*, p. 91.
47. Giorgio Agamben, 'The Work of Man', in Matthew Calarco and Steven DeCaroli (eds), *Giorgio Agamben: Sovereignty and Life* (Stanford: Stanford University Press, 2007), p. 6.
48. Agamben, *The Kingdom and the Glory*, p. 91.
49. Thomas Aquinas, *Of God and His Creatures*, trans. Joseph Rickaby (Grand Rapids, MI: Christian Classics Ethereal Library, 2000).
50. Aquinas, *Of God and His Creatures*, p. 115.
51. Aquinas, *Of God and His Creatures*, p. 128.
52. Agamben, *The Kingdom and the Glory*, p. 90.
53. Agamben, *The Kingdom and the Glory*, pp. 53–4.
54. Aquinas, *Of God and His Creatures*, p. 128.
55. Agamben, *The Kingdom and the Glory*, p. 56.
56. Agamben, *The Kingdom and the Glory*, p. 56.
57. For a reading of Agamben's account of the way this paradigm was transferred into modern political thought by Rousseau, see Jessica Whyte '"The King Reigns but He Doesn't Govern": Thinking Sovereignty and Government with Foucault, Agamben

and Rousseau', in Tom Frost (ed.), *Giorgio Agamben: Legal, Political and Philosophical Perspectives* (Abingdon: Routledge, 2013).
58. Aristotle, *De Anima (On the Soul)*, trans. Hugh Lawson Tancred (London: Penguin, 1986).
59. Giorgio Agamben, 'Absolute Immanence', in *Potentialities: Collected Essays in Philosophy*, trans. Daniel Heller-Roazen (Stanford: Stanford University Press, 1999), p. 230.
60. Giorgio Agamben, *Remnants of Auschwitz: The Witness and the Archive*, trans. Daniel Heller-Roazen (New York: Zone Books, 1999), p. 147.
61. Thomas Aquinas, *Summa Theologica* (Raleigh: Hayes Barton Press, 1952), 3869–70.
62. Ludwig Feuerbach, *Thoughts on Death and Immortality*, trans. James A. Massey (Berkeley: University of California Press, 1980), p. 111.
63. Breckman, *Marx, the Young Hegelians, and the Origins of Radical Social Theory*, p. 10.
64. Feuerbach, *Thoughts on Death and Immortality*, pp. 6–12.
65. Feuerbach, *Thoughts on Death and Immortality*, p. 11.
66. Feuerbach, *Thoughts on Death and Immortality*, p. 12.
67. Feuerbach, *Thoughts on Death and Immortality*, p. 101.
68. Feuerbach, *Thoughts on Death and Immortality*, p. 112.
69. Ludwig Feuerbach, 'Introduction to the Essence of Christianity', in *The Fiery Brook: Selected Writings*, trans. Zawar Hanfi (London: Verso, 2012), p. 99.
70. Max Stirner, *The Ego and His Own*, trans. Steven T. Byington (Cambridge: Cambridge University Press, 2002), p. 33.
71. Stirner, *The Ego and His Own*, p. 34.
72. Althusser, 'The Humanist Controversy', p. 258.
73. Althusser, 'The Humanist Controversy', p. 258.
74. Marx, *Economic and Philosophic Manuscripts of 1844*, p. 71.
75. Feuerbach, 'Introduction to the Essence of Christianity', p. 124.
76. Marx, *Economic and Philosophic Manuscripts of 1844*, p. 71.
77. Marx, *Economic and Philosophic Manuscripts of 1844*, p. 72.
78. Louis Althusser, 'On Feuerbach', in *The Humanist Controversy and Other Writings*, p. 122.
79. Marx, *Economic and Philosophic Manuscripts of 1844*, p. 72.
80. Giorgio Agamben, *Means without End: Notes on Politics*, trans. Vincenzo Binetti and Cesare Casarino (Minneapolis: University of Minnesota Press, 2000), p. 82.

81. Giorgio Agamben, *Profanations*, trans. Jeff Fort (New York: Zone Books, 2007), p. 81.
82. Karl Marx, 'Theses on Feuerbach', in Karl Marx with Friedrich Engels, *Collected Works, Vol. 5*, trans. Clemens Dutt et al. (London: Lawrence & Wishart; New York: International Publishers; and Moscow: Progress, 1976), p. 4. For Althusser, Marx's transition from the critique of religion to the critique of politics is not a *theoretical* shift but only the addition of another object to be analysed with the help of Feuerbach's theory. Yet, this underestimates the importance of the shift from the criticism of the heavens to the criticism of earth (see Althusser, 'The Humanist Controversy', p. 245).
83. Marx, 'Theses on Feuerbach', p. 4.
84. Marx, 'Theses on Feuerbach', p. 4.
85. Karl Marx and Friedrich Engels, 'The German Ideology', in Marx with Engels, *Collected Works, Vol. 5*, p. 64.
86. Marx, 'Theses on Feuerbach', p. 5.
87. Althusser, 'The Humanist Controversy', p. 265.
88. Althusser, 'The Humanist Controversy', p. 289 (original emphasis).
89. Althusser, 'The Humanist Controversy', p. 289.
90. Althusser, 'The Humanist Controversy', p. 265.
91. Althusser, 'The Humanist Controversy', p. 289.
92. Althusser, 'The Humanist Controversy', p. 289.
93. Karl Marx, *Grundrisse*, trans. Martin Nicolaus (Harmondsworth: Penguin, 1973), p. 83.
94. Marx, *Grundrisse*, p. 83.
95. Marx, *Grundrisse*, p. 87.
96. Marx, *Grundrisse*, p. 104.
97. Karl Marx, *Capital Volume 1*, trans. Ben Fowkes (Harmondsworth: Penguin, 1976), p. 988.
98. Marx, *Capital Volume 1*, p. 899.
99. Wood, *Democracy against Capitalism*, p. 41.
100. Giorgio Agamben, *The Time That Remains: A Commentary on the Letter to the Romans*, trans. Patricia Dailey (Stanford: Stanford University Press, 2005), p. 30.
101. Agamben, *The Time That Remains*, p. 31.

5

Liturgical Labour: Agamben on the Post-Fordist Spectacle
Daniel McLoughlin

Agamben has described contemporariness as 'a singular relationship with one's own time, which adheres to it and, at the same time, keeps a distance from it'.[1] He suggests that the way that one maintains such a disjunction to the present is by 'perceiving the indices and signatures of the most archaic in the most modern'.[2] The archaic does not, however, simply mean that which is chronologically distant: it is what is 'close to the origin', an *arche* that remains an operative force within historical becoming.

The Kingdom and the Glory attempts to perceive the archaic amidst the 'current triumph of economy and government over every other aspect of social life'.[3] It does so through a genealogy of the thought and practice of the Church. The first half of the book traces the use of the term *oikonomia* from its Greek roots in the art of household management, through Christian theology, up to its influence on modern political concepts and governmental practices. The last three chapters develop a genealogy of rituals of glorification, from the acclamation of magistrates in Republican Rome, to the liturgical rituals of the Church, the mass rallies of fascism and the society of the spectacle. Drawing these two analyses together, Agamben argues that power in 'the West' has assumed the form of a governmental machine whose 'ultimate structure' lies 'in the relation between *oikonomia* and glory'.[4]

The early volumes of *Homo Sacer* were often criticised for focusing too much on sovereignty and failing to analyse capitalism and the forms of liberal governmentality central to the contemporary operation of power.[5] Agamben's 'theological genealogy' of economy and government is, then, a major development in his political thought, deepening his account of the operation of power, and addressing contemporary capitalism for the first time within the confines of the *Homo Sacer* project. However, there appear to be some important limits to any attempt to understand the contemporary victory of economy through Agamben's genealogy of economy. *The Kingdom and the Glory* says little directly about the present world, apart from its comments about the society of the spectacle, which are rather brief. This is quite unlike the early volumes of *Homo Sacer*, which drew on Greek philosophy and Roman law to discuss contemporary political problems such as security politics, mass populations of refugees and Guantánamo Bay. A number of critics have also argued that Agamben's archaeology obscures what is specific to the political economy of capitalism. Alberto Toscano, for example, criticises Agamben for analysing the economy through the 'managerial paradigm' of *oikonomia*: what is more relevant to understanding the contemporary economy, he argues, is the logic of accumulation without limit (*chrematistics*) made possible by money, which in contemporary capitalism 'threatens to generate an entirely unmanageable economy'.[6] Jessica Whyte has argued that, by tracing the paradigm of economy from Ancient Greece through to modern capitalism, Agamben effaces the differences between modes of production and conflates the labour of the slave and the proletarian. This is problematic, she argues, because 'what is definitive of labour under capitalism is *not* that the labourer is subjected to the will of another, but that he or she is subjected to the impersonal domination of capital'.[7]

This chapter responds to the relative absence of an explicit engagement with contemporary capitalism in Agamben's theological genealogy as well as his ostensible erasure of the specificity of the capitalist mode of production. I argue that, while Agamben's work on economy and government does not address the capitalist mode of production as a whole, it can and should be fruitfully read as a response to the mutation of capitalism that has emerged since the 1970s: what I call the 'Post-Fordist spectacle'. I do so by tracing the development of Agamben's theological reading of contemporary capitalism. Agamben's early analyses of the spectacle emphasise the analogy between sacrificial separation and the fact that spectacular capitalism separates things from their use value. However, this analysis tends to marginalise the role of production in the commodity form and, as a result, underplays the Marxian insight that estrangement arises from the 'free' activity of those subject to exploitation. *The Kingdom and the Glory* does contain echoes of this Marxian critique of estrangement under capitalism.

Agamben on the Post-Fordist Spectacle   93

Yet the work is underpinned by a statist model of government that makes it problematic for the purposes of analysing political economy. In *The Highest Poverty*, however, Agamben outlines a monastic practice of self-government and work that simultaneously produces and acclaims the divine order. This 'liturgical labour' helps us to theorise the nature of estrangement in contemporary capitalism, which directly exploits our communicative capacities. I make this argument by reading Agamben's analyses of monasticism and the spectacle in conjunction with the account of immaterial production developed by post-workerist theorists.

Agamben on the spectacle and the commodity

In the early chapters of *Capital Volume 1*, Marx argues that the commodity form is comprised of both use value – the utility of the object to the individual – and exchange value – the value that it has on the market. He rejects the argument that exchange value is determined by supply and demand and argues, instead, that it arises from the quantity of abstract labour time involved in the production of any commodity, or what he simply refers to as value. The value of a commodity is inherently social, as it is not determined simply by the time expended in production, but by the time that is necessary given existing social conditions including the technological means and relations of production. But, while the value of a commodity arises from labour, it can only be realised through an act of exchange, which renders different forms of labour commensurable and thereby makes it possible to conceive of labour-power in the abstract (as opposed to the particular concrete forms of labour that go into producing the use values of particular objects). Yet, precisely because of this, the production of goods for exchange gives rise to fetishism, in which commodities take on an appearance of autonomy from the power that created them:

> The labour of the private individual manifests itself as an element of the total labour of society only through the relations which the act of exchange establishes between the products and, through their mediation, between producers. To the producers, therefore, the social relations between their private labours appear as what they are, i.e. they do not appear as direct social relations between persons in their work, but rather as material relations between persons and social relations between things.[8]

Marx famously uses a theological analogy to illuminate this estrangement: the commodity form masks the human power that produced the object in the same way that, in religion, 'the products of the human brain appear as independent beings endowed with life, and entering into relation both with one another and the human race'.[9]

Marx's critique of political economy described the emergence of the capitalist mode of production in early modern Europe. By the mid-twentieth century, however, capitalism had spread across the globe and intensified its hold on countries of the capitalist core: and, 'in those societies in which modern conditions of production prevail', Guy Debord would write in 1968, 'all of life presents itself as an immense accumulation of spectacles'.[10] In the society of the spectacle, the estrangement characteristic of the commodity form is radicalised as the commodity attains the 'total occupation of social life'.[11] 'Separation is', Debord writes, 'the alpha and omega of the spectacle.'[12] This is because, in the society of the spectacle 'everything that was directly lived has moved away into a representation'.[13] The spectacular representation of life is separate from the life that it represents, 'a pseudo-world apart, an object of mere contemplation [. . .] the "concrete inversion of life"'.[14] The individual in the society of the spectacle experiences his or her world through the mediation of the spectacle and, as a result, is separated from his or her own life and reduced to the status of a passive observer. Finally, the spectacle separates people from each other, producing all those subjected to it as 'atomised masses'[15] who can only find unity in and through the common flow of images.

Debord's work is fundamental for Agamben's analysis of capitalism and his diagnosis of the contemporary world. His first treatment of Debord appears in *The Coming Community*. What particularly interests him here is the relationship between the spectacle and language: indeed, 'the spectacle is language, the very communicativity or linguistic being of humans'.[16] By commodifying human sociality and displaying it in a separate sphere, the spectacle separates us from our communicative essence: a 'fuller Marxian analysis' should, he writes, take account of the fact that capitalism now expropriates not only 'productive activity' but also language itself.[17]

Agamben deepens his account of this spectacular capitalism in the essay 'In Praise of Profanation', which extends Marx's analogy between the commodity and theology by reading Debord through two different lenses: the problem of sacrifice; and a fragment from Walter Benjamin entitled 'Capitalism as Religion'. Agamben has a longstanding concern with the social and political role of sacrificial praxis.[18] The infamous figure of *homo sacer* first appears in the closing pages of *Language and Death*, which notes that the sacred man may be killed without committing a crime because he has been excluded from the community. Immediately prior to this discussion, however, Agamben offers the following observation:

> at the centre of the sacrifice is simply a determinate action that has been invested with a series of prohibitions and ritual proscriptions. Forbidden action, marked by sacredness, is not, however, simply excluded: rather, it is now accessible only for certain people and according to determinate rules. In this way it provides society and its ungrounded legislation with the fiction of a beginning: that which is excluded from the community is, in fact, that on which the entire life of the community is founded.[19]

According to Agamben, then, sacrificial activity provides the ever renewed foundation for law and authority by (re)producing the fundamental boundary between sacred and profane and masking its origins in social praxis through the fiction of an 'immemorial beginning'.[20] One consequence of this division is the sacred man, who can be 'killed but not sacrificed', because he has been separated from the profane but not taken into the sacred order. A second consequence is the granting of legal authority to a certain class of people who have access to separated things and whose role is to regulate the relationship between the sacred and the profane according to 'determinate rules'.[21]

The link between sacrificial praxis and separation that Agamben first articulates in *Language and Death* allows him, many years later, to read capitalism in religious terms. Benjamin's 'Capitalism as Religion' claims that not only does capitalism serve 'to satisfy the same worries, anguish and disquiet formerly answered by so-called religion'[22] but that it is the most extreme religious cult ever to exist: it has no particular dogma, only cultic practice; this cultic practice is permanent (rather than being confined to festive days); and the cult aims to produce guilt and blame rather than atoning for them.[23] 'In Praise of Profanation' reads Benjamin's account of the capitalist cult through Agamben's analysis of sacrificial separation: the commodity form turns objects into an 'an ungraspable fetish'[24] and the process of commodification thereby 'generalizes in every domain the structure of separation that defines religion'.[25] The development of capitalism gradually exacerbates this problem: as the sphere of commodities expands, objects are increasingly encountered in the realm of consumption (which is a separate sphere in which everything is ultimately equivalent) rather than in the sphere of use (which is both immediate and characterised by qualitative differences). The extreme outcome of this process is the society of the spectacle, which, unlike the regulated sacrificial practice of traditional religions, involves a 'single, multiform, ceaseless process of separation that assails every thing, every place, every human activity in order to divide it from itself'.[26]

Agamben conceives his analysis of the commodity as a corrective to the analytical tendencies of orthodox Marxism which, in the 1960s, 'foolishly abandoned'[27] the problem of the commodity form. However, as Jessica Whyte points out in a critique of Agamben's analysis of contemporary capitalism, the central problem of the commodity form is not that it eclipses use value, but that it both refers to and masks value.[28] In Marx's mature critique of political economy, then, he follows the analysis of commodity fetishism with a comprehensive account of the particular mode in which production is organised in order to accumulate capital. The most important form of separation for Marx is thus that between social labour and the exchange value to which it gives rise. In Agamben's early analysis of the spectacle, by contrast, the analysis of labour and the mode of production are marginalised by his focus on the hollowing out of use value by exchange.[29]

Agamben's early elision of production stands in marked contrast to the thought of his contemporaries, post-workerists such as Antonio Negri and Paolo Virno, who focus on the transformation of production since the 1970s and the rise of what they call 'immaterial labor'. This analysis of Post-Fordist production has done much to illuminate the political economy of contemporary capitalism, and we will soon return to this work. However, as David Eden has argued, the problem with this focus on production is that, at least in Hardt and Negri's work, it leads to the marginalisation of exchange value. As Eden points out, this is problematic, because it obscures the type of estrangement that arises from commodity production. The proletarian sells his or her labour as a commodity to a capitalist who provides him or her with means of production.[30] This allows the proletarian to actualise his or her productive capacity through a cooperative effort with other workers. However, by valorising capital, this labour also entrenches the conditions for the worker's domination and exploitation: as Marx points out, 'the more the worker exerts himself in his work, the more powerful the alien, objective world becomes which he brings into being over against himself'.[31] Capitalism thus gives rise to a very particular form of estrangement that is 'freely' produced by those who are subjected to exploitation. By concealing the social labour that produces the commodity, exchange value also conceals the fact that capital lives off the productive activity of workers. Interestingly, Eden turns to Agamben's analysis of the spectacle as a way of illustrating the importance of estrangement, as a counter to Hardt and Negri's emphasis on production. But, while Agamben does argue that the spectacle involves the expropriation of our linguistic capacities, Whyte is correct to argue that the problem of production is marginalised in Agamben's early account of spectacular capitalism. While Debord himself links the development of the spectacle to the productive efforts of human labour,[32] Agamben's reading of Debord underplays the fact that we freely produce the spectacle through our linguistic activities, and instead tends to cast the spectacle as a destructive force to which humanity is being subjected.

By illuminating the relationship between exchange value and value, Marx was able to illuminate the circuits through which value is accumulated in a capitalist economy, and to illustrate the particular nature of estrangement that emerges from commodity production: the fact that, as John Holloway puts it, 'people not only accept the miseries of capitalism but also actively participate in its reproduction'.[33] As we have seen, both Agamben's early analysis of the spectacle and the post-workerist analysis of immaterial labour provide somewhat one-sided accounts of contemporary capitalism, by emphasising exchange in the first case and production in the latter. To adequately mobilise Marx's insights into the fetishism of the commodity, the analysis of contemporary capitalism needs to grapple with the fact that exchange value and value are distinct yet related aspects of a commodity economy. In the remainder of this chapter I argue that Agamben's recent work on economy does help us to theorise the operation of commodity fetishism under the particular conditions of contemporary capitalism by emphasising the relationship between (immaterial) production and (spectacular) exchange value. *The Kingdom and the Glory* develops an account of democratic political power as a form of estrangement, one that is produced and sustained by people subjecting themselves to the exercise of power through glorification. *The Highest Poverty* then builds on this analysis through an account of monastic liturgy, a form of glorification through labour, which helps cast light on the economy of the Post-Fordist spectacle.

Glory and the spectacle

There is little need to dwell upon the details of Agamben's genealogies of economy and glory as they have been ably outlined by others in this volume. Nonetheless, a quick sketch of their most salient features is important to address the way that *The Kingdom and the Glory* develops upon Agamben's previous analyses of capitalism and the spectacle.

The theoretical core of the genealogy of *oikonomia* is an ontological transformation produced by the doctrine of the Trinity. In classical ontology divine action was thought to be grounded in divine nature. However, in response to the challenge of heresy, the early Church Fathers began to argue that God was singular at the level of his being but multiple in his 'economy' – that is, his activity of governing the world. This introduced a fracture between being and praxis into the history of metaphysics: the Christian God is inoperative at the level of being (that is, he is radically transcendent with respect to the world and so cannot act directly upon it); and for this reason he requires an immanent government (Christ, the Holy Spirit and the hosts of angels) that can put his will and laws into effect. Trinitarian theology is thus characterised by a 'vicarious and effectual' ontology, in which the action of government produces order by putting the divine law to work, thereby rendering it operative.

Agamben's genealogy of glory turns from the theory of divine economy to a particular practice central to its operation. Glory involves a call and response between two forms of practice: the 'objective' dimension of glory is the majestic appearance of power through signs or insignia (as, for example, when God appears to the Jews as consuming fire, or the Roman emperor displays himself resplendent in crown and purple toga); the 'subjective' aspect of glory is the popular acclamation through which people respond to objective glory (such as when a stadium cheers an actor or athlete, or the people acclaim a magistrate or emperor). *The Kingdom and the Glory* draws on the Catholic theologian Erik Peterson to illuminate the role played by such rituals in the life of the Church. In Roman law the public celebration of power could, in certain circumstances, produce a juridical effect, such as when troops acclaimed their commander as Caesar; or senators acclaimed the emperor as a substitute for them voting. Peterson draws on this history to argue that the liturgy, which is one long song in praise of God, constitutes the Church as a theological-political community: by expressing the consent of the faithful to God's sovereignty, it binds them to his law and turns the 'impolitical' mass of believers into citizens of the celestial city.

The crux of Agamben's archaeology of glory appears when he asks why the Christian liturgy is so full of acclamations: 'Why', he writes, 'must God be continually praised?'[34] Drawing on Marcel Mauss, he characterises sacrifice and prayer as 'effective actions', oral or gestural practices through which individuals seek to influence the gods. One of Mauss's formative influences, an 1899 study by Sylvian Levi, argues that Brahmanic practices of sacrifice are not simply an attempt to influence the Vedic gods, but rather constitute them as such. As Mauss summarises Levi's findings, the theologians of the Vedic era believed that 'the gods, like the Demons, are born from sacrifice. It is thanks to it that they have ascended to the heavens, in the same way as the one who carries out a sacrifice still does.'[35] The conclusion that Agamben draws from this is that the Christian God does not demand that the faithful glorify him because he is glorious; instead, God needs the practice of glorification because he would not exist without it.

For Christian theologians, then, order derives from God who, as sovereign over the world, creates a divine government that produces that order on his behalf. In *The Kingdom and the Glory* (and its sequel *Opus Dei*) the Catholic Church provides the model for this political apparatus: the Church claims to be part of a cosmic hierarchy charged with giving effect to God's law and its liturgical rituals glorify God, constituting the Church as a political community, and granting authority to its hierarchy to act on God's behalf. For Agamben, by contrast, the order of this world does not originate in the 'immemorial beginning' of a transcendent sovereign will and the law that it lays down. Order is, rather, a product of social praxis – what Agamben calls, in good Foucauldian terms, 'the techniques and strategies of government and power'.[36] The legitimacy of this order derives from a fictional presupposition that is produced and maintained through rituals, carefully managed by the governmental hierarchy, through which believers freely subject themselves to the power of the Church.

Agamben draws out the political implications of this theological analysis through a reading of Carl Schmitt, who takes up Peterson's thesis to argue that 'acclamation is an eternal phenomenon of all political communities. There is no state without a people, and no people without acclamations.'[37] Schmitt's analysis is aimed at the liberal democracy of the Weimar state, whose individual secret ballot is, he claims, an expression of liberal individualism. 'True democracy' only appears when the people express their constituent power through acclamation: '"people" is a concept that becomes present only in the public sphere [. . .] the people only appear in public; and they first produce the public generally'.[38]

In the sphere of politics, then, government is legitimated by a sovereign fiction produced through acclamation by the citizens assembled as a 'people'. The most obvious contemporary expression of Schmitt's rather authoritarian version of direct democracy is the mass rallies of twentieth-century fascism.[39] But, while rituals play a minimal political role in liberal democracies, and public acclamation of leaders has all but disappeared, Schmitt argues that acclamations nonetheless survive in such states in the attenuated form of public opinion.[40] Drawing on this suggestion, Agamben claims that the spectacle is the contemporary sphere of acclamation. Although he does not flesh out the argument in detail, it is clear that the spectacle involves the three aspects of political glorification outlined in Schmitt's article. First, the spectacle unifies people (albeit in a very different way from the maximum of presence and identity described by Schmitt) by producing an atomised mass of individuals who are brought together, in a purely mediated fashion, by their consumption of the same spectacle. Second, the spectacle legitimates the existing order and thereby reproduces itself as a social relation: 'the attitude which it demands', Debord writes, 'is passive acceptance which in fact it already obtained by its manner of appearing without reply, by its monopoly of appearance'.[41] Finally, the legitimacy that the spectacle gives to the prevailing order is founded on a fiction: as Debord writes, the spectacle is 'the common ground of the deceived gaze and of false consciousness'.[42]

The Kingdom and the Glory thus articulates a form of estrangement in which the free activity of those subjected to power produces and masks the conditions of their own domination. Agamben's analysis therefore has certain affinities with Marx's account of the fetishistic structure of commodity production. Yet the two thinkers are concerned with different activities taking place in different spheres: for Marx the 'bewitched and distorted world'[43] of commodities masks its roots in social labour, while Agamben's account of 'economic' estrangement focuses on a linguistic activity that produces and sustains political power.

As such, Agamben's genealogy of economy seems to have little to say about the problem of commodity production that is central to the Marxist analysis of political economy. Indeed, Agamben's examples of the modern relevance of the governmental machine tend to focus on the state. When *The Kingdom and the Glory* illustrates the impact that the theology of *oikonomia* has had on modern thought and practice it identifies Rousseau's theory of popular sovereignty and the separation between executive and legislative powers as secularised versions of the economic paradigm. Agamben's analysis of modern glorification also centres on the political problem of the constitution of a people and the legitimation of institutional power, while his brief analysis of contemporary capitalism rests on an analogy between Schmitt's analysis of acclamation and the society of the spectacle, thereby focusing on the role that it plays in legitimating the existing order, and saying nothing about the processes of production and exchange that we associate with political economy. Finally, when Agamben does look to the theory of modern political economy, he examines the theological origins of Adam Smith's concept of the free market. Yet one of the central points of *Capital Volume 1* is that, to understand the nature of capitalism, we need to look beyond the 'noisy sphere' of distribution and exchange and turn instead to the 'hidden abode of production. Here we shall see, not only how capital produces, but how capital is produced. We shall at last force the secret of profit making.'[44]

At first glance, then, Agamben's analysis of economic theology seems to be vulnerable to the same criticisms that have been levelled at his earlier work: a focus on the political at the expense of the economic, and an emphasis on exchange at the expense of production. Appearances can be deceiving, however, particularly as Agamben has a taste for addressing contemporary political problems in an oblique and archaeological fashion. As Jason E. Smith points out, at the very time that Agamben was formulating the *Homo Sacer* project, he was also 'developing a kind of alliance or convergence with certain aspects of the post-workerist Italian tradition'.[45] In the key essay 'Form-of-Life', which maps out many of the coordinates for the project, Agamben makes a clear reference to immaterial labour when he writes that 'the contemporary phase of capitalism, the society of the spectacle' is characterised by the 'massive inscription of social knowledge into the productive process'.[46] This suggests that, by the time he writes *Homo Sacer*, the society of the spectacle remains the primary framework for Agamben's account of twentieth-century capitalism, but that his understanding of *contemporary* capitalism filters this through the problem of Post-Fordist production.

The characterisation of contemporary capitalism as a Post-Fordist spectacle allows us to rethink the stakes of Agamben's archaeological response to the 'current triumph' of economy and government. In order to do this, the next section outlines the post-workerist diagnosis of contemporary production, while the final section shows how Agamben's account of glory can be read in this context.[47]

Post-Fordism and production

One of the central theses of post-workerism is that the mode of production and the state form began to undergo a 'great transformation' in the 1970s in response to pressure from workers' struggles against the Fordist organisation of labour. This revolutionary process was driven by ostensibly marginal social subjects, those who were 'educated, uncertain, mobile [...] hated the work ethic and opposed, at times head on, the tradition and the culture of the historical left'.[48] One of the decisive factors in the eventual victory of capital was the fact that it adopted the propensities of these subjects – 'exit from the factories, indifference to steady employment, familiarity with learning and communications networks'[49] – and turned them into the basis for a renewed cycle of capital accumulation through the package of strategies now familiar to us in the age of neo-liberal globalisation: the extraction of value outside the factories; making labour more 'flexible' and precarious; and the use of knowledge and communication to drive innovation. The cornerstone of this

Post-Fordist economy is a new form of work: the 'immaterial labor' that 'produces the informational and cultural content of the commodity'.[50] This labour takes two forms: first, technologically developed industrial production began to integrate cybernetics and computer control requiring advanced linguistic and cognitive skills; second, the development of the tertiary (or service) sector extended wage labour beyond the factory and saw the rise of affective and intellectual forms of work.[51] According to the post-workerists, immaterial labour now plays a hegemonic role in the global economy: the production of immaterial goods has become a crucial means for making profit; the computerisation of the assembly line means that material production is often guided by immaterial labour;[52] and the demand for material commodities is increasingly driven by image and branding that are products of immaterial labour.[53]

The rise of immaterial labour transforms the capitalist mode of production in a number of important ways. Industrial capitalism valorised capital by extracting surplus value from workers who produced material commodities within factories. A portion of these commodities were sold back to workers so that they could replenish their bodily existence and sell their labour-power to the capitalist again the next day. The increased scale of production under Fordism required more consumption by workers and gave rise to consumer capitalism and the society of the spectacle. With the development of Post-Fordism, however, the commodification of culture is no longer simply an after-effect of abundant material production. This is because the product of immaterial labour is 'first and foremost a social relation', the raw material of which is 'subjectivity and the "ideological" environment in which it lives and reproduces'.[54] If immaterial production has indeed become hegemonic, then the most important commodity for contemporary capitalism is the life world, and culture and communication provide the means for its manufacture.

Post-workerists such as Virno and Negri argue that the communicative and political nature of immaterial labour offers the potential to develop a new form of radically democratic political organisation that emancipates life from the command of capital and the state.[55] However, the insidious side of the Post-Fordist politicisation of labour is an increased interest in the regulation of subjectivity. The capitalist was crucial to innovation and the organisation of work in the industrial phase of capitalism as he or she provided the means of, and plan for, production. In the Post-Fordist economy, by contrast, workers are:

> expected to become 'active subjects' in the co-ordination of the various functions of production, instead of being subjected to it as simple command. [. . .] a collective learning process becomes the heart of productivity, because it is no longer a matter of finding different ways of composing or organizing already existing job functions, but of looking for new ones.[56]

The response of capital to this increased worker autonomy is the attempt to assure command over labour through the management of subjectivity: 'capital wants a situation where command resides within the subject him- or herself, and within the communicative process'.[57]

Negri argues that the Post-Fordist intensification of subjective regulation is a decisive moment in the development of biopower (a form of power that 'regulates social life from its interior, following it, interpreting it, absorbing it').[58] Industrial capitalism was characterised by a relatively clear distinction between the site at which value was extracted and spheres that were not directly productive.[59] The extraction of value from the industrial workforce was dependent upon the operation of disciplinary power, which produced the docile bodies necessary for work on the assembly line.[60] By contrast, the immaterial production characteristic of Post-Fordism takes place across the social field. This gives rise to a 'social factory'[61] that transforms all of life into work: 'living and producing tend to become indistinguishable. Insofar as life tends to be completely invested by acts of production and reproduction, social life itself becomes a productive machine.'[62] Because the Post-Fordist 'factory' is the totality of social relationships, the rise of immaterial labour corresponds to a generalised transformation in the relationship between power and subjectivity with the evolution from disciplinary society to the 'society of control'.[63] Where discipline produces a series of fixed identities in particular institutions, mechanisms of control are diffused in a network across the social field and constantly respond to the particularities of a situation. Denizens of the society of control thus constantly undergo processes of subjectification that give rise to hybrid and overlapping subjectivities 'produced simultaneously by numerous institutions in different combinations and doses'.[64]

Post-workerists argue that the rise of immaterial labour has made language and communication central to production and the accumulation of capital. The consequences of this transformation in production include the intensification of subjective regulation, the extension of mechanisms of biopolitical governance across the social field, the transition from the society of discipline to one of control, and the setting of the totality of life to work. How, then, might the post-workerist analysis of contemporary production help us to think through the nature and stakes of Agamben's archaeology of economy? And how might Agamben's archaeology contribute, in turn, to our understanding of Post-Fordist capitalism?

Liturgical labour and the Post-Fordist spectacle

Agamben's analysis of the governmental machine in *The Kingdom and the Glory* builds upon his earlier account of sacrifice in *Language and Death*: the Eucharist, which lies at the centre of the Church service, is thought to repeat Christ's sacrifice,[65] and this sacrificial act is bound up with and constitutive of a series of determinate separations: the sacrifice could only be administered by a Priest according to particular rules and at determinate times; the Church hierarchy is separated from and rules over the laity; the person of the priest is separated from his Office; and the exercise of the Office is separated from periods of labour and rest. The ecclesiastical model of liturgy is thus a juridical and statist one in which the governing authority is separated from the rest of society and rules over it: it 'extracts a liturgy from life' but constitutes it 'in a separate sphere, whose proprietor was the priest'.[66] However, as I have already observed, the emphasis on the state is problematic from the perspective of understanding the political economy of capitalism. It is also of questionable relevance to the diagnosis of contemporary power, given Agamben's own argument for the crisis of the modern state and his observation that, with the exception of totalitarianism and fascism, practices of glorification involving the presence of a public and a governmental hierarchy have diminished in importance.

In *The Highest Poverty*, however, Agamben presents a very different model of liturgy through an analysis of monasticism. Foucault notes that monastic life was 'actually the point of departure and matrix of discipline',[67] as the monk's time was completely occupied by a schedule of prayer, reading and manual labour that regulated both body and soul. For Agamben, however, what is particularly important about monasticism is that its disciplinary organisation was part and parcel of a radical new form of liturgical practice: as the monk and theologian John Cassian writes in his study of Egyptian monasticism, 'the whole purpose of the monk and indeed the perfection of his heart amount to this – total and uninterrupted dedication to prayer'.[68] Even the monk's manual labour came to be seen as a kind of 'spiritual work' that should be attended to with the same devotion as his prayer: 'every gesture of the monk, all the most humble manual activities become a spiritual work and acquire the liturgical status of an *Opus Dei*'.[69]

In the monastery, then, the activity of government is no longer the province of a separate organisation charged with ruling over a laity but is, rather, spread throughout the community. This generalised self-government accompanies (and makes possible) a practice of manual and spiritual (or immaterial) work that occupies the totality of monastic life. The monk was thought to be an instrument of God and his disciplinary labour was thought to be divine work, a practice that put to work (or rendered operative) God's will and his law (although in practice it simply reproduced the order of the monastic community). This disciplinary labour was, in turn, understood as an acclamation, in part because it was accompanied by prayer, and in part because work itself was seen as giving glory to God.

There is a strong analogy between this monastic liturgical paradigm and the operation of the government in Post-Fordist capitalism. The first arm of the governmental machine that Agamben outlines is an activity that (re)produces order. While Agamben's work identifies a crisis of law and state, this does not mean that the activity of governing has ceased. In an essay that emerged alongside his research into *oikonomia*, Agamben describes the current phase of capitalism as a 'massive accumulation and proliferation of apparatuses'[70] that seek to govern human beings. He has also repeatedly connected the crisis of law to the development of liberal governmentality and, more recently, to the emergence of the society of control.[71] For Agamben, then, the contemporary government of subjects does not occur primarily through a separate authority that imposes its law upon its subjects, as per ecclesiastical liturgy, but rather arises from apparatuses that are immanent to the social terrain, our language and our subjectivities.⁷² As the post-workerists identify, the development of this decentralised form of government (and in particular, the rise of the society of control) has facilitated the colonisation of the totality of life by work – just as self-disciplinary labour occupies the whole monastic community for the entirety of its time. While the contemporary activity of productive self-government is not thought to realise a divine order, it is nonetheless responsible for (re)producing, putting to work or rendering operative the social, economic and political order of capitalism, which is often treated as being as immutable as if it were put in place by a divine will.

The second arm of the governmental machine is the practice of glorification, which celebrates the appearance of sovereignty and thereby binds the subjects of governmental activity to its power. As we have seen, Agamben's initial analysis of glory treats liturgy as a political and statist problem and then argues that the society of the spectacle is the contemporary form of glorification. In the society of the spectacle, however, the glorification that gives legitimacy to the activity of governing no longer occurs in a Church service (or, in its secular equivalent, a mass rally), but is, rather, produced through our continuous participation in a spectacle that permeates our existence.⁷³ Glorification in the society of the spectacle is thus closer to monastic liturgy, which turns all of life into a celebration of the divine, than it is to ecclesiastical liturgy, which is separated from the rest of life. Where the analogy between the spectacle and monastic liturgy breaks down, however, is in the role played by work: in the monastery, liturgical glorification is inseparable from the continuous exercise of office through work; in the society of the spectacle, by contrast, the spectacular glorification that colonises life is an after-effect of practices of a material production that remain confined to the time and place of the factory. The analogy between the spectacle and the monastery only properly holds with the rise of immaterial labour: as Paolo Virno writes, the spectacle has now become 'the reigning productive force, something that goes beyond the domain of its own sphere, pertaining, instead, to the industry as a whole, to *poiesis* in its totality'.⁷⁴ The Post-Fordist spectacle integrates the apparatuses of production and glorification, and thereby collapses the distinction between the fetishisation that arises from commodity production and the estrangement that characterises the governmental machine.

Contemporary capitalism directly exploits communicative

capacities for the purposes of both production and consumption. The practices of immaterial production and the spectacular display of exchange value have largely taken over the political functions of government and glorification from the state and deeply woven them into the fabric of our everyday existence. Denizens of the Post-Fordist spectacle are, like the monks, office-holders in a governmental hierarchy, busily engaged in a liturgical labour that occupies the totality of life, a work that both reproduces and acclaims the order to which we are subjected. This helps to explain the peculiar combination of political passivity and relentless activity that characterises the contemporary political and economic situation, as incessant work now coincides directly with the production of 'the empire of modern passivity' that is the spectacle – which, as Debord puts it, 'covers the entire surface of the world and bathes endlessly in its own glory'.[75]

Notes

1. Giorgio Agamben, *What Is an Apparatus? and Other Essays*, trans. David Kishik and Stefan Pedatella (Stanford: Stanford University Press, 2009), p. 41.
2. Agamben, *What Is an Apparatus?*, p. 50.
3. Giorgio Agamben, *The Kingdom and the Glory: For a Theological Genealogy of Economy and Government*, trans. Lorenzo Chiesa with Matteo Mandarini (Stanford: Stanford University Press, 2011), p. 1.
4. Agamben, *The Kingdom and the Glory*, p. xii.
5. For such criticisms from a Marxist perspective, see Michael Hardt and Antonio Negri, *Commonwealth* (Cambridge, MA, and London: Harvard University Press, 2009), p. 4; Steven Colatrella, 'Nothing Exceptional: Against Agamben', *Journal for Critical Education Policy Studies*, vol. 9, no. 1 (2011), p. 97.
6. Alberto Toscano, 'Divine Management: Critical Remarks on Giorgio Agamben's *The Kingdom and the Glory*', *Angelaki*, vol. 16, no. 3 (2011), p. 130. Anthony Adler has endorsed this critique of Agamben's managerial paradigm: see Anthony Adler, 'Managing the Unmanageable: Agamben's *The Kingdom and the Glory* and the Dance of Political Economy', *Concentric: Literary and Cultural Studies*, vol. 40, no. 2 (September 2014), p. 163.
7. Jessica Whyte, '"Man Produces Universally": Praxis and Production in Agamben and Marx', in J. Habjan and J. Whyte (eds), *(Mis)read-*

ings of Marx in Continental Philosophy (London and New York: Palgrave Macmillan, 2014), pp. 191–2.
8. Karl Marx, *Capital: A Critique of Political Economy, Volume 1*, trans. Ben Fowkes (London: Penguin, 1990), p. 166.
9. Marx, *Capital Volume 1*, p. 166.
10. Guy Debord, *Society of the Spectacle* (London: Rebel Press, 1983), p. 1.
11. Debord, *Society of the Spectacle*, p. 42.
12. Debord, *Society of the Spectacle*, p. 25.
13. Debord, *Society of the Spectacle*, p. 1.
14. Debord, *Society of the Spectacle*, p. 2.
15. Debord, *Society of the Spectacle*, p. 7.
16. Giorgio Agamben, *The Coming Community*, trans. Michael Hardt (Minneapolis: University of Minnesota Press, 1993), p. 79.
17. Agamben, *The Coming Community*, p. 79.
18. The relationship between the sacred and violence appears in a 1970 essay entitled 'On the Limits of Violence', which is Agamben's earliest translated work: Giorgio Agamben, 'On the Limits of Violence', trans. Lorenzo Fabbri, *diacritics*, vol. 39, no. 4 (2009) pp. 103–11. I have gone back as far as *Language and Death* as this is the work in which the threads of the analysis of the sacred that I am most concerned with in this essay – separation and authority – first appear.
19. Giorgio Agamben, *Language and Death: The Place of Negativity* (Minneapolis and Oxford: University of Minnesota Press), p. 105.
20. Agamben, *Language and Death*, p. 105.
21. Agamben's later analysis of the sacred man complicates the analysis in *Language and Death*. *Homo Sacer* argues that the sacred man can be 'killed but not sacrificed' because he is excluded from both sacred and profane law, but is nonetheless included in the community through his exclusion. Further, where *Language and Death* argues that the sacred is an 'ambiguous and circular concept' (p. 105), *Homo Sacer* criticises the ambiguity of the sacred as a *mythologeme*. As we will later see, *The Kingdom and the Glory* returns to and develops upon the analysis of sacrifice and authority first articulated in *Language and Death*.
22. Walter Benjamin, 'Capitalism as Religion', trans. Rodney Livingstone, in *Selected Writings, Volume 1: 1913–1926*, ed. Marcus Bullock and Michael W. Jennings (Cambridge, MA: The Belknap Press of Harvard University Press, 2004), p. 259.
23. Benjamin, 'Capitalism as Religion', p. 259.

24. Giorgio Agamben, 'In Praise of Profanation', in *Profanations*, trans. Jeff Fort (New York: Zone Books, 2007), p. 81.
25. Agamben, 'In Praise of Profanation', p. 81.
26. Agamben, 'In Praise of Profanation', p. 81.
27. Giorgio Agamben, *Means without End: Notes on Politics*, trans. Vincenzo Binetti and Cesare Casarino (Minneapolis: University of Minnesota Press, 2000), p. 75; Agamben, *The Coming Community*, p. 78.
28. Jessica Whyte, *Catastrophe and Redemption: The Political Thought of Giorgio Agamben* (Albany: State University of New York Press, 2013), p. 132.
29. For Whyte, this gives rise to problems in Agamben's account of contemporary political economy, which casts the homogenous planetary petit bourgeoisie as the end point of capitalist development, and pays insufficient attention to the problem of uneven geographical development. For my critique of Whyte's reading, see Daniel McLoughlin, 'Rethinking Agamben: Ontology and the Coming Politics', *Law and Critique*, vol. 25, no. 3 (2014), pp. 319–29.
30. Obviously the freedom involved in labour under capitalism is purely formal and is profoundly limited in fact: as Marx writes, the 'free labourer' is free 'in the double sense, that as a free individual he can dispose of his labour-power as his own commodity, and that on the other hand, he has no other commodity, i.e. he is rid of them, free of all the objects needed for the realization of his labour-power' (Marx, *Capital Volume 1*, pp. 272–3).
31. Karl Marx, 'Economic and Philosophical Manuscripts', in *Early Writings* (London: Penguin, 1992), p. 324. Marx makes this point in connection to alienation, rather than fetishism, and the relationship between the earlier and later analyses is contested. Nonetheless, the particular point he makes here still holds good for the later analysis of political economy.
32. See, for example, Debord, *Society of the Spectacle*, p. 42.
33. John Holloway, *How to Change the World without Taking Power: The Meaning of Revolution Today* (London: Pluto Press, 2002), p. 53.
34. Agamben, *The Kingdom and the Glory*, p. 224.
35. Marcel Mauss, *Œuvres*, vol. 1 (Paris: Editions de Minuit, 1968), p. 353, quoted in Agamben, *Kingdom and the Glory*, p. 226.
36. Agamben, *The Kingdom and the Glory*, p. 259.
37. Carl Schmitt, *Volksentscheid und Volksbegehren: Ein Beitrag zur Auslegung der Weimarer Verfassung und zur Lehre von der unmit-*

telbaren Demokratie (Berlin: Walter de Gruyter, 1927), p. 34, quoted in Agamben, *The Kingdom and the Glory*, p. 172.
38. Carl Schmitt, *Constitutional Theory* (Durham, NC, and London: Duke University Press, 2008), p. 254.
39. For Schmitt, the people cannot discuss, they can only shout yes or no to proposals that are put to them. Schmitt, *Constitutional Theory*, p. 338.
40. Schmitt, *Constitutional Theory*, p. 275.
41. Debord, *Society of the Spectacle*, p. 12.
42. Debord, *Society of the Spectacle*, p. 3.
43. Marx, *Capital: Volume III*, trans. David Fernbach (London: Penguin, 1991), p. 966.
44. Marx, *Capital Volume 1*, p. 280
45. Jason E. Smith, 'Form-of-Life: From Politics to Aesthetics (and Back)', *The Nordic Journal of Aesthetics*, no. 44–5 (2012–13), p. 66.
46. Agamben, *Means without End*, p. 155.
47. Post-workerism is a varied body of thought involving thinkers with a range of theoretical perspectives. What is common to post-workerist thought is, however, the attempt to grapple with the implications of the autonomist social struggles of the 1960s–70s for the development of capitalism and the categories of radical thought. This chapter focuses on the two thinkers whose ideas Agamben has most explicitly engaged: Paolo Virno and Antonio Negri (although my account of immaterial labour also draws heavily on Maurizio Lazzarato).
48. Paolo Virno, *Grammar of the Multitude* (Cambridge, MA, and London: Semiotext(e), 2004), p. 99. While this insurrection took place across the Western world, it is in Italy that the process of political innovation and theoretical experimentation was the most sustained. For a comprehensive analysis of this movement and its roots, see Sergio Bologna, 'Tribe of Moles', in Sylvère Lotringer and Christian Marazzi (eds), *Autonomia: Post-Political Politics* (Los Angeles: Semiotext(e), 2007), pp. 36–61.
49. Virno, *Grammar of the Multitude*, p. 99.
50. Maurizio Lazzarato, 'Immaterial Labor', in Paolo Virno and Michael Hardt (eds), *Radical Thought in Italy: A Potential Politics* (Minneapolis and London: University of Minnesota Press, 1996), p. 132.
51. Lazzarato, 'Immaterial Labor', p. 132.
52. The practice of relocating production from advanced capitalist countries to places such as Taiwan, China, India and Bangladesh threw

something of a spanner in the works of this aspect of the post-workerist analysis. The price of material labour proved to be so cheap in many of these countries that it was not profitable to automate the production process. Recently, however, the price of labour has been increasing in China (in part due to worker militancy) and a range of companies have begun to introduce robots to replace workers: see, for example, Dexter Roberts, 'The March of Robots into Chinese Factories', *Bloomberg Business*, 29 November 2012, available at <http://www.bloomberg.com/bw/articles/2012-11-29/the-march-of-robots-into-chinese-factories> (last accessed 15 March 2014).
53. The diagnosis of the contemporary economy in terms of the hegemony of immaterial labour is, however, certainly open to question. Badiou, for example, argues that there is nothing 'post-modern' about contemporary capitalism and that we are, rather, seeing a particularly noxious return to the capitalist development of the nineteenth century (Badiou, *The Rebirth of History: Times of Riots and Uprisings*, trans. Gregory Elliott (London: Verso, 2012), pp. 9–15). Others have criticised the category of immaterial labour for being too elastic (see Aufheben, 'Keep on Smiling: Questions on Immaterial Labour', *Aufheben*, vol. 14, available at <https://libcom.org/library/aufheben/aufheben-14-2006/keep-on-smiling-questions-on-immaterial-labour> (last accessed 23 November 2015)) or for being Eurocentric (see Ricardo Antunes, *The Meanings of Work: Essay on Affirmation and Negation of Work*, trans. Elizabeth Molinari (Leiden: Brill, 2013), p. 166). On the other hand, Marxist geographer David Harvey, whose work is a fairly orthodox form of Marxist political economy, has recently emphasised the role that immaterial labour plays in the contemporary economy (David Harvey, *Seventeen Contradictions and the End of Capitalism* (London: Profile Books, 2014), pp. 135–8). The point of the analysis here is not, however, to resolve this debate one way or the other, but rather to illustrate the conceptual and political problems that I believe Agamben is responding to, and hence how his thought might enrich the analysis of contemporary capitalism.
54. Lazzarato, 'Immaterial Labor', p. 142.
55. This is because labour now involves the capacity to manage productive cooperation meaning that workers are capable of the kinds of self-organisation required for genuinely democratic self-governance. See Virno, *Grammar of the Multitude*, pp. 61–3; Hardt and Negri, *Commonwealth*, pp. 352–3.
56. Lazzarato, 'Immaterial Labor', p. 134.

57. Lazzarato, 'Immaterial Labor', p. 135.
58. Michael Hardt and Antonio Negri, *Empire* (Cambridge, MA, and London: Harvard University Press, 2000), p. 24.
59. Labour that was productive of value did, however, clearly rely upon other forms of labour, such as reproductive labour, that did not directly produce value for capitals.
60. On the relationship between industrial capitalism and disciplinary power, see Michel Foucault, *Discipline and Punish: The Birth of the Prison*, trans. Alan Sheridan (London: Penguin, 1977), pp. 220–1.
61. Hardt and Negri, *Empire*, p. 196. This is due to the rise in importance of forms of labour not based in factories, as well as the particular nature of immaterial production, in which there is no clear distinction between productive and non-productive time. For example, communicative labour continues after the worker has clocked off as, for example, when the academic wakes in the middle of the night with a new idea, or the barista hones his or her service skills in every social interaction. Immaterial production is also parasitic on forms of life that exist outside the wage relationship: for example, the music industry profits by packaging whole subcultures for sale, and Facebook relies on the unpaid labour of all its users.
62. Michael Hardt and Antonio Negri, *Multitude: War and Democracy in the Age of Empire* (London: Penguin Press, 2004), p. 148.
63. This analysis draws heavily on Gilles Deleuze, 'Postscript on the Societies of Control', *October*, vol. 59 (Winter 1992), pp. 3–7.
64. Michael Hardt and Antonio Negri, *Empire* (Cambridge, MA, and London: Harvard University Press, 2000), p. 331.
65. Agamben, 'In Praise of Profanation', p. 79.
66. Giorgio Agamben, *The Highest Poverty: Monastic Rules and Form-of-Life*, trans. Adam Kotsko (Stanford: Stanford University Press, 2013), p. 83.
67. Michel Foucault, *Security, Territory, Population: Lectures at the Collège de France, 1977–1978*, ed. Michel Senellart, trans. Graham Burchell (Houndmills: Palgrave Macmillan, 2008), p. 46.
68. Jean Cassien, *Conferences*, ed. Pichery, Sources Chrétiennes series, no. 64, vol. 3 (Paris: Cerf, 1959). English translation: John Cassian, *Conferences*, trans. Colm Luibheid (New York: Paulist Press, 1985), pp. 40/101, quoted in Agamben, *The Highest Poverty*, pp. 22–3.
69. Agamben, *The Highest Poverty*, p. 23.
70. Agamben, *What Is an Apparatus?*, p. 50.
71. For the link to liberal governmentality, see Giorgio Agamben, 'Security and Terror', *Theory & Event*, vol. 5, no. 4, pp. 1–6; Giorgio

Agamben 'From the State of Control to a Praxis of Destituent Power', Public lecture in Athens, 16 November 2013, available at <http://www.chronosmag.eu/index.php/g-agamben-for-a-theory-of-destituent-power.html> (last accessed 12 December 2014). For the link to the society of control, see Agamben, 'From the State of Control'. For discussion of the relationship between the normalisation of the exception and the rise of government, see Daniel McLoughlin, 'Giorgio Agamben on Security, Government and the Crisis of Law', *Griffith Law Review*, vol. 23, no. 1 (2012), pp. 680–707.

72. There is, however, an important difference between the two insofar as a post-workerist thinker such as Negri emphasises the production of subjectivity, where Agamben emphasises the way that contemporary governmental apparatuses produce desubjectivation (Agamben, *What Is an Apparatus?*, pp. 19–21).

73. One of the problems with Agamben's genealogy of glory is that it can give the misguided impression that there is a genetic continuity between the theological-political lineage of glorification and the practices of the spectacle. The glorious display that is celebrated in the spectacle is, however, nothing more than exchange value that has congealed and turned into an image. The rituals of spectacular glorification do not derive from Church and state, but rather arise from the fetishistic structure of the commodity that is involved in the particular conditions of capitalist production. The spectacle's origin in the commodity form is the reason for the radical transformation of the practice of glory that it involves.

74. Virno, *Grammar of the Multitude*, p. 60.

75. Debord, *Society of the Spectacle*, p. 13.

6

An Alogical Space of Genetic Reintrication: Notes on an Element of Giorgio Agamben's Method
Justin Clemens

The Heavenly Circuit: Berenice's Hair;
Tent-pole of Eden; the tent's drapery;
Symbolical glory of the earth and air!
The Father and His angelic hierarchy
That made the magnitude and glory there
Stood in the circuit of a needle's eye.

Some found a different pole, and where it stood
A pattern on a napkin dipped in blood.
                      W. B. Yeats, 'Veronica's Napkin'[1]

I

In an extraordinary recent encounter, the French thinkers Alain Badiou and Jean-Claude Milner divide strenuously over the sense of contemporary political action. For Milner, we must now recognise that 'the heart of the question of politics' is 'the issue of bodies and their survival'.[2] Accepting this 'hard kernel' of the political entails that we adopt a sceptical position vis-à-vis political action, in which a certain kind of pragmatism should order our actions. For Badiou, by contrast, such a position is tantamount to an abandonment of political militancy as such. As is well known, he instead proposes a reconstruction of 'the communist hypothesis', that is, that politics must be undertaken as a situated local struggle to correlate equality and freedom at the level of the community. Hence Badiou can assert 'Politics is the real of communism.'[3] Their exchange is all the more salutary in that, in its very sharpness, it brings out certain limits and positional constraints of political thinking today. On the one hand, Milner offers a kind of disenchanted minimalist dialectic in which the survival of communities becomes the extimate kernel of the political. Contingencies affecting the natural substrate of humanity – such as plagues, earthquakes, environmental catastrophes, and so on – both found and threaten the political, in such a way as to render all utopian propositions both unduly local and essentially delusory. For its part, the state, through its monopoly on violence, at once opens a space for genuine politics that is based not on killing but on confrontations of discourse, yet thereby operates as an anti-political power.

By contrast, Badiou attempts to identify and affirm what remains today of the great modern revolutionary programmes as the 'communist hypothesis' – which can only be a 'hypothesis' precisely because the motif of revolution that governed modernity is now ruined. As he elsewhere writes: 'We don't know today what a revolution or the figure of the State corresponding to this could be.'[4] One can immediately see how the two thinkers occupy contemporary poles of thought on this matter. Yet there is also a kind of shared diagnosis at the heart of this dissent. Badiou names it explicitly: *biopolitics*. Whether you are 'for' or 'against' biopolitics is pragmatically and philosophically irrelevant. The political stakes of our time can only take their orientations from a global terrain sculpted and saturated by the routines of its governance. In doing so, they must also acknowledge the 'obscurity' and 'desuetude' – two terms of Mallarmé's poetry that are given a key *political* importance by Badiou – of all traditional forms of radical politics.

2

It is in this context that Giorgio Agamben offers strong correctives for the thinking of contemporary politics. His analyses are not resigned to the biopolitical revelation, but nor do they seek simply to restitute allegedly anti-biopolitical operations. Agamben is concerned to avoid the repetition of received or familiar modes of political action, for a number of reasons. Most such modes have now shown their complicity with biopolitics, proven unactionable or failed utterly. Rather, by undertaking a series of constantly renovated genealogies and archaeologies of biopolitics itself, its key historical figures, events and switching-points, Agamben establishes a strong and singular account of the becoming of our contemporary political predicament. He further shows how certain ancient philosophical concepts are integrally implicated in

Notes on an Element of Giorgio Agamben's Method 117

biopolitics, not least ontology itself, the Aristotelian distinction between potential and actual, as well as the inherited distributions of modal categories (possible, necessary, impossible, contingent). His project is therefore highly challenging in a number of senses: in provoking intellectual difficulties (for example, the very language we use is at once compromised yet non-derogable), practical difficulties (for example, the historical struggles against biopolitical extension have also enjoyed a complicity with their nominal enemy) and imaginative difficulties (for example, given our own implication in these phenomena, how can we possibly evade or neutralise their hold?). In this chapter, I will discuss Agamben's work through an analysis of one of his recurrent techniques: the genealogical interlacing of apparently antithetical concepts. I will examine this technique of Agamben's in some detail, with particular reference to what it enables him to adopt from and reshape in the work of Michel Foucault. In doing so, I give some justifications for Agamben's procedure in quite abstract philosophical terms, before showing how the challenges it raises are anything but abstract. I further show how this technique functions as a kind of motor for Agamben's work, driving him to extend and revisit his own theses on biopolitics. I conclude with a remark on its recent redeployment in *The Kingdom and the Glory*, where it enables a further rearticulation of familiar political oppositions, such as those between thought and action, power and glory, and repressive and ideological state apparatuses. Finally, I suggest that it is this intellectual operation of Agamben's that gives us an orientation towards the challenges of radical politics today, as well as itself being a mode of pursuing such a politics.

3

One of Agamben's characteristic rhetorical techniques is to identify concepts that, having been constructed independently of one another – even, sometimes, having been constructed in opposition to one another – can be rearticulated in such a way that they come to exhibit a singular, intelligible co-dependency. Such codependency is never, however, a simple resolution or reduction: it must rather be formalised as a kind of paradox, such that the paradoxical nature of this co-dependency also turns out to be integral to the secret of its functioning. Through such a rearticulation, Agamben generates new genealogies of concepts, their imbrication, application and implications, which not only illuminate certain opacities in the historical or intellectual record, but open further, hitherto under-examined or unexpected lines of inquiry in and for the present. Agamben's procedure has undoubtedly proven its suppleness and fecundity in a number of modalities, perhaps most notoriously in the great complex of works that bear the series title *Homo Sacer*, which traverse and re-examine certain decisive Western philosophical, theological and poetic events from the Ancient Greeks to the present. Certainly, like Foucault, Agamben is concerned to orient his researches with respect to the question of 'the ontology of the present'; yet the problem of what is itself 'present', and how it comes to be so, is significantly reconfigured in the course of his researches.

4

Agamben's relationship to Foucault's analyses of governmentality is evidently central to this project. Foucault's work on governmentality, initially polemically broached as a kind of reproach to legalistic theories of sovereignty and the state, can therefore help to illuminate some puzzles about Agamben's methods. Although Foucault goes to some trouble to explain that, in his account, sovereignty is not simply thereby surpassed or forgotten, but subsists, even extends, its fiction of dominance in the regime of governmentality, for him these dispensations of power, or, more precisely, power-relations, are and must be essentially disjoint. There was and is no necessity to the emergence of either sovereignty or biopower, so they remain in practice, in principle, and in reason independent. One must describe their aetiology and symptomatology according to entirely different forms of evidence. Finally, these different forms of power retain a temporal marking that is irreversible.[5] Whatever the complexities of their historical becoming, Foucault himself – as well as his most reputable commentators – understands the different dispensations of power as themselves *marking time*.[6] Hence, to the extent that Foucault offers a general theory of power, or, rather, new forms of attentiveness to the productive conversions of power-relations, an integral part of his work is dedicated to exposing radical fractures and transformations in received frames of interpretations. With regard to specific situations, he essays to show how a variegated site of power-relations with often only nominal consistency can come to subsist as a shell of itself, fade before another, come to be transformed by supplementation, or even by straightforward supplantation – and that one must deal with such specificities on a case-by-case basis.[7]

5

Foucault's genius for revelatory juxtapositions is justly famous. Perhaps there is no more striking instance of this than the disturbing opening of *Discipline and Punish*, in which the public torture and execution of the regicide Damiens in 1757 is set against a model, meticulous schedule of a new incarceratory regimen. It is by means of the shock of this juxtaposition, in some ways not unlike the 'before and after' photographs that remain a marketing staple of contemporary corporeal regimens from diet to plastic surgery, that Foucault proceeds to anatomise certain key – and often sudden – transformations in the nature of penal repression. For Foucault, infractions against the sovereign of the Ancien Régime were necessarily punished by a spectacular version of a personal vendetta upon the perpetrator, one which at once exaggerated and reversed the crime in a kind of hyperbole of corporeal atrocity. But the new world of post-Enlightenment *carceri* is something altogether different. Punishment starts to hide more and more away from public view; it becomes less physical and more spiritual, less a matter of tormenting a body than rectifying a soul; it is no longer undertaken as an exercise in vengeful glory but as an ugly necessity; it exerts itself as a form of continuing monitorial treatment rather than as a punctual riposte to particular transgressive acts; it becomes the object of a swarm of subsidiary experts rather than the subject of an exceptional legal algorithm. We are no longer in the realm of 'glorious', personalised, death-dealing events, but involved in the continuously extended disciplinary power over life. As is perhaps too well known, Bentham's panopticon becomes one of Foucault's privileged emblems of this radical shift in the modern diagram of power, whereby spectacle is superseded by surveillance, mythic violence by administrative knowledge, sovereign power by biopower.

6

The disjunctions identified and described by Foucault cannot be separated from his methodological innovations. The turn to micro-practices, to an unprecedented range of evidence, to a pluralisation of zones and a problematisation of situations, is coupled with his polemical call to abandon received ideas regarding, say, the mutual exclusivity of power and knowledge. I will return to the power–knowledge coupling shortly, but for the moment want to mark a related aspect of this project, which bears directly upon the thought of dis-continuity. In a superb summation of the philosophical import of Foucault's methods – which are themselves of course self-confessedly extensions of Friedrich Nietzsche's and Martin Heidegger's studies into the archaeology and genealogy of concepts and practices – Jean-Claude Milner notes that 'Foucault's program thus constructs a general typology of every possible discursive cut: a sort of topology of the concept', whereby the project of 'archaeology' becomes consubstantial with the hypothesis that 'a discontinuity is necessarily covered over by a stratum that masks it'.[8] So Foucault writes:

> within the very judicial modality of judgement, other types of assessment have slipped in, profoundly altering its rules of elaboration [...] A whole set of assessing, diagnostic, prognostic, normative judgements concerning the criminal have become lodged in the framework of penal judgement.[9]

For Foucault, then, there must be a multiplication of such almost-imperceptible cuts in the institutional corpus, in such a way that even contemporaneous transformations across institutions are not necessarily causally linked, nor even homologous with each other.

Perhaps paradoxically, then, what Milner names as Foucault's 'absolute nominalism' entails the reintroduction of temporal markers of incomparability and incompossibility into every analysis. Foucault starts to reconsider 'history' as a sequence of indiscernible 'cuts' that falsify all and any attempts to ground a general continuity. To give a single example: the 'history of madness', which might initially look like it could provide a great transhistorical continuity and foil to the story of reason, turns out to be rather a disjointed abstraction; instead, we find an astonishing heterogeneity of institutional and conceptual operations at work from the European Middle Ages on, in which so-called 'madness' is constituted, explained and treated in an enormous range of different ways. The name of madness (or, as elsewhere, 'the clinic', 'sexuality' or 'the prison', etc.) turns out to bear on a range of completely different materials, aims and procedures, whose essential disunity is to some extent masked by the apparent consistency of the name. What appeared a continuity is a morass of incompatible multiplicities. The general theory of the cut, identified by Milner as one of Foucault's contributions, is simultaneously a conceptual affirmation of the temporal self-positioning and situation of the absolutely non-equivalent.

7

Despite the complexities of his analyses of the transformations of power-relations, which seek to dismantle and rebuke all and any grand ground-concepts (including any 'whole' or totality, de facto or de jure) that would supposedly gather and regulate the social field, Foucault retains a conviction regarding the temporal succession of the various practices to which he attends. In the examples already invoked, a false continuity – the abiding thinking of power according to any of the variant available articulations of sovereignty–law–exception – is exposed as dissimulation and misunderstanding. It is *dissimulation* insofar as it masks the real operations of power-relations; it is *misunderstanding* insofar as power-relations no longer have much to do with the form of law itself. In what might even be considered a moment of attenuated Kantian critique, Foucault returns a limited pertinence to the analyses of sovereignty (they do have something to say about certain punitive practices of early modern European principalities), as he condemns them for surpassing their legitimate field of operations (they succumb to a kind of historical subreption which treats the phantoms of sovereignty as if they were still real). 'To cut the head off the king at the level of theory' is one of Foucault's great slogans from his later work, and it impels him to the astonishingly detailed and wide-ranging reconstructions of strictly modern routines of biopower – which examine economics, administration, philosophy, theology, sexuality, epidemiology, and so on – now familiar from his later seminars and published texts.[10] Different organisations of power-relations constitute utterly different kinds of object with utterly different kinds of technique.

8

At once with and against Foucault, Agamben asserts at the beginning of the eponymous volume of *Homo Sacer* (which, moreover, bears the crucial subtitle *Sovereign Power and Bare Life*) that 'the two analyses [of sovereign power and biopolitics] cannot be separated', and that:

> the inclusion of bare life in the political realm constitutes the original – if concealed – nucleus of sovereign power. *It can even be said that the production of a biopolitical body is the original activity of sovereign power* [...]. Placing biological life at the center of its calculations, the modern State therefore does nothing other than bring to light the secret tie uniting power and bare life, thereby reaffirming the bond (derived from a tenacious correspondence between the modern and the archaic which one encounters in the most diverse spheres) between modern power and the most immemorial of the *arcana imperii*.[11]

Whereas Foucault, as we have briefly seen, thinks of biopower as an emblematically modern phenomenon, essentially foreign to the operations of ancient political practices, Agamben wants to re-bind the two. He is objecting that, rather than considering government as an autonomous configuration irreducible to the operations of sovereignty, the two should be conceived of as being born together, as conjoined biopolitical twins. As the extract above outlines, it is not simply that sovereignty is covertly supplanted by biopower while the ashy, ashen ghosts of the former persist as misdirecting markers, but that, for Agamben, *the moment of the exposure of biopower as such allows it to be shown to be the very origin and essence of sovereignty that sovereignty had itself originally and essentially dissimulated as an integral component of its operations*. Where Foucault sees a misleading overlapping supersession, Agamben wants to see a kind of motivated indistinction of the precision of the articulation, whereby, for example, a juridico-political phenomenon comes to be misunderstood under the heading of 'the original ambivalence of the sacred', by a 'scientific mythologeme' 'itself in need of explanation'.[12] Another example: the dazzling glory of kingship occludes in its very brightness its integral identity with allegedly derivative administrative operations (I will come back to this point below). For Agamben, part of the difficulty in confronting the work of biopolitics is that the terms in which it has historically been understood have, for essential reasons, found themselves misled by its inherent dissimulations: here, Agamben takes up, just as Foucault did but with a different inflection, Martin Heidegger's analyses of the history of metaphysics as destined by a 'forgetting of the forgetting of the question of being'. It is only with the closure of the epoch of metaphysics that its limits emerge as such – a closure which is not an end, but rather shows itself *in* the fullness of its reign – and thereby, at the moment of its greatest extension and domination, offers a chance for its displacement. For Agamben, this means that such concepts as 'the original ambivalence of the sacred' have missed the precise ways in which the operations of sovereignty have at once separated and articulated the 'high' and the 'low', at the very moment that such 'concepts' fail to live up to the criteria of the 'science' that they allegedly exemplify. Something analogous holds for Agamben's account of biopolitics. So we are confronted with a different sort of inquiry by Agamben, which scrambles the chronology, character and constitution of the concepts at stake in order to rearticulate them anew. Agamben functions, in this regard, at a significantly more abstract level of analysis than Foucault, if, in his very hypertrophy of abstraction, he by no means repudiates the Foucauldian demonstrations and discoveries.

9

From Agamben's perspective, the very 'necessity' on Foucault's part to divide and multiply his 'object' in order to analyse it – a necessity which is bound up, as we have briefly seen, with the latter's radical methodological transformations – is itself testimony to the essential difficulty of thinking this object (and therefore is not a simple intellectual 'failure' or mere 'oversight' of Foucault's). Leaving aside the immediate rhetorical appeal of Agamben's operation, which, in repudiating invidious personal criticisms also evades some of the identificatory perils of exegesis, it also enables Agamben to establish *an alogical space of genetic reintrication*. This establishment is tantamount to reconstructing a sequence on the basis of the becoming-indistinct of the in-separated. If analyses of religion, law and politics have been analytically and practically separated throughout their history (and Foucault's division of biopolitics and sovereignty unwittingly repeats such a separation), such 'separations' have themselves been established on the basis of a covert 'inseparation'; that is, the originary compact between sovereignty and biopolitics. It is only, paradoxically, when such in-separated elements start to evince their indistinction across a range of contemporary phenomena that a reconstruction of their operations can finally be established. For Agamben, the fact that biopolitics was always already inscribed in the sovereignty that it seems to supplant does not mean that radical changes in power-relations and their forms have not occurred. It is rather that their temporality and differences must now be redescribed, as an urgent politico-ontological task. Otherwise we will be condemned to repeat the unliveability of biopolitics in the guise of novelty. As Agamben asserts in 'What Is the Contemporary?': 'the entry point to the present necessarily takes the form of an archaeology; an archaeology that does not, however, regress to a historical past, but returns to that part within the present that we are absolutely incapable of living'.[13] One of the immediate shocks released by such a procedure is therefore a *time-shock*: what seems to be contemporary is in fact fated by the most archaic. And if that is the case, then the problematic of the *event(s) of dissimulation-revelation* also needs to be rethought.

Yet if Agamben's intervention contravenes the peculiar time-marking qualities of Foucault's analyses, this contravention may immediately seem to reintroduce the very teleology with which Foucault wished to dispense. Indeed, Catherine Mills (and many other commentators) accordingly maintains that, 'for Agamben, the Nazi genocide was indicative of a hidden logic intrinsic to Western politics, and the paroxysms of World War II merely brought this logic to light in an unprecedented way'.[14] In its straightforwardly teleological forms, this perception is misplaced. Rather, for Agamben, what happens is *retroactively revelatory*: it is at once a genuine event, a novelty, yet one that thereby also exposes and reactivates previously unsuspected limits destined by a still-not-fully-unveiled-origin. This is undoubtedly why he likes to cite Benjamin: 'the historical index contained in the images of the past indicates that these images may achieve legibility only in a determined moment of their history'.[15] It is crucial for Agamben to maintain the priority of events as bound at least *in nuce* to a genuine novelty. It is therefore incorrect to consider that Agamben states or implies that the death camps were a necessary outcome of Western metaphysics, politics or pragmatics: the camps were not 'necessary' at all. But we cannot continue to act as if they did not happen. As Agamben notes of 'Auschwitz', in a critique of the Nietzschean doctrine of eternal return: '*One cannot want Auschwitz to return for eternity, since in truth it has never ceased to take place; it is always already repeating itself.*'[16] Indeed, this remark enables us to specify something further regarding Agamben's general doctrine of events: an event is something which, having happened, and which, being contingent, could always also not have happened, introduces and inscribes a new limit in a situation which at once impels us to re-examine its historical preconditions and urgently attempt to transform that limit in its turn. The historicity of events for Agamben involves the identification and elaboration of a sequence of moments or figures, that is, singularities or events, in which each always already incessantly and irremediably repeats itself, and in which each reverberates with as it extends its predecessors' limits.

10

These 'moments or figures' are not always the ones might expect. If one merely blandly lists the sorts of things to which Agamben pays attention, we find such oddities as the medieval word '*corn*', the *Muselmann*, pornography, cartoons, the halo, Bartleby the Scrivener, gesture, the face – that is, often marginal, unclassifiable or bizarre phenomena which together do not seem to partake in a critical, consistent or coherent procedure, except, perhaps, as the divagatory *trouvailles* of whimsy or arbitrariness. But this very appearance of oddity is surely essential to the work of 'study' that Agamben discusses in *Idea of Prose* in a kind of methodological self-portrait, that study which delivers an illuminating 'shock' in its presentation of strange assemblages.[17] Moreover, one could find diverse quasi-synonyms of this procedure operative throughout Agamben's work: the figures of the collector, the constellation or the fetishist drawn from Walter Benjamin, in which, as disparity is gathered and presented on a single plane, new organisations at once material, perceptible and conceptual can be discerned; the model metaphors of the 'experiment' and 'the laboratory', out of which new creatures and concepts come; the resolute focus on examples as modes of 'means without end'. This is why Agamben can legitimately announce that:

> In the course of my research, I have written on certain figures such as *Homo sacer*, the *Muselmann*, the state of exception, and the concentration camp. While these are all actual historical phenomena, I nonetheless treated them as paradigms whose role was to constitute and make intelligible a broader historical-problematic context.[18]

One should add that, despite his adverting to 'actual historical phenomena' here, Agamben ultimately makes no principled distinction between allegedly 'real', 'empirical' events or 'fictional', 'poetic' or 'phantasmatic' ones. The same essay from which the above citation is drawn concludes with a fragment of a poem of Wallace Stevens, after weaving through a series of short remarks on persons and *topoi* as different as Foucault, Thomas Kuhn, Sextus Pompeius Festus, Aristotle, Enzo Melandri, Immanuel Kant, the regulae of the early monastic orders, Victor Goldschmidt, grammatical declensions, Plato, the hermeneutic circle and Aby Warburg. One should also add that Agamben's clear and present 'influences', including Heidegger, Benjamin and Foucault, are almost never simply relied upon or cited without comment, whether explicit or implicit. Rather, as I have suggested vis-à-vis Foucault, he tries to place himself at the limits of their thinking – not least to show thereby that no such limit can itself be an end.

II

So teleology is not thereby wished away by Agamben; nor is it simply reinscribed or reaffirmed. On the contrary, he induces us to acknowledge that it is sovereign power itself which is *essentially* teleological, at least in a certain perverse sense. Sovereign power in the history of its solidarity with biopolitics bills itself as its own end and justification; the paradoxes of exceptionality consistently provide power with the alibi of necessity-as-end, in which the sense of *telos* as 'end' has been radically separated from that of *telos* as 'fulfilment', and that separation covered over. If we turn to Agamben's remarks on *telos* in *The Time That Remains*, we find a significant inversion and displacement of this separation-veiling. In this rereading of St Paul, Agamben notes that: 'Only to the extent that the Messiah renders the *nomos* inoperative, that he makes the *nomos* no-longer-at-work and thus restores it to the state of potentiality, only in this way may he represent its *telos* as both end and fulfilment.'[19] If this operation of rendering-inoperative is the messianic gesture par excellence, we ourselves have only been bequeathed a '*weak* messianic power' (as Benjamin puts it). It is with this in mind that Agamben explicitly pursues the messianic restoration of *telos* throughout his later work. As we have already seen, an event can be analysed to expose ciphered background conditions qua unveiling-of-limits, as it simultaneously introduces another chance of transformation. For such a transformation, a limit must be parlayed into a threshold – I will return to this problem below – but this cannot be done willy-nilly; moreover, it cannot be done according to the very phenomena and processes that have now been exposed as complicit with sovereignty.[20]

12

'Don't start with the good old things but the bad new ones', Brecht advises Benjamin, and it is just such advice that Agamben rigorously takes up.[21] As a glance at Agamben's work will confirm, he is incessantly identifying and enumerating the 'bad new things' of our times: the *Muselmann*, pornography and advertising, the society of the spectacle, and so on. If critics continue to misrepresent such a form of attention in a number of ways – sometimes even as an 'aestheticization' or a form of 'contextual narrowness' – Agamben's resolute commitment to 'the new' is irreducible to such critiques.[22] It is only the new that has the chance of escaping the repetitions of inheritance. Yet what is new is also always by definition on the verge of slipping away unrecognised, if not of being confounded with the old. This is also one reason why Agamben's philosophy is and must be strictly characterised as 'experimental', that is, positioned at the limits of knowledge, treating of limit-phenomena, 'brought to experimental and non-canonical use in a thoroughly profane universe', in Sergei Prozorov's felicitous summation.[23] This is also where the problematic of contingency, explicitly designated as such by Agamben throughout his work, communicates with its *also-always-can-not-have-happened*. As he remarks in a powerful essay titled 'Bartleby, or On Contingency': 'if Bartleby is a new Messiah, he comes not, like Jesus, to redeem what was, but to save what was not'.[24] Novelty is the redemption of whatever-could-have-been-but-was-not, beyond the repetitions of inheritance.

13

I have no hesitation in identifying this procedure – which I began, perhaps misleadingly, by calling a 'rhetorical technique' – as the matrix of what Agamben variously nominates 'profanation', 'gesture' or even, after Benjamin, 'weak messianic power'. As Anton Schütz notes, 'To profane is to lift the barriers of separation in solemn forms religious as well as secular, in order to give them back to use.'[25] Because the sacred that requires profanation is not usually available in an easily accessible or demonstrable presentation, as a recognisable figure, form or formation, Agamben seeks it in the overlooked, the underestimated or the aporetic detail. Why? Because an aporia, for example, is a sign at once of separation or division, as it is also a sign of the unsettled nature of that division; moreover, an aporia is, by definition, unavailable for use. It is therefore also still potentially 'new' in a particular sense of this term; or at least negatively designates a site at which the new can still have occurred. If, as we proposed above, Agamben's analysis of sovereignty unleashed a 'time-shock', whereby the apparently modern directly communicates with the archaic in a surprising way, he will also maintain that what is apparently archaic can directly communicate with the new – if itself in a singular and asymmetrical way. As he puts it, once again alluding to the Pauline doctrine, 'the being-contemporary with the Messiah' is "the time of the now" (*ho nyn kairos*)'.[26] The new is the now – but also a fracturing of times that simultaneously relates now-time to then-time. What I have denominated the 'time-marking' character of Foucault's objects is radically complicated by Agamben, whose research thus refuses or rather overgoes the conceptual, empirical and temporal limits given these objects by Foucault.[27]

14

Agamben very often treats Foucault this way: for example, regarding the relative lack of attention paid by the French thinker to modern totalitarian states or to the concentration camps.[28] In 'The Author as Gesture', Agamben takes up Foucault's famous disquisition on the author, in order to show how Foucault thereafter exacerbates the distinction between 'the author-individual and the author-function', without ever satisfactorily answering his critics.[29] In doing so, Foucault produces an 'enigmatic' 'aporia' which he himself never satisfactorily resolves. Once again, Agamben first shows how Foucault keeps subtly changing his position regarding the aporia, itself an indication that more is going on than an effective distinction; and then second provides a way of rephrasing Foucault's distinction in a way that Foucault himself did not, yet which can thereby rearticulate the division instituted between life and function, 'where the living being, encountering language and putting itself into play in language without reserve, exhibits in a gesture the impossibility of its being reduced to this gesture'.[30] We meet once again the same abstract move on Agamben's part with respect to his objects. We find the identification of an apparent antagonism as the operation of a sacred complicity; we find a process of reconstruction in the analysis of a paradoxical unity; we find the injunction to profanation patent in this very exposure, incarnating a gesture towards a return of the aporia to the realm of use. What prevents this abstract recurrence of Agamben's thought from being a mere intellectual parlour trick is that it is always also tied to the singularity of its objects, engaging a long, slow, protracted process of study that reconstructs the minutiae of sequences such as, say, the genealogical fate of the ancient term *oikonomia* in the early Christian writers.[31] Or, to modify the vocabulary in accordance with Agamben's own terms, such a practice is not simply a practice of the philosophical concept, but of the signature; a signature is to be discriminated from a concept insofar as the former is essentially a *transmission* device bearing upon the functional articulation of signs.[32] In such terms, philosophy becomes the study of signatures, which tracks a genetic sequence of contingent rerouting devices (signatures) that over time come to construct and consolidate a thought-machine (a paradigm) whose functioning establishes and regulates a particular segment of human practice. Agamben's procedure might be denigrated as 'mere erudition' if you like, but that would be to miss the fact that, as Agamben's conceptual armature becomes more and more abstract, it also becomes more and more material. It becomes more material in a number of senses, but let us simply cite the most basic and immediate sense: the materiality of language itself, down to the disposition of letters and words. Since Agamben's inquiries always proceed according to rigorous philological criteria, it is no surprise that at every point he gives minute attention to even the most minimal linguistic variations – minimal variations that often have maximal effects. As Aby Warburg said, in a phrase approvingly quoted by Agamben himself, 'Der liebe Gott steckt im Detail.'[33] Without the painstaking provision of such philological details, Agamben's procedure would have neither pertinence nor purchase.[34] These details are often of the order of Foucault's own 'little question, What happens?' if given a different inflection or different frame.[35] For Agamben, 'what happens?' is as dependent upon often-unperceived literal displacements as upon unexpected institutional repurposings of existing political techniques or grand historical events.

15

What is also notable in this context is that what I have called Agamben's construction of 'an alogical space of genetic reintrication', is itself sometimes reinjected by Agamben into materials that he himself had previously treated. As I have noted, he works upon Foucault to reintricate biopower and sovereignty, the author-individual and the author-function, the structure of the death camps with the political analyses that mention these only briefly. In doing so, however, another 'sacred' division de facto emerges: between (to put it briefly) 'the political' and 'the economic'. Foucault's own work was itself elaborated partially as a riposte to Marxist theory, in which the relationship between the political and the economic – however variously it was thought in and by that tradition – was itself foundational, consecrated in the fundamental syntagm 'political economy' crucial to the Marxist enterprise. In response, Foucault's many different analyses through the course of his career have to be interpreted as consistently trying to circumvent and undermine any self-evidence to this syntagm. In *The Order of Things*, the modern episteme of the 'empirico-transcendental doublet' co-conditions economics alongside biology and linguistics; in studies such as *History of Madness* or *Discipline and Punish*, the economic is not extensively addressed, and certainly not as a determining factor in the power–knowledge mutations there tracked by Foucault; in *The History of Sexuality: Volume 1*, Foucault even seems to imply in passing that the triumph of modern capitalism was in fact itself dependent on prior developments in power–knowledge relations.[36] It is certainly not that Foucault ignores the economy, but that, as his seminars attest, a significant part of his programme is clearly to dissolve its priority in the order of things, to reconsider 'the economy' within a 'general economy' of power-relations.[37] For a philologist, however, this substitution still begs the question: why and how is it that power-relations can come to be thought of as an *economy* at all?

16

With entirely different references and with different techniques, this turns out too to be a line that Agamben follows. Yet he continues to do so according to the operation I have been outlining. Having reconstructed the bond between biopower and sovereignty, the state of exception, the production of bare life, and the sequence of political innovations that culminates in the camps, he has more recently turned his attention to a genealogy of the concept of the 'economy' itself. His extraordinary treatise *The Kingdom and the Glory* in fact opens with an announcement regarding the 'paradigms' of thought that have proved decisive in the genealogy of the modern West. I will not have time to examine the substance of Agamben's painstaking demonstrations of the development of *oikonomia* in *The Kingdom and the Glory* here; I want only to underline a new kind of repetition of his own characteristic operation, with respect to the identification and rebinding of political and economic paradigms. For there are now two paradigms simultaneously at stake: first, that of the political, which founds the operations of sovereignty; second, that of the economy, which founds the operations of government.

17

The Kingdom and the Glory opens by explicitly situating itself, once again, in the wake of Foucault's researches into government. Once again, too, Agamben does not fail to note that he himself is undertaking a kind of work of fulfilment of something that Foucault announced, but could not complete 'for internal reasons'. The messianic identification is stringently if covertly underlined. These reasons also pick up on precisely the temporal elements I have been attempting to identify here: 'in this study, the shadow that the theoretical interrogation of the present casts onto the past reaches well beyond the chronological limits that Foucault assigned to his genealogy'.[38] Here, in his return to the early development of Christian Trinitarian doctrine, Agamben once again identifies a dehiscence in the materials. The separation is no longer between law and exception but between *oikonomia* and glory, management and ceremony, the meta-organisational techniques of organisation, and the operations of power's self-acclamation. Agamben announces:

> One of the theses that we shall try to demonstrate is that two broadly speaking political paradigms, antinomical but functionally related to one another, derive from Christian theology: political theology, which founds the transcendence of sovereign power on the single God, and economic theology, which replaces this transcendence with the idea of an *oikonomia*, conceived as an immanent ordering.[39]

Agamben orients his reconstruction of the coming-to-be of this division according to the Peterson–Schmitt 'debate' regarding the status of political theology. For Peterson, there cannot be a Christian political theology due to the fact of the Trinity: political theology can only have a meaning for Jews and pagans. For Schmitt, on the contrary, there must of course be a Christian political theology. The dispute hinges on the very different locales that the reactionary thinkers assign to the *katechon*, the power that inhibits the *eschaton*. For Peterson, the *katechon* is the refusal of the Jews to convert; for Schmitt, it is the Empire. Instead of the Second Coming, then, we get the Catholic Church. What becomes clear for Agamben in his return to some of the ancient sources of this debate, such as Tertullian, is that another term, *oikonomia*, is at play, which is recurrently and explicitly linked to the functions of *monarchia*. But such a bond suggests a certain strain, too. How is it that this bond between economy and monarchy came to be established and resolved in and by the early Christian writers?

18

Picking up on the development of the sense and reference of *oikonomia* (economy, domestic management) from Plato, Aristotle and Xenophon, Agamben tracks how this term – which first of all designates not a science, but a practice – comes to be taken up in St Paul, whose language to designate the messianic community is drawn from the semantic penumbra of domestic economy with its slaves, servants and administrators, as well as in Stoic rhetoric, which makes of the economy not only a disposition or division but a participation in an order. Paul even uses the phrase 'the economy of the mystery' (Eph. 3: 9), which evinces that there has already been a degradation of the Aristotelian opposition between *oikos* and *polis*. Yet Paul's decisive role in the establishment of Christian messianism also means that his deployment of the term serves to reset the metaphorical and practical inheritance of Christianity around the community that is the 'house of God'. Moreover, the early Christian thinkers are struggling not only with Gnostic adversaries but rival monotheists in their attempts to fix a properly Christian dispensation. As Agamben writes:

> Both Hippolytus and Tertullian are engaged in a confrontation with adversaries (Noetus and Praxeas) who adhere to a rigorous form of monotheism – and are defined, for this reason, Monarchians – and see the personal distinction between the Father and the Word as in danger of relapsing into polytheism. The concept of *oikonomia* is the strategic operator that, before the elaboration of an appropriate philosophical vocabulary – which will take place only in the course of the fourth and fifth centuries – allows a temporal reconciliation of the trinity with the divine unity.[40]

In this struggle, the Pauline phrase 'economy of the mystery' is inverted, becoming instead 'the mystery of the economy'. What for Paul had been a kind of domestic ordering for a community's orientation towards the Messiah became itself struck by an indecomposable, recalcitrant opacity. This fateful inversion has further extraordinary consequences: for theses on angelology, providence, history, the separation of being and praxis, and so on. If there is no space to examine Agamben's demonstrations in any further detail, the new proto-doctrine of the economy created by the inversion of Paul's syntagm under pressure of doxological polemic has, however, one more serious consequence that we must mention here. Given that 'the classical cosmos – its "fate" – is based on the perfect unity of being and praxis', then 'the doctrine of the *oikonomia* radically revokes this unity'.[41] The problem for the Christians is this: God must be good; God must be creative (active, volitional); evil can be neither of God Himself nor a foreign competing principle. Whereas the pagans, philosophers, Gnostics and Jews all have consistent responses to this aporia – for instance, by not acknowledging a division between being and act, by considering that 'God' is a bungling or evil demiurge, that the gods are irrelevant or indifferent to us, or that God is an active caretaker – the Christians can only resolve the difficulty by means of an economising of the Trinity. If God is indivisible in substance, his praxis is triune.

19

A notable fact regarding Agamben's analysis of the determining function of economy in early Christianity is how closely it resembles his own gesture of genetic reintrication I have been discussing here. Confronted by a tormenting aporia of division, under pressure of established religions on the one side and rival emergent sects on the other, and without any assured reference points, these writers repurposed the term 'economy' in order to resolve these separations, without reduction, in the name of salvation. Yet 'economy' in Christian theology also simultaneously operates according to the imbrication of mass management and marketing techniques through forms of mystification, in its binding of the mystery of the Trinity to the glory of God. The angels of yesterday show their continuity with the porn stars of the present, in collusion with the sovereign who takes power over life by abandonment. It is here that Agamben's gesture – as infinitesimally close to the intellectual inventions of the early Christians as it may be – radically departs from it. Their operations diverge on the place of *temporality*: where the Church's position is founded on deferral, Agamben's messianic gesture is directed towards the activation of the messianic now-time.

20

While it would be of the utmost interest to further track the emergence and development of this operation in Agamben's work – which may well already be secreted, for instance, in the linked essays that comprise *The Man without Content* or the components of *Stanzas*[42] – all I have sought to do in this context is to identify, isolate and (to some extent) explicate the deployment of and justifications for one of his signature methodological operations. This operation of genetic reintrication is one that Agamben ultimately comes to reapply to his own work in order to rebind the paradoxical articulated separations of the political and the economic; in doing so, his work can be seen to force itself beyond itself, that is, beyond its own previously unthought separations. I believe that this operation must be given its full import and its full modesty as self-consciously messianic, that is, weak, impoverished and profane, to pick up on the terms that Agamben has himself explored elsewhere, and which I have briefly touched on above. It is 'weak', in that it draws upon neither violence nor established legitimacies in its elaboration; it is 'impoverished', in that it does not offer clear directives or managerial interventions as a guide, or any commodity or glory as reward; it is 'profane', in that it confronts sacral separations at their root.

21

Agamben's thought is a committed thought, resistant to any sense of the triumph of capital, democracy or human rights. As an ongoing 'act', in its inherently public nature and its self-transforming continuation, it is tantamount to an act of witnessing along the very lines Agamben himself analyses, resisting, to invoke Jacques Rancière, the determined dissolution of 'norm into fact'.[43] In an obscure epoch in which traditional forms of political action have shown their complicity or failure, Agamben proposes and practises new ways of approaching and thinking through this obscurity. Yet such thinking-through is not opposed to nor in lieu of 'real action'. His work exposes and elaborates some of the ways in which new forms of thoughtfulness are absolutely necessary if one is to cut across the regularised repetitions of the worst. There is no institution that is not comprised as much of brains as it is of bricks, and it is surely an integral aim of the reactionary attacks on 'mere theory' or the 'pretensions of philosophy' to neutralise or negate the integral threat that thinking constitutes for established or emergent powers. In fact, the ancient distinction between 'theory' and 'practice' is itself complicit with such powers insofar as the thinker is thereby destined to oscillate between the positions of absolute mastery, contemplative withdrawal and engaged intellectual henchman. Not one of Agamben's figures, whether 'real' or 'fictional', solitary or communal – whether Paul of Tarsus, the mediaeval melancholic, Bartleby the Scrivener or the community of Franciscan monks – fails to disrupt this distinction. On the contrary, all find a different use for things. The operation I have investigated here must, therefore, be accorded the status of an act of radical politics along just such lines, even if it must also simultaneously run the risk of appearing impotent or irrelevant – when it appears at all. Study and scholarship may be not much as acts, but they are not altogether nothing. If they issue no commandments, they describe, in all senses of this word, unheralded forms-of-life.

Notes

1. William Butler Yeats, 'Veronica's Napkin', in *Collected Poems* (London: Picador, 1990), p. 270.
2. Alain Badiou and Jean-Claude Milner with Philippe Petit, *Controversies*, trans. Susan Spitzer (Cambridge: Polity, 2014), p. 12.
3. Badiou and Milner, *Controversies*, p. 23.
4. Alain Badiou with Fabien Tarby, *Philosophy and the Event*, trans. Louise Burchill (Cambridge: Polity, 2013), p. 37.
5. The *locus classicus* for this aspect of Foucault's work is of course Michel Foucault, *Discipline and Punish: The Birth of the Prison*, trans. Alan Sheridan (New York: Vintage, 1979).
6. For example, note the terms in which Gilles Deleuze attends to this very issue: 'What is Foucault trying to say in the best pages of *The History of Sexuality*? When the diagram of power **abandons** the model of sovereignty in favour of a disciplinary model, when it becomes the "bio-power" or "bio-politics" of populations, controlling and administering life, it is indeed life that emerges as the **new** object of power. At that point law increasingly **renounces** that symbol of sovereign privilege, the right to put someone to death (the death penalty), but allows itself to produce all the more hecatombs and genocides: not by returning to the **old** law of killing, but on the contrary in the name of race, precious space, conditions of life and the survival of a population that believes itself to be better than its enemy, which it **now** treats not as the juridical enemy of the **old** sovereign but as a toxic or infectious agent, a sort of "biological danger."' I have made bold 'abandons', 'new', 'renounces', 'old', etc., as evidence of how, in the end, the two different forms of power are not only irreducible but one supplants the other historically. See Gilles Deleuze, *Foucault*, trans. Sean Hand, with a foreword by Paul Bove (Minneapolis: University of Minnesota Press, 1988), p. 92.
7. For a clear instance of this specifying mania on Foucault's part, see Ben Golder's remarks on Foucault's theses regarding rights discourses, 'Foucault's Critical (Yet Ambivalent) Affirmation: Three Figures of Rights', *Social and Legal Studies*, vol. 20, no. 3 (2011), pp. 283–312.

8. Jean-Claude Milner, *L'Œuvre claire: Lacan, la science, la philosophie* (Paris: Seuil, 1995), pp. 79–80.
9. Foucault, *Discipline and Punish*, p. 19.
10. See *inter alia* Michel Foucault, *Security, Territory, Population: Lectures at the Collège de France, 1977–1978*, ed. Michel Senellart, trans. Graham Burchell (Houndmills: Palgrave Macmillan, 2004); Michel Foucault, *The Birth of Biopolitics: Lectures at the Collège de France, 1978–1979*, ed. Michel Senellart, trans. Graham Burchell (Houndmills: Palgrave Macmillan, 2008).
11. Giorgio Agamben, *Homo Sacer: Sovereign Power and Bare Life*, trans. Daniel Heller-Roazen (Stanford: Stanford University Press, 1998), p. 6 (original emphasis).
12. See Agamben, *Homo Sacer*, pp. 75–83.
13. Giorgio Agamben, 'What Is the Contemporary?', in *What Is an Apparatus? and Other Essays*, trans. David Kishik and Stefan Pedatella (Stanford: Stanford University Press, 2009), p. 51. As a complementary instance of Agamben's convictions in this regard, see also his remarks on fashion in the same essay.
14. Catherine Mills, *The Philosophy of Agamben* (Stocksfield: Acumen, 2008), p. 84. See also some of the essays collected in Andrew Norris (ed.), *Politics, Metaphysics and Death: Essays on Giorgio Agamben's* Homo Sacer (Durham, NC, and London: Duke University Press, 2005), for example those by Erik Vogt and Peter Fitzpatrick; Mathew Abbott, *The Figure of this World: Agamben and the Question of Political Ontology* (Edinburgh: Edinburgh University Press, 2014). In a very different vein, Andrew Benjamin argues that Agamben is wrong about the Greek dispensation, as well as about its implications for the present: Andrew Benjamin, *Place, Commonality, and Judgment: Continental Philosophy and the Ancient Greeks* (London and New York: Continuum, 2010).
15. Agamben, *What Is an Apparatus?*, p. 53.
16. Giorgio Agamben, *Remnants of Auschwitz: The Witness and the Archive*, trans. Daniel Heller-Roazen (New York: Zone Books, 1999), p. 101 (original emphasis). For Agamben's other remarks about Nietzsche, see also *Homo Sacer*, p. 48; Giorgio Agamben, *The Man without Content*, trans. Georgia Albert (Stanford: Stanford University Press, 1999), p. 92.
17. See Giorgio Agamben, *Idea of Prose*, trans. Michael Sullivan and Sam Whitsitt (Albany: State University of New York Press, 1995), p. 63. See my own note on this procedure in Justin Clemens, *Psychoanalysis*

is an Antiphilosophy (Edinburgh: Edinburgh University Press, 2013), pp. 98–9.
18. Giorgio Agamben, *The Signature of All Things: On Method*, trans. Luca D'Isanto with Kevin Attell (New York: Zone Books, 2009), p. 9.
19. Giorgio Agamben, *The Time That Remains: A Commentary on the Letter to the Romans*, trans. Patricia Dailey (Stanford: Stanford University Press, 2005), p. 98.
20. This is why Jessica Whyte is correct to discern a dialectic of 'catastrophe and redemption' at work in Agamben, but incorrect insofar as her critique targets Agamben's putative teleology, his apparent refusal to provide guidelines for action, or his recourse to singular (weak, compromised, fictional?) figures such as Bartleby. See Jessica Whyte, *Catastrophe and Redemption: The Political Thought of Giorgio Agamben* (Albany: State University of New York Press, 2013), and the review essay by Daniel McLoughlin of Whyte and Mathew Abbott's book, 'Rethinking Agamben: Ontology and the Coming Politics', *Law and Critique*, vol. 25, no. 3 (2014), pp. 319–29.
21. Walter Benjamin, 'Conversations with Brecht', *New Left Review*, vol. 1, no. 77 (1973), p. 1.
22. See Jay M. Bernstein, 'Bare Life, Bearing Witness: Auschwitz and the Pornography of Horror', in *Parallax*, vol. 10, no. 1 (2004), pp. 2–16; Nicholas Chare, 'The Gap in Context: Giorgio Agamben's "Remnants of Auschwitz"', *Cultural Critique*, no. 64 (2005), pp. 40–68. Although I believe Chare is in one sense correct about Agamben's 'contextual narrowness' here (and his article makes a number of excellent points about Agamben's work more generally), Agamben is not attempting to account for all the problems of holocaust witnessing, but identifying a significant lapsus in the historiography and interpretation of the figure of the *Muselmann*; second, such a focus on Agamben's part is also a necessary restriction to draw out the implications of the figure.
23. Sergei Prozorov, 'Profanation in the Political Philosophy of Giorgio Agamben', *Theory, Culture & Society*, vol. 28, no. 4 (2011), pp. 71–95.
24. Giorgio Agamben, 'Bartleby, or On Contingency', in *Potentialities: Collected Essays in Philosophy*, trans. Daniel Heller-Roazen (Stanford: Stanford University Press, 1999), p. 270.
25. Anton Schütz, 'Profanation', in Alex Murray and Jessica Whyte (eds), *The Agamben Dictionary* (Edinburgh: Edinburgh University Press, 2011), p. 164.

26. Agamben, *What Is an Apparatus?*, p. 52.
27. This feature is often explicitly noted by Agamben, for example: 'in this study, the shadow that the theoretical interrogation of the present casts onto the past reaches well beyond the chronological limits that Foucault assigned to his genealogy' (Giorgio Agamben, *The Kingdom and the Glory: For a Theological Genealogy of Economy and Government*, trans. Lorenzo Chiesa with Matteo Mandarini (Stanford: Stanford University Press, 2011), p. xi).
28. See Agamben, *Homo Sacer, passim.*
29. Giorgio Agamben, 'The Author as Gesture', in *Profanations*, trans. Jeff Fort (New York: Zone Books, 2007), p. 63.
30. Agamben, *Profanations*, p. 72. In the most recent and final instalment of the *Homo Sacer* series, *L'uso dei corpi* (Vicenza: Neri Pozza, 2014), *passim*, Foucault continues to play a comparable role.
31. See Agamben, *The Kingdom and the Glory*.
32. See Agamben, *The Signature of All Things*, pp. 33–80.
33. 'The good God hides in the details.' Agamben riffs extensively upon Warburg's expression – which itself is a twist on the common German idiom *Der Teufel steckt im Detail* (the devil's in the details) – in the essay 'Aby Warburg and the Nameless Science', in *Potentialities*, pp. 89–103; see also p. 32.
34. A great early example of Agamben's philological talents can be found in the chapter titled '*Corn*: From Anatomy to Poetics', in *The End of the Poem: Studies in Poetics*, trans. Daniel Heller-Roazen (Stanford: Stanford University Press, 1999), pp. 23–42, where, after listing a sequence of (often bizarre) theories regarding the significance of this enigmatic term, he offers an absolutely stunning conceptual resolution to the problem which is *literally* more material (and certainly more persuasive) than any of his erudite predecessors.
35. Michel Foucault, 'Afterword: The Subject and Power', in Hubert L. Dreyfus and Paul Rabinow, *Michel Foucault: Beyond Structuralism and Hermeneutics* (Brighton: Harvester Press, 1982), p. 217.
36. We can discern Foucault's delimitations of the determinations of the economic in such statements as 'Comte and Marx both bear out the fact that eschatology (as the objective truth proceeding from man's discourse) and positivism (as the truth of discourse defined on the basis of the truth of the object) are archaeologically indissociable: a discourse attempting to be both empirical and critical cannot but be both positivist and eschatological; man appears within it as a truth both reduced and promised' (Michel Foucault, *The Order of Things: An Archaeology of the Human Sciences* (New York: Pantheon

Books, 1970), p. 320). See also Michel Foucault, *The History of Sexuality: Volume 1, The Will to Knowledge*, trans. Robert Hurley (Camberwell: Penguin, 2008), and Agamben's comments on this in *Homo Sacer*, for example, p. 3.
37. Hence Foucault will easily use the phrase 'general economy' to speak of, for instance, the global interrelationship of various discourses, or 'market economy' or 'welfare economy' in regards to particular moments of his studies, as he will reopen questions regarding, say, the specific conditions pertaining to the development of the field of 'political economy' itself from the eighteenth century, for example, 'the intellectual instrument, the type of calculation or form of rationality that made possible the self-limitation of governmental reason was not the law. What is it, starting from the middle of the eighteenth century? Obviously, it is political economy' (Foucault, *The Birth of Biopolitics*, p. 13).
38. Agamben, *The Kingdom and the Glory*, p. xi.
39. Agamben, *The Kingdom and the Glory*, p. 1.
40. Agamben, *The Kingdom and the Glory*, p. 36.
41. Agamben, *The Kingdom and the Glory*, p. 54.
42. See Giorgio Agamben, *Stanzas: Word and Phantasm in Western Culture*, trans. Ronald L. Martinez (Minneapolis: University of Minnesota Press, 1993).
43. See Jacques Rancière, *Aesthetics and Its Discontents*, trans. Steven Corcoran (Cambridge: Polity, 2009), p. 110.

7

Zoē aiōniōs: Giorgio Agamben and the Critique of Katechontic Time

Nicholas Heron

Only rarely has it been recalled that Erik Peterson's bracing critique of political theology was effectively carried out, not on one, but on two fronts.[1] On the one hand, there was the well-known argument that with the proclamation of the orthodox dogma of the Trinity, early Christianity's brief flirtation with a political theology founded on the model of Hellenistic Judaism was brought to an abrupt and definitive end (for the reason that the triune God, unlike the 'monarchical' God of the Jews, had no analogue in the created world). On the other hand, however, there was the lesser-known, but no less significant, argument (and potentially even more devastating for its implicit target in Carl Schmitt) concerning the triumph of St Augustine's theology of peace over the prevailing interpretation of the Pax Romana as the fulfilment of the messianic prophecies of the Old Testament.[2] According to this second perspective – which is treated only very briefly in the text, yet whose significance is underscored by the dedication to Augustine which graces the treatise's opening page – any peace, whether Roman or otherwise, which would be realised politically (and hence appear immanent to history) must necessarily be an illusion, because true, authentic peace is to be attained only at the end of time, only in eternity.[3] The significance of the first of these claims for Giorgio Agamben's recent reconstruction of the paradigm of economic theology requires little comment. It is starting from Peterson's critique, to be sure, that he undertakes to rehabilitate Schmitt's concept, even while submitting it to a profound structural overhaul, by showing how the ante-Nicene Church Fathers responsible for the first articulation of the doctrine of the Trinity had in fact sought to reconcile the received theological-political notion of divine monarchy with the unprecedented elaboration of a divine economy.[4] The significance of the second of these claims for Agamben's project, on the other hand, is anything but obvious. Yet it is only against the backdrop of this argument regarding Augustine's theology of peace with its eschatology of deferral, I want to suggest, that the precise sense of his intervention with respect to the debate between the theologian and the jurist becomes fully intelligible.

Agamben's appraisal of the debate in fact encompasses three distinct levels.[5] On the surface, there is the dispute regarding the admissibility or inadmissibility of a specifically Christian political theology, which Peterson had called radically into question. Beneath the surface of the dispute, however, there is a secret solidarity between the two adversaries, which is reflected in a shared orientation to the philosophy of history, which Agamben (invoking the unidentified entity or figure which the Second Letter to the Thessalonians depicts as forestalling the end of time) describes as 'katechontic'. Finally, at a tertiary level, there is a second, more or less concealed dispute – which for Agamben constitutes the true stakes of the debate – concerning the nature and identity of the *katechōn* itself, that is, of the force responsible for delaying and even eliminating concrete eschatology.[6] If Schmitt's use of the figure of the *katechōn* has attracted significant scholarly interest,[7] Peterson's own invocation of it, by contrast – from which Schmitt probably derived his – has received comparatively little attention. Yet it is the interpretation that Peterson gives to this figure that guides Agamben's appraisal of the particular experience of time concomitant with the elaboration of an economic theology. If it is true, however, that the experience of time in question here remains incomprehensible except against the backdrop of the Augustinian theology of peace that underpins it, it nonetheless cannot be said to coincide with it completely. Rather, it constitutes a particular perversion of it, whose sense we shall have to construe. And in this perspective the precise nature and identity of the *katechōn* becomes absolutely decisive.

In what follows, then, we shall seek to specify the particular conception of time consubstantial with Agamben's economic theology, by situating it in relation to the broader philosophical history of reflections on time, at least insofar as the latter may be said to inform the Augustinian theology of peace whose perversion it represents. Crucially, as we shall see, within this history time is defined for the most part only negatively, only as against that which is not time, namely, eternity. The philosophical history of time is thus to a large extent determined by the philosophical history of eternity, whose inferior image time is understood to be. As we shall nonetheless see, it is precisely this hierarchy that the katechontic orientation to time effectively overturns. Henceforth, it is time that as it were conquers (and even, according to very particular means, annexes) eternity. But it is only against the backdrop of this diagnosis, we shall suggest in closing, that Agamben's otherwise surprising reclamation of the biblical figure of 'eternal life' may be understood.

Aiōn: from immanence to transcendence

The curious semantic history of the Greek term *aiōn*, from which the modern vocabulary pertaining to 'eternity' derives, has long fascinated scholars.[8] For example, in the eighth-century *summa* of Eastern theology known to tradition as *De fide orthodoxa*, John of Damascus could distinguish no fewer than five distinct meanings for the term. The life of each human being, he wrote, is called an *aiōn*, as is a period of a thousand years. But the whole present life is also termed an *aiōn*, as is the future immortal life after the resurrection. Finally, in what is undoubtedly the most intriguing meaning of the term, *aiōn* is said to coincide neither with time itself, nor even with a part of it, being instead to eternal things what time is to temporal things: coextensive with them, 'as it were the movement and space of time'.[9] Perhaps nowhere, as in this sequence, is the radical polysemy and even heterogeneity of the term so clearly attested: here *aiōn* names, by turns, the duration of an individual life; that of a period which far exceeds the duration of an individual life, up to the point of encompassing the entire present age and even that of the one to come; and finally, most drastically, the measure particular to things which are outside of time altogether. According to a curious paradox, *aiōn* is thus, for John, simultaneously the measure of what is inside time *and* of what is outside time – indeed, as God, who in one sense made the *aiōnes*, is in another sense said to be of the *aiōn* himself.

In truth, of course, what appears in John in the simultaneity of the list is but the concatenation in a single place of a semantic evolution that took place over the course of centuries. In a sequence which has given linguists and philologists much work to do, Aristotle, in addition to clearly indicating the direction in which this evolution had advanced, had already sought to account for it through recourse to the practice of a singular form of etymology. According to him, the ancients must have been divinely inspired when they coined the word *aiōn*. 'The total time', he wrote, 'which circumscribes the length of life of every creature, and which cannot in nature be exceeded, they named the *aiōn* of each. By the same analogy', he continued, 'also the sum of existence of the whole heaven, the sum which includes all time even to infinity, is *aiōn*, taking the name from *aei einai* [literally, "is always"], for it is immortal and divine.'[10] For Aristotle, then, the inspired word already contained within itself the seed of its later development, thus accounting for the otherwise inexplicable passage – amounting to nothing less than a complete overhaul of its meaning – from signifying something of limited duration to something of unlimited duration. In his commentary on this passage, A. J. Festugière has nonetheless provided a far more prosaic explanation. For him, even in the latter instance – in which its meaning, to be sure, first begins to approximate that of 'eternity' – *aiōn* still retains the initial significance of 'duration of an individual life'. Only here it refers to a life, no longer of finite, but of infinite duration: namely, the life of a god.[11]

Festugière's elegant explanation is nonetheless complicated by the fact that the very original meaning of the word on whose basis Aristotle seeks to account for its later extension, is itself representative of a relatively late stage in its semantic history. Far from explaining anything, it must first itself be explained. As Émile Benveniste has shown, above all through the examination of its numerous appearances within the Homeric corpus, *aiōn* – like the corresponding Indo-Iranian form *āyu* – originally had nothing whatsoever to do with duration. It signified life, not in its temporal, but in its so to speak vital aspect: not 'life-time' (as the Liddell–Scott–Jones lexicon would have it, for example), but 'life-force'.[12] And, in this respect, it has a specifically human connotation, which makes its later development all the more striking. If the frequent association between *aiōn* and *psychē* (as in the use of the syntagm *psychē te kai aiōn*, where it appears more or less as a synonym[13]) were not already indication enough, Benveniste's thesis is confirmed by a very particular acceptation of the term that lexicographers have been at a loss to explain. At the beginning of Book 19 of the *Iliad*, when Achilles expresses concern that flies may enter the wounds of Patroclus and breed worms inside that would disfigure his corpse, the qualification he immediately adds to this – *ek d'aiōn pephatai*, 'for the life is slain in him'[14] – has been seen, by ancient and modern commentators alike, to entail such a concrete image of *aiōn* as to necessitate its translation, in accordance with later attestations where the reference is manifest, with 'spinal marrow'. In the Homeric Hymn to Hermes, for example, the eponymous hero is described as killing two cows by rolling on them and piercing their spinal marrow (*di' aiōnas tetorēsas*); and in one of Pindar's fragments the recipient of blows from Heracles' rough club is depicted as having his marrow shattered throughout his bones (*aiōn de di hosteōn eraisthē*).[15] As Benveniste argues, however, nothing obliges one to translate the passage from the *Iliad* in like manner. For *aiōn* could not have acquired this later, anatomical significance, he maintains, had it not first denoted the force of life itself (for which, as we have seen, there is already ample evidence elsewhere in the Homeric corpus). If it comes subsequently to denote a particular part of the body, then, the latter must be understood to coincide with the very place in which that force was thought to reside.[16]

It is, as such, only starting from this 'quasi-physical' connotation, Benveniste contends, that the subsequent dislocation of *aiōn* on to a temporal register may be understood.[17] 'Because *aiōn* is the internal principle which keeps the human being alive', he writes, 'it is the persistence of *aiōn* that will measure the duration of life; so long as the *aiōn* of a human being remains intact, he or she shall live.'[18] Still, even in this preliminary step, *aiōn* will refer to a strictly delimited portion of time in general (*chronos*); according to the beautiful definition of Festugière, it will be 'the *chronos* of a particular life'.[19] But this makes its ultimate extension by analogy to the unlimited lifetime of the gods, which is already accomplished in a celebrated sequence of Plato's *Timaeus*, even more remarkable than Aristotle's recourse to the practice of an 'inspired' etymology would suggest. The principle of life itself – 'the force which animates the being and makes it live'[20] – *aiōn* is what must perpetually renew itself, even as it is continually extinguished.[21] It is, accordingly, life's incessant recreation of the force that nourishes it, which, for Benveniste, ultimately 'suggests to thought the most immediate image of what endlessly maintains itself in the freshness of the ever new'.[22] In short: the image of eternity. And yet, once installed, this image will be responsible for instituting the most striking of conceptual reversals. Initially, the notion of eternity was imaged on the model of a strictly delimited portion of *chronos* ('the *chronos* of a particular life'). By the time of the *Timaeus*, however, the situation has been completely overturned: it is now *chronos* itself, in its entirety, with its division into past, present and future, which has become, in Plato's felicitous expression, 'the moving image of eternity [*eikō* (...) *kinēton tina aiōnios*]'.[23] Henceforth, *aiōn* is what is properly outside of time and of the world altogether, being instead its very paradigm. And with this extraordinary shift, Benveniste observes, the 'conversion' is complete: a principle immanent to life itself, whose 'seat' was even located in a particular part of the body, has now finally come to be identified with that which completely transcends it, and with respect to which, from this point on, it will be wholly subjected.[24]

The moral degradation of time

An important concomitant effect of this conversion is the beginning of what has been memorably described as the 'moral degradation of time'.[25] In the very place in which he confirms the Platonic disaggregation of *aiōn* and *chronos*, we already find Aristotle identifying the passage of time with a destructive power. Things that are contained in time, he writes, are also in turn affected by it. But when we say that something has been affected by time, he adds, we do not speak of it being made more youthful or beautiful; we speak of it wasting away in time, of it growing old through time and of it being forgotten with time: 'for we regard time in itself as destroying rather than producing, for what is counted in time is movement, and movement dislodges whatever it affects from its present state'.[26] It follows that things that exist always (*aei*), are not, as such, in time (*ouk estin en chronoi*). They are neither contained by time, nor measured by time, and hence are not in any way affected by time.[27]

It is with Plotinus, however, that time's emergence comes to be presented in terms of a veritable fall. That what is in question here is a decline from an ideal state, is marked, above all, by his singular petition to the Muses, in an apparent paraphrase of Plato's own uptake of the Homeric device, 'to tell of how time first came out', where *chronos*, time, is simply substituted for *stasis*, civil war.[28] Since one cannot call upon the Muses to answer such a question, he writes, because they did not yet exist, one might instead ask time itself to give an account of how it first came into being. 'It might say something like this about itself', he begins:

> [T]hat before, when it had not yet, in fact, produced this 'before' or felt the need of the 'after', it was at rest with eternity in real being; it was not yet time, but itself, too, kept quiet in that. But since there was a restlessly active nature which wanted to control itself and be on its own, and chose to seek for more than its present state, this moved, and time moved with it; and so, always moving on to the 'next' and the 'after', and what is not the same, we made a long stretch of our journey and constructed time as an image of eternity. For because Soul had an unquiet power, which wanted to keep transferring what it saw there to something else, it did not want the whole to be present to it all together; and, as from a quiet seed the formative principle, unfolding itself, advances, as it thinks, to largeness, but does away with the largeness by division and, instead of keeping its unity in itself, squanders it outside itself and so goes forward to a weaker extension; in the same way Soul, making the world of sense in imitation of that other world, moving with a motion which is not that which exists There, but like it, and intending to be an image of it, first of all put itself into time, which it made instead of eternity, and then handed over that which came into being as a slave to time, by making the whole of it exist in time and encompassing all its ways with time.[29]

In this remarkable passage, the emergence of time – time's self-genesis, as it were – is clearly seen to coincide with the passage from a perfect to an imperfect state: quiet gives way to restlessness, unity to division, being to becoming, thereby confirming Plato's elevation of *aiōn* to a position of absolute transcendence with respect to *chronos*. Not for nothing does Plotinus declare *aiōn* to be identical with God in an earlier sequence.[30] Yet his account nonetheless maintains a number of distinctive features with respect to that of his master, which in a sense makes it, rather than Plato's, the text that would exert the determining influence over the Christian elaboration of these concepts.

Most importantly, as far as the generation of time is concerned, Plotinus's account eliminates the mediation of the Platonic demiurge. Here, very distinctly, it is Soul which plunges itself into time, indeed which 'temporalises' itself and hence which makes of *itself* the moving image of eternity. Time is not created: it is the eternal Soul's self-alteration that is itself generative of time.[31] If this means, on the one hand, that time is what results from the Soul's descent into multiplicity and distension, it is also nonetheless the case that, in precisely this way, it is thereby rejoined to eternity. Precisely because time is defined here by the *diastasis zōēs*, the 'stretching out of life' ('the life of the Soul in a movement of passage from one to another', he writes, 'is time'[32]), it is also possible for the Soul – such is the necessary implication – to arrest this movement and to return to the unity whence it came, and hence to abolish time.[33] It is the great Neoplatonic thinker himself who is thus responsible for re-suturing the great rift between time and eternity that his master had instituted.[34]

Liberatio a tempore

When we turn, finally, to the Christian tradition, whose principal spokesperson is Augustine, time comes to be impressed with a fundamental, and perhaps ineradicable, ambivalence. On the one hand, it is a creation of God. Like the heaven and the earth, like the sun and the moon, like the plants and the beasts, like the human being itself – time, too, according to Augustine, was created. The response to the improper question par excellence demands that this be so. No time can have elapsed before God created the world, during which he would have been unoccupied, he maintains, because time itself had not been created. God – or rather, his Word – created time, not before, but together with the world ('there can be no doubt', he writes, 'that the world was created not in time but with time'[35]), such that there is a necessary relationship between the two: not only is the world necessarily temporal, but time itself is also in turn essentially worldly. As a creature, then, time must be good in and of itself. As we read in Genesis: 'God saw everything that he had made, and indeed it was very good' (Gen. 1: 31). And yet, it is also, indeed pre-eminently, that which is changeable (*mutabile*), and hence serves as the sign par excellence of sin. Like earthly existence itself – which, in a well-known passage, Augustine vacillates between describing as a 'mortal life' (*vitam mortalem*) and a 'living death' (*mortem vitalem*)[36] – time exists only in the sense that it tends toward non-existence. The very cause of its being, he memorably records, is that it will cease to be.[37] Indeed, so strong is this identification of time with sin and death, that Augustine will come to speak of the Word becoming flesh precisely in order to liberate man from time (*liberatio a tempore*).[38] Perhaps the most striking example comes from his tractates on the Gospel of John, in which both senses of time can be seen to coexist alongside one another without this entailing any contradiction. In time, nothing stands still, nothing remains fixed. 'And so', he implores, 'we ought to love him through whom times were made, that we may be freed from time and fixed in eternity where there is no longer any alteration of time [*per quem facta sunt tempora ut libremur a tempore, et figamur in aeternitate, ubi iam nulla est mutabilitas temporum*].'[39] It is not only that he who made time is also the one who liberates us from time; it is that he who made time is himself made of what he made, in order to liberate us from it: 'For he was made what he had made; he who made man was made man, so that what he had made might perish [*factus est enim quod fecerat; factus est enim homo qui hominem fecerat, ne periret quod fecerat*].'[40]

The specific time from which the faithful must be liberated is what Augustine famously describes with the phrase *distentio animi*.[41] Since what one measures when one measures time cannot be the future (which does not yet exist), nor the present (which has no extension), nor the past (which is no longer), it follows that for Augustine time can only be a distention of the soul itself.[42] There is here, to be sure, more than an echo of the Plotinian *diastasis zōēs*. At the moment I begin to recite a psalm I know, he writes, 'the life of this action of mine' is stretched in two directions simultaneously: 'into the memory as what I have just said and into the expectation as what I am about to say'. Even still, my attention is fixed on what is present, which actively transfers the future (expectation) into the past (memory), up until the point that all expectation has been consumed and absorbed in the memory.[43] But what holds for the psalm in its entirety, he continues, holds also for each of its constituent parts and even for each of its individual syllables. But the same holds also in the inverse direction: for the larger action of which the recitation of the psalm itself would be but a part. Indeed, in a gesture which effectively collapses at least one of the significations of the Greek *aiōn* into *chronos*, Augustine will extend this paradigm to the 'whole life' (*tota vita*) of an individual human being and, indeed, even to the 'whole age' (*tota saeculo*) of human history.[44] From the shortest to the longest, the life of any action whose future is absorbed by its past thus entails time.

But the Augustinian *distentio* is also traversed by another movement which sharply distinguishes his vision from that of Plotinus. As Gerard O'Daly has observed, the distinctly moral use of the term in the concluding paragraphs of Book 11, where it carries the sense of fragmentation and dispersal, makes it difficult to square the earlier usage with a definition of time (in accordance with which it could be rendered simply with 'extension').[45] And indeed, as he proceeds to demonstrate, there are two scriptural references that make such an understanding highly problematic. In the first instance, *distentio* is already employed in the Old Latin Bible in a sense also well attested among classical authors, where it simply means 'preoccupied, busy, distracted'. Thus, for example, at Ecclesiastes 3: 10, God is said to have given human beings 'great business' to be 'preoccupied' with (*deus distensionem magnam dedit hominibus, ut distendantur in ea*).[46] Much more important, however, is the opposition that Augustine himself forges between *distentio* and *extentio* on the basis of his exegesis of Philippians 3: 12–14; a text which, as O'Daly notes, serves as a kind of 'leitmotif' is his discussions of the *liberatio a tempore*.[47] The decisive text, which furnishes the contrast with Plotinus, is *Confessions* 11, 29, 39:

> 'Your right hand upheld me' in my Lord, the Son of man who is mediator between you the One and us the many, who live in a multiplicity of distractions by many things; so 'I might apprehend him in whom also I am apprehended', and leaving behind the old days I might be gathered to follow the One, 'forgetting the past' and moving not toward those future things that are transitory but to 'the things which are before me', not stretched out in distraction but extended in reach, not by being pulled apart but by concentration [*non distentus sed extentus, non secundum distentionem sed secundum intentionem*]. So I 'pursue the prize of the high calling' where I 'may hear the voice of praise' and 'contemplate your delight' which neither comes nor goes.[48]

The sense of O'Daly's intervention should now be clear: not only is *distentio* already relatively widely attested among classical sources, including importantly in the Old Latin Bible that Augustine would have had before him, thus making the supposition of a translation of the Greek *diastasis* altogether unnecessary; but it cannot be rendered with 'extension' in any case, for the apparently simple reason that *extentio* in fact names the very counter-movement whereby the soul reaches beyond the ravages of time to that which 'neither comes nor goes'. His analysis nonetheless stops short of registering the decisive shift that Augustine's exegesis of Philippians 3: 12–14 represents for the history of the philosophical reflection on the categories of time and eternity. 'Forgetting the past and reaching forward to what lies ahead': as with Plotinus, time for Augustine remains clearly linked to eternity; but while for Plotinus, as we have seen, the return from multiplicity to unity was premised upon the arrest of movement and even the reversal of time, the irreversibility of time after the Fall means that for Augustine it must instead be sought solely in what lies ahead. With Augustine, eternity (and the true, authentic peace that attends to it) comes, curiously enough, to be situated in the future.[49]

Economy and eschatology

By virtue of a striking paradox, then, it is the *liberatio a tempore* itself which gives time its sense and its direction, which impresses upon it the distinctive features with which we still appraise it today: its rectilinearity, its irreversibility and its unrepeatability. It is the way out of time that in effect defines time. Or at least that gives it a particular value. In this sense, it has been rightly observed that Christianity is a historical religion, in the double sense of the term:

> [N]ot only is it born at a precise moment in history, and not only does both its foundation and its faith rest upon a person (Jesus) whose historicity, despite the efforts of 'mythologists', is not in any doubt; but also, and above all, it gives time a concrete value and attaches to its development, understood as unidirectional and irreversible, a soteriological significance. Moreover, it binds its own fate to history; it conceives itself and interprets itself according to a historical perspective; it brings with it, more or less implicitly, and very soon elaborates, a kind of philosophy or, better, theology of history.[50]

That this 'theology of history' unfolds under the sign of an essentially economic paradigm is, to be sure, one of the major theoretical discoveries to result from Agamben's recuperation of economic theology. The theology of history entails an economy (and vice versa): such is Agamben's important insight. And yet, for him, the sense of this theology remains unclear so long as economy in question here is understood simply 'as a synonym for the providential unfolding of history in accordance with an eschatological design'.[51] And not least because it serves to obscure the historical separation, in the first instance internal to Christianity itself, between 'economy' and 'eschatology' – which is to say, between its orientation toward time and the world, on the one hand, and its orientation toward the end of time and eternity, on the other – whose ultimate resolution will be singularly determining for the modern legacy of economic theology.

What is at issue here is the supposition of a distinctly theological meaning of the Greek term *oikonomia* understood to have been conferred upon it by the apostle Paul and then adopted by the early Church Fathers, whose actuality Agamben has nonetheless sought to emphatically contest. In a well-known sequence of his letter to the Ephesians, which would come to serve as a genuine *topos* in the discourse of the early Church Fathers, the apostle (or whomever its author might have been) had evoked the curious figure of an *oikonomia tou mystēriou*, an 'economy of the mystery', hidden for the ages in God, which he had been entrusted as God's emissary to reveal.[52] Notwithstanding numerous instances both within the Pauline corpus itself and in the New Testament more broadly where its application is perfectly consistent with its everyday secular use – in which it referred more or less exclusively to the administration and management of the antique household[53] – patristic scholars have almost universally understood this striking construction to have marked a new point of departure in the semantic history of the term. Henceforth – so the standard account runs – *oikonomia* would acquire the highly specialised significance of 'divine plan of salvation', particular to its use within the theological sphere. As Agamben has argued, however, the supposition of such a dramatic shift cannot be justified either from a conceptual or from a linguistic perspective. Indeed, the insistence upon the emergence of a new and specifically theological meaning for the term, he suggests, is but the result of a later theoretical projection onto the semantics of a term that retained the eminently pragmatic sense it had in the profane sphere. Only the latter has now been displaced onto a new, hitherto undemonstrated, field of application.[54] For Agamben, both in Paul and in the Church Fathers (who, importantly, were responsible for inverting the juxtaposed terms of the Pauline syntagm), the economy of the mystery names not the divine plan of salvation but the salvific activity of God in time and in the world – in a word, his government.[55] Only in this way, he argues, may the two, apparently incompatible applications for the term, between which the nascent Trinitarian theology of the first centuries appears to oscillate – the one which would refer to the internal articulation of the divinity, the other to its historical manifestation in time – be shown to cohere in a unitary paradigm.

Whether it refers to the administration of his own apostolic vocation or, more broadly, to the divine administration of the cosmos, the use of *oikonomia* (and related terms) in Paul thus remains intimately connected to the eschatological events whose witness he pre-eminently is.[56] It is only with the subsequent suspension of concrete eschatology, according to Agamben – which, for Peterson, as we shall see, grounds the very historical existence of the Church itself – that the theological economy will gradually come to be detached from the eschatological perspective in which it was first elaborated. And with this detachment, we would like to suggest, we witness a second great decoupling of the figures of time and eternity, where Plotinus and Augustine had relinked them. Only that here it is now time which emerges as transcendent with respect to eternity, even to the point of eliminating it altogether.

The paradox of the Church

The name that Agamben gives to the experience of time that results from the theological economy's transcendence of its eschatological context is katechontic time.[57] Ever since Carl Schmitt renewed an antique tradition, which extends back as far as Tertullian and Lactantius, by employing it as a metaphor for the state,[58] the enigmatic entity or person tasked with holding back the 'mystery of lawlessness', which the eschatological excursus of the Second Letter to the Thessalonians (2: 3–8) famously terms the *katechōn*, has occupied a privileged position within the discourse of political theology – even to the point of being identified with it entirely.[59] Here we nonetheless propose that this pregnant symbol be read as an emblem of economic, rather than political, theology.

In a sense, this identification is not without historical precedent. For the tradition to which Schmitt refers in fact constitutes but one side of the range of patristic interpretations pertaining to this obscure figure. Indeed, already in the first decades of the fifth century, Augustine, while himself confessing that the meaning of the verses in question ultimately eluded him, could present the field of possible readings as if divided into two distinct camps. There were those, he writes, who argued that Paul referred here to the Roman Empire; but there were others again, he continues, who maintained that the apostle referred instead to the Church itself, or at least to the *malis et fictis* who form a necessary part of it, up until the moment that they attain a number large enough to constitute a *magnum populum* for the Antichrist.[60] Although he remains unidentified in the text, the author from whom Augustine draws this second interpretation, as Agamben has demonstrated, is the fourth-century North African theologian Tyconius, whose doctrine of the 'bipartite body' of the Church would exert a significant and well-documented influence over the formation of Augustine's own thought.[61] According to this curious doctrine, which is at once ecclesiological and eschatological, the Church under present conditions is composed of two distinct, yet inseparable parts – a 'dark' part and a 'beautiful' part, as he interprets a verse from the Song of Songs – which correspond respectively to the bodies of Satan and Christ. And it will remain so until the end of time, when, in accordance with the eschatological drama described in 2 Thess. 2, the two necessarily commingled bodies will finally separate: 'Now this goes on from the time of the Lord's passion until the Church, which keeps it in check,' he writes, 'withdraws from the midst of this mystery of lawlessness so that godlessness may be unveiled in its own time, as the apostle says.'[62]

With this striking reading, Tyconius, according to Agamben, was the first to advance the provocative thesis that, by functioning as the *katechōn*, the Church (or rather, its 'bipartite body') also actively contributed, in accordance with the immunitary logic which defines the katechontic,[63] to delaying the second coming of Christ and the advent of the Kingdom of God. This thesis would of course receive its most extreme formulation in Ivan Karamazov's 'little poem' on the Grand Inquisitor, in which the katechontic function of the Church, in having become permanent, now no longer truly withholds the appearance of the Antichrist, precisely because it coincides with it entirely.[64] But it also finds a particular expression in the work of the very author whose searching critique of Schmitt's political theology, as we have seen, served as the point of departure for Agamben's genealogy of the paradigm of economic theology.[65] In an important 1929 essay, which precipitated his own conversion to Catholicism, the German theologian Erik Peterson introduced a striking – if disquieting – variation to the tradition which Tyconius had inaugurated.[66] In his account, which is grounded in an extended reading of Romans 9–11 pursued elsewhere,[67] it is the non-belief of the 'people of God' in the messianic status of Jesus, which in truth functions as the *katechōn*. Yet, surprisingly, this non-belief in turn founds, and indeed promotes, the very historical existence of the Church.[68] For Peterson, then, the Church lives only in the space opened by the suspension of the concrete eschatological: so long as the Jews persist in refusing to recognise Jesus as the Messiah, the Church too shall continue to exist.[69] It follows that for him Alfred Loisy's celebrated dictum according to which 'Jésus annonçait le Royaume, et c'est l'Église qui est venu' holds to the letter, albeit in a sense altogether different from what the French theologian must have had in mind. For Peterson, the fact that Jesus announced the Kingdom and it is the Church that came, means just this: that Jesus' proclamation was, for the Jews, unambiguously eschatological, indeed concrete eschatological; but that it was precisely on the basis of their unbelief that the 'Twelve' decided to depart Jerusalem in order to go to the Gentiles, thereby founding the Church, at least in part, as a 'demonstration' against the concrete eschatological.[70]

It is important to observe the seemingly radical thesis that is implicit in this reading. According to Peterson, the Church owes its existence – both in the historical and in the theological sense – not to the prognostications of Jesus himself, but solely to the irrevocable decision of the 'Twelve'. The Church, that is to say, is not the Church of Christ but only the Church of the Apostles.[71] And in the indefinitely adjourned time that coincides with this 'demonstration', the acts of worship, the *leitourgia*, conducted within the Church come to acquire a genuinely public and even political status, in the absence of whose binding character – such is Peterson's conviction – the Church would cease to be at all.[72] It is precisely here that the profound connection between Peterson's ecclesiology and the political-theological injunction formulated in his polemic with Schmitt begins to become perspicuous. It is the suspension of the concrete eschatological which, by deferring the end of history and the advent of the Kingdom of God, in effect makes secular politics possible; yet this politics, he maintains, remains the unique prerogative of the Church and of the Church alone.

But the paradox of a distinctly Christian politics – a politics, that is to say, of the Church qua *instrumentum* of the theological economy – also immediately begins to become apparent here. For the Church in its very historical becoming, as we have seen, finds itself suspended between two inextricable, and yet ultimately incompatible, tendencies: its orientation toward time and the world, on the one hand (economy), and its orientation toward the end of time and eternity, on the other (eschatology). And, as Agamben has observed, it cannot truly fulfil the one except by relinquishing the other. 'The paradox of the Church', he writes, 'is that, from the point of view of eschatology, it must renounce the world; yet it cannot do so because, from the point of view of the economy, it is of the world and cannot renounce the latter without renouncing itself.'[73] What results from the impossible reconciliation of these two conflicting orientations appears before us today in full view: the complete eclipse of the former in favour of the latter; the renunciation, not of time and of the world, but of the end of time and of eternity. And, together with this, the instauration of something like an infinite economy – which, by definition, must be at once interminable and directionless ('blind' and 'derisory' is how Agamben describes it).[74] The mere instrument of an activity whose animating intention completely transcends it is thus curiously emancipated from the very divine principle that would define it. And yet, it is precisely in this way that – far from representing an antagonistic force with respect to it – the Church, in its katechontic aspect, can be seen to have laid the foundations for the emergence of the modern state. A state, that is to say, in which economic and political activities no longer appear as distinct and even opposed, as in the tradition that issues from Aristotle, but in which it becomes possible to speak, without falling into contradiction, of a 'political economy', precisely. It is only to the extent that the Church first assumed the prerogative of a 'State' – and hence, in a very precise sense, *temporalised* its own spiritual power – that the modern state could in turn assume the prerogative of a Church.

Eternal life

It is perhaps less surprising, in this light, that in the concluding pages of *The Kingdom and the Glory* Agamben should seek to reclaim the biblical figure of 'eternal life' (*zōē aiōnios*).[75] The grounds for such a recuperation already appears intimated elsewhere in his striking description of katechontic time – which, for him, articulates nothing less than 'the theological structure of the time in which we live' – as a 'blocked messianism' (*messianismo bloccato*).[76] 'By suspending and withholding the end', he writes,

Agamben and the Critique of Katechontic Time   157

the *katechōn* inaugurates a time in which nothing can really happen, because the sense of historical becoming, which finds its truth only in the *eschaton*, is now indefinitely deferred. What happens in the suspended time of the *katechōn* is, in this sense, an undecidable, which happens, so to speak, without really happening, because its futurity, the *eschaton* which alone could give it meaning, is now incessantly deferred and adjourned.[77]

And yet, nothing could be further from Agamben's intention than to suggest that the figure of eternal life he evokes is to be understood, according to a purely temporal register, simply as what the blessed will receive in the age to come. Indeed, the analysis of glory, which forms the second part of his book, had demonstrated the striking continuity that insists between the conception of eternal life consonant with the doctrine of the glorious bodies of the blessed and the katechontic logic that articulates the theological economy. According to this reading, glory would be the form in which the theological economy prolongs and even survives its own constitutive finitude.[78] In this sense, the invocation of eternal life must be read as the attempt to restore the messianic status of the very figure whose future promise served as the strategic operator par excellence in the institutionalisation of that messianic community which the Church purports to be. 'Eternal' (*aiōnios*) here would not in any sense denote a future condition (as in the longstanding tradition inaugurated by Augustine); but rather – perhaps recalling the early semantic history of the term reconstructed by Benveniste – the special 'quality' that life assumes on account of being placed in relation with the messianic event.[79]

It is certainly significant, in this sense, that the technical expression for messianic time in the Pauline letters in Agamben's interpretation – *ho nyn kairos*, 'the now-time' – entails an entirely different temporal register again: that of *kairos*.[80] As R. B. Onians has shown, *kairos* originally carried a specifically spatial meaning: it denoted the aperture in a warrior's breastplate, through which a weapon (whether sword, lance or arrow) might fatally pass. It thus referred to the brief opening that must be seized in the critical moment, and only as such did it acquire its later temporal significance (an etymology which, Onians suggests, is carried over even to the Latin *opportunus*, which preserves the reference to a passage).[81] In the same way – so Agamben seems to infer – the *ho nyn kairos* would articulate the breach, internal to time itself, of eternity. *Kairos*, in this sense, would coincide neither with time (*chronos*) nor with eternity (*aiōn*); it would be instead, as Agamben writes, a 'seized *chronos*',[82] which is to say, precisely what *connects* it to *aiōn*, precisely what *attaches* it to eternity.

Eternal life thus entails a qualitative transformation of lived chronological time. It does not infer another time, a supplementary time that would succeed lived chronological time, but effects a pulsing, so to speak, internal to it. As distinguished from our *bios*, the life *that* we live (what theologians call the *vita quam vivimus*), eternal would be that life (*zōē*) *through which* we live (the *vita qua vivimus*): that which makes our life liveable.[83] According to Paul, this is the life of Jesus – the *zōē tou Iēsou* – which the faithful make visible in their mortal flesh.[84] But again, this life would not be another life with respect to the life that we live; it would be that life, and none other; yet as marked, Agamben writes, 'by a special indicator of inoperativity':[85] the opening of the Sabbath rest in the present.

Notes

1. See Michael J. Hollerich, 'Introduction', in Erik Peterson, *Theological Tractates*, ed. and trans. Michael J. Hollerich (Stanford: Stanford University Press, 2011), p. xxiv.
2. Erik Peterson, 'Monotheism as a Political Problem: A Contribution to the History of Political Theology in the Roman Empire', in *Theological Tractates*, pp. 68–105.
3. See Peterson, 'Monotheism as a Political Problem', pp. 103–4. Although Peterson here curiously references *De civitate Dei*, 3, 30, the theological justification appears much later in the same work. 'While this Heavenly City', Augustine writes in Book 19, for example, 'is on pilgrimage in this world, she calls out citizens from all nations and so collects a society of aliens, speaking all languages. She takes no account of any difference in customs, laws, and institutions, by which earthly peace is achieved and preserved [. . .] provided that no hindrance is presented thereby to the religion which teaches that the one supreme and true God is to be worshipped. [. . .] In fact [the Heavenly City] relates the earthly peace to the heavenly peace, which is so truly peaceful that it should be regarded as the only peace deserving the name, at least in respect of the rational creation; for this peace is the perfectly ordered and completely harmonious fellowship in the enjoyment of God, and of each other in

God. When we arrive at a state of peace, there will be no longer a life that ends in death, but a life that is life in sure and sober truth; there will be no animal body to "weigh down the soul" in its process of corruption; there will be a spiritual body subdued in every part of the will.' Augustine, *De civitate Dei*, 19, 17; *Concerning the City of God against the Pagans*, trans. Henry Bettenson (London: Penguin, 2003), p. 878. Cf. also 19, 27, pp. 892–3.

4. See Giorgio Agamben, *The Kingdom and the Glory: For a Theological Genealogy of Economy and Government*, trans. Lorenzo Chiesa with Matteo Mandarini (Stanford: Stanford University Press, 2011).
5. See Agamben, *The Kingdom and the Glory*, pp. 6–8. Cf. also pp. 15–16.
6. Agamben, *The Kingdom and the Glory*, p. 7.
7. The literature on this subject is vast. For recent examples, see Théodore Paléologue, *Sous l'œil du Grand Inquisiteur: Carl Schmitt et l'héritage de la théologie politique* (Paris: Cerf, 2004); Massimo Maraviglia, *La guerra penultima: Il concetto di katechon nella dottrina dell'ordine politica di Carl Schmitt* (Milan: LED, 2006); Peter Hohendahl, 'Political Theology Revisited: Carl Schmitt's Postwar Reassessment', *Konturen*, vol. 1 (2008), pp. 1–28; Julia Hell, '*Katechon*: Carl Schmitt's Imperial Theology and the Ruins of the Future', *The Germanic Review: Literature, Culture, Theory*, vol. 84, no. 4 (2009), pp. 283–326.
8. For an overview, see Éric Alliez, 'Aiōn, Chronos', trans. Steven Rendall, in Barbara Cassin (ed.), *Dictionary of Untranslatables: A Philosophical Lexicon* (Princeton: Princeton University Press, 2014), pp. 24–31.
9. John of Damascus, *De fide orthodoxa*, 2, 1; *Writings*, trans. Frederick H. Chase, Jr. (Washington, DC: Catholic University of America Press, 1958), p. 203 (trans. modified).
10. Aristotle, *De caelo*, 279a22–8; *On the Heavens*, trans. W. K. C. Guthrie (London: William Heinemann, 1971), p. 93.
11. A. J. Festugière, 'Le sens philosophique du mot LIWN: A propos d'Aristote, *De caelo* I 9', *La parola del passato*, vol. 11 (1949), pp. 172–89.
12. Émile Benveniste, 'Expression indo-européenne de l'"éternité"', *Bulletin de la Société de Linguistique de Paris*, vol. 38 (1937), p. 107. Cf. s.v. *aiōn*, in *A Greek-English Lexicon*, comp. Henry George Liddell and Robert Scott, rev. Henry Stuart Jones (Oxford: Clarendon, 1996), p. 45.
13. See Homer, *Iliad*, 16, 453; *Iliad, II: Books 13–24*, trans. A. T.

Murray (rev. William F. Wyatt) (Cambridge, MA: Harvard University Press, 1999), pp. 196–7. Cf. Homer, *The Odyssey*, 9, 523; *The Odyssey, I: Books 1–12*, trans. A. T. Murray (rev. George E. Dimock) (Cambridge, MA: Harvard University Press, 1995), pp. 354–5.
14. Homer, *Iliad*, 19, 17; II; p. 337.
15. *Homeric Hymns*, 4, 125; *Homeric Hymns; Homeric Apocrypha; Lives of Homer*, ed. and trans. Martin L. West (Cambridge, MA: Harvard University Press, 2003), pp. 122–3. Pindar, fr. 111; *Pindar, II: Nemean Odes, Istmian Odes, Fragments*, ed. and trans. William H. Race (Cambridge, MA: Harvard University Press, 1997), p. 345.
16. Benveniste, 'Expression indo-européenne de l'"éternité"', p. 109.
17. Benveniste, 'Expression indo-européenne de l'"éternité"', p. 111.
18. Benveniste, 'Expression indo-européenne de l'"éternité"', p. 109.
19. Festugière, 'Le sens philosophique du mot LIWN', p. 189.
20. Benveniste, 'Expression indo-européenne de l'"éternité"', 111.
21. It is perhaps for this reason that, in a striking passage of his *De Anima*, Aristotle will speak of the two principal activities of the nutritive soul – reproduction and nutrition – as what enables all living things to 'share in the eternal and the divine' (*tou aei kai theiou metechosin*). See Aristotle, *De Anima*, 415a30; *On the Soul; Parva Naturalia; On Breath*, trans. W. S. Hett (Cambridge, MA: Harvard University Press, 1957), pp. 86–7. For an illuminating discussion of this passage, see Miguel Vatter, *The Republic of the Living: Biopolitics and the Critique of Civil Society* (New York: Fordham University Press, 2014), pp. 280–1.
22. Benveniste, 'Expression indo-européenne de l'"éternité"', p. 111.
23. Plato, *Timaeus*, 37d; *Timaeus; Critias; Cleitophon; Menexenus; Epistles*, trans. R. G. Bury (London: William Heinemann, 1961), pp. 76–7 (trans. slightly modified).
24. Benveniste, 'Expression indo-européenne de l'"éternité"', p. 112.
25. Ernst H. Kantorowicz, *The King's Two Bodies: A Study in Mediaeval Political Theology* (Princeton: Princeton University Press, 1957), p. 275.
26. Aristotle, *Physics*, 221a30–b2; *The Physics, I*, trans. Philip H. Wicksteed and Francis M. Cornford (London: William Heinemann, 1957), p. 405.
27. Aristotle, *Physics*, 221b3–7; I, p. 405.
28. Plotinus, *Enneads*, 3, 7, 11: 7; *Plotinus, III: Enneads III. 1–9*, trans. A. H. Armstrong (Cambridge, MA: Harvard University Press, 1967), p. 337. Cf. Plato, *The Republic*, 545d–e; *The Republic, II: Books*

VI–X, trans. Paul Shorey (London: William Heinemann, 1956), pp. 244–5.
29. Plotinus, *Enneads*, 3, 7, 11: 11–34; pp. 336–9.
30. Plotinus, *Enneads*, 3, 7, 5: 18–19; pp. 310–11.
31. As has been observed, Plotinus indeed coined the transitive verb *chronoō*, unattested either before or after him, in order to express this self-temporalisation. See, for example, Hans Jonas, 'The Soul in Gnosticism and Plotinus', in *Philosophical Essays: From Ancient Creed to Technological Man* (Englewood Cliffs: Prentice-Hall, 1974), p. 332.
32. Plotinus, *Enneads*, 3, 7, 11: 44–5; p. 341.
33. See Plotinus, *Enneads*, 3, 7, 12: 20–2; p. 345.
34. This point has been stressed by Reiner Schürmann in his *Broken Hegemonies*, trans. Reginald Lilly (Bloomington: Indiana University Press, 2003), p. 154: 'What separates Plotinus not only from the authors of Greek antiquity but also from those of Hellenic antiquity is his understanding of time as tied to eternity.'
35. Augustine, *De civitate Dei*, 11, 6; p. 436.
36. Augustine, *Confessiones*, 1, 6, 7; *Confessions*, trans. Henry Chadwick (Oxford: Oxford University Press, 1991), p. 6.
37. Augustine, *Confessiones*, 11, 14, 17; p. 231.
38. See Roland J. Teske, 'Vocans temporales, faciens aeternos: St. Augustine on Liberation from Time', *Traditio*, vol. 41 (1985), pp. 29–47.
39. Augustine, *In Iohannis Evangelium*, 31, 5; *Tractates on the Gospel of John, 28–54*, trans. John W. Rettig (Washington, DC: Catholic University of America Press, 1988), p. 34.
40. Augustine, *In Iohannis Evangelium*, 31, 5; p. 34.
41. The most incisive commentary remains that of Paul Ricoeur, *Time and Narrative*, vol. 1, trans. Kathleen McLaughlin and David Pellauer (Chicago: The University of Chicago Press, 1984), pp. 5–30.
42. Augustine, *Confessiones*, 11, 24, 33; p. 240.
43. Augustine, *Confessiones*, 11, 28, 38; p. 243 (trans. modified).
44. Augustine, *Confessiones*, 11, 28, 38; p. 243.
45. Gerard J. P. O'Daly, 'Time as *Distentio* and St. Augustine's Exegesis of *Philippians, 3, 12–14*', *Revue des études augustiniennes*, vol. 23, no. 3–4 (1977), pp. 265–71.
46. See O'Daly, 'Time as *Distentio*', p. 267.
47. See O'Daly, 'Time as *Distentio*', p. 269.
48. Augustine, *Confessiones*, 11, 29, 39; pp. 243–4. Cf. also 9, 10, 23; pp. 170–1.

49. See Hannah Arendt, *Love and Saint Augustine*, ed. Joanna Vecchiarelli Scott and Judith Chelius Stark (Chicago: The University of Chicago Press, 1996), pp. 9–33.
50. Henri-Charles Puech, 'Temps, histoire et mythe dans le christianisme des premiers siècles', in *En quête de la Gnose, I: Le Gnose et le temps et autres essais* (Paris: Gallimard, 1978), p. 1.
51. Agamben, *The Kingdom and the Glory*, p. 44. Such an equivocation is reflected even in Puech's essay, which we have cited above. See Puech, 'Temps, histoire et mythe', p. 13.
52. Eph. 3: 8–9. Cf. also Eph. 1: 8–10 and Col. 1: 24–5.
53. See Agamben, *The Kingdom and the Glory*, pp. 21–3, for examples from Paul; and, for a more extensive examination, J. Reumann, '*Oikonomia*-Terms in Paul in Comparison with Lucan *Heilgeschichte*', *New Testament Studies*, vol. 13 (1966), pp. 147–67.
54. See Agamben, *The Kingdom and the Glory*, pp. 20–1.
55. A use of the term that is already attested prior to Paul, both in the Stoic sources as well as in those of Hellenistic Judaism. See Reumann, '*Oikonomia*-Terms in Paul', pp. 150–3. It is important to note, moreover, that when Hippolytus and Tertullian come to speak of a 'mystery of the economy', even there the meaning of the term remains largely unchanged. What has changed, however, is the sense of the activity in question, which, on account of its having been identified with what it must reveal, has now itself become mysterious and even inscrutable. And hence which now must be *interpreted*. See Agamben, *The Kingdom and the Glory*, pp. 38–9; Giorgio Agamben, *Il mistero del male: Benedetto XVI a la fine dei tempi* (Bari: Laterza, 2013), p. 32.
56. See Agamben, *Il mistero del male*, p. 32. Particularly significant, in this regard, is Col. 1: 25–6, in which both senses are clearly operative in the one and the same verse: 'I became [the Church's] minister (*diakonos*), according to God's commission (*oikonomian tou theou*), to fulfil the word of God, the mystery hidden throughout the ages and generations but which has now been revealed to his saints.'
57. For the term itself, see Giorgio Agamben, 'Introduction to Carl Schmitt', *Un giurista davanti a se stesso: Saggi e interviste*, ed. Giorgio Agamben (Vicenza: Neri Pozza, 2005), p. 17. Given the particular prominence that the figure of the *katechōn* has come to assume in Agamben's thought subsequent to this publication, it seems legitimate to treat it as a genuine 'paradigm' in the specific sense that he has given to this term. See Giorgio Agamben, *The Signature of All*

Things: On Method, trans. Luca D'Isanto with Kevin Attell (New York: Zone Books, 2009), pp. 31–2.
58. The key text is Carl Schmitt, *The* Nomos *of the Earth in the International Law of the* Jus Publicum Europeaum, trans. Gary L. Ulmen (New York: Telos Press, 2006), pp. 59–66; but cf. also Schmitt, 'Three Possibilities for a Christian Conception of History', trans. Mario Wenning, in *Telos*, vol. 147 (2009), pp. 167–70, which is especially pertinent in the present context.
59. See, most recently, Massimo Cacciari, *Il potere che frena: Saggio di teologia politica* (Milan: Adelphi, 2013); Roberto Esposito, *Two: The Machine of Political Theology and the Place of Thought*, trans. Zakiya Hanafi (New York: Fordham University Press, 2015), 76–82.
60. Augustine, *De civitate Dei*, 20, 19; p. 933.
61. See Agamben, *Il mistero del male*, pp. 10–13, 27–8.
62. Tyconius, *Liber regularum*, 7; *The Book of Rules*, trans. William S. Babcock (Atlanta: Scholars Press, 1989), pp. 122–3, quoted in Agamben, *Il mistero del male*, pp. 10–11, 28.
63. See Roberto Esposito, *Immunitas: The Protection and Negation of Life*, trans. Zakiya Hanafi (Cambridge: Polity, 2011), pp. 63–4.
64. See Fyodor Dostoevsky, *The Brothers Karamazov: A Novel in Four Parts and an Epilogue*, trans. David McDuff (London: Penguin, 2003), pp. 322–44.
65. See Agamben, *The Kingdom and the Glory*, pp. 1–16.
66. Erik Peterson, 'The Church', in *Theological Tractates*, pp. 30–9.
67. Cf. Peterson, 'The Church from Jews and Gentiles', in *Theological Tractates*, pp. 40–67.
68. See Peterson, 'The Church', p. 32.
69. In a recent article, which considers Agamben's reading of Peterson, Christoph Schmidt has rightly criticised Agamben for inferring a repudiation of Israel from Peterson's remarks and hence for imputing a distinctly Catholic anti-Semitism to him on these grounds. Indeed, as a close reading of Peterson's writings from this period clearly shows, Peterson's emphasis on the Church from Jews *and* Gentiles was expressly directed, however problematically, against the prevailing anti-Semitic sentiment both within the Church and without. See Christoph Schmidt, 'The Return of the Katechon: Giorgio Agamben contra Erik Peterson', trans. Andrew German, *The Journal of Religion*, vol. 94, no. 2 (2014), pp. 182–203. To the extent that Schmidt's article is premised on the curious notion that Agamben discerns a contradiction between Peterson's rejection of political theology and his insistence on the political character of

the Church, he completely misconstrues the sense of Agamben's intervention. Among other things, we have attempted to demonstrate here that precisely the opposite is true.
70. See Peterson, 'The Church', p. 32.
71. It is important to observe that by emphasising the function of the Twelve, Peterson expressly excludes the apostolic legitimacy of Paul. He belongs to the 'charismatic' order of the apostles, but not to the 'legal' order of the Twelve. See Peterson, 'The Church', pp. 35–6.
72. See Peterson, 'The Church', pp. 36–8.
73. Agamben, *Il mistero del male*, p. 17.
74. See especially Giorgio Agamben, *The Church and the Kingdom*, trans. Lelend de la Durantaye (Calcutta: Seagull Books, 2012), pp. 35–41. Of course, as Agamben has underscored, it is not simply the case that the eschatological perspective has disappeared altogether, on account of having been abandoned by the Church itself; rather, it returns in a secularised and parodic form in the generalised sense of imminent crisis that is announced in almost every sphere and which in each instance must be *managed*.
75. See Agamben, *The Kingdom and the Glory*, pp. 247–9.
76. Agamben, 'Introduction to Carl Schmitt', pp. 16–17. Cf. also Giorgio Agamben, *The Time That Remains: A Commentary on the Letter to the Romans*, trans. Patricia Dailey (Stanford: Stanford University Press, 2005), p. 103.
77. Agamben, 'Introduction to Carl Schmitt', p. 16.
78. See especially Agamben, *The Kingdom and the Glory*, p. 249; but cf. also pp. 159–63.
79. See Agamben, *The Kingdom and the Glory*, p. 248.
80. See Agamben, *The Time That Remains*, pp. 59–78. For the relevant uses of this expression in Paul, cf. Rom. 3: 26; 11: 5; 13: 11; 1 Cor. 7: 29; 2 Cor. 6: 2.
81. See R. B. Onians, *The Origins of European Thought* (Cambridge: Cambridge University Press, 2000), pp. 343–8.
82. Agamben, *The Time That Remains*, p. 69.
83. Agamben, *The Kingdom and the Glory*, pp. 248–9. Cf. Giorgio Agamben, *L'uso dei corpi* (Vicenza: Neri Pozza, 2014), p. 288.
84. 2 Cor. 4: 11.
85. Agamben, *The Kingdom and the Glory*, p. 248 (trans. modified).

8

Agamben, Badiou and Affirmative Biopolitics

Sergei Prozorov

Agamben and Badiou are rarely discussed together, especially in the context of politics. Even though both authors reached the height of their international fame at the same time and represented the next wave in continental philosophy after the predominance of 'post-structuralism', the difference of their interests, influences and, not the least, styles often makes it difficult to see what common tendency these authors exhibit. While a number of studies have addressed affinities between Agamben and Badiou in terms of their interest in formalism and the problems of reference,[1] the discussions of the two authors have generally tended to accentuate the differences between them, even when they are addressing the same theme, for example, Pauline messianism.[2]

This is easy to understand, since the differences in question appear so evident as to form pedagogically helpful oppositions, between, for example, Badiou's rehabilitation of grand systematic philosophy and Agamben's reinvention of the fragmentary genre, Badiou's daring abandonment of the linguistic and discursive focus of French philosophy and Agamben's insistence on the ontological significance of language, Badiou's reaffirmation of radical emancipatory politics and militant activism and Agamben's wariness of communism and revolutionary politics as complicit in the biopolitical tendency of the West. In this chapter we will challenge at least the latter opposition, not because it is incorrect as such but because it occludes an important proximity between the two authors in the ontopolitical dimension. The elucidation of this proximity will also help render the contribution of both authors to radical politics more intelligible, offering a more nuanced interpretation of Badiou's alleged overcoming of nihilistic biopolitics in favour of militant communism and a more explicitly political reading of Agamben's often arcane meditations on the form-of-life.

We shall begin by addressing the two areas of explicit disagreement between Agamben and Badiou in order to demonstrate that the two authors' positions are in fact much closer than they themselves cared to admit. Firstly, we shall address Agamben's criticism of Badiou's interpretation of Paul as a universalist and his alternative interpretation of Pauline messianism in terms of the logic of the remnant. We shall argue that Agamben's critique would only be valid if Badiou affirmed a traditional hegemonic notion of universalism, which he definitely does not. In contrast, his account of universality in generic and indiscernible terms accords with Agamben's interpretation of Paul in a number of important ways. We shall also show that while Agamben is reluctant to deploy the concept of universalism (as well as many other central concepts of the Western political tradition), he has shown a persistent interest in rethinking universality in generic terms from his early writings onwards. Agamben's criticism of Badiou in *The Time That Remains* thus fails to recognise his proximity to his own position.

Secondly, we shall address the reverse case of Badiou misrecognising the proximity of Agamben's stance to his own. In his extended note in *Logics of Worlds* Badiou accused Agamben of the valorisation of weakness and passivity in his account of bare life, which contrasts sharply with his own affirmation of militant activism of the subject of the truth procedure. The figure of Bartleby, which Agamben discusses appreciatively and Badiou curtly dismisses, offers a good illustration of what is at stake in this discussion. We shall show that despite Badiou's interest in historical sequences of 'grand politics' as examples of his politics of truth, his own militant practice is much closer to the Bartleby-politics of inoperativity associated with Agamben. The presentation of the two authors' stances as a simple opposition of activity/passivity, strength/weakness, militancy/victimhood is therefore too simplistic and does justice to neither of them.

These two instances are important not merely as the most explicit points of disagreement between Agamben and Badiou. They also serve as a starting point for our more general and provocative argument about a more fundamental affinity between the two authors in the context of biopolitics. While Agamben considers the biopolitical problematic the sole remaining site for thinking politics and Badiou rejects the biopolitical lexicon as part of nihilistic 'democratic materialism', we shall argue that both authors are working through the possibility of an affirmative biopolitics that would not negate life in the name of its protection or transformation. By retracing the account of the generation of truths in Badiou's meta-ontology we shall demonstrate a striking similarity of his concept of the *body of truth* to Agamben's notion of the *form-of-life*.

Of course, this similarity does not efface the differences between the two authors that remain important. The task of this chapter is not to argue that the political philosophies of Agamben and Badiou are alike, let alone identical. Our argument is rather that the reconstitution of an ontopolitical orientation common to both authors permits us to relocate these differences into the more appropriate context of methodology, style or even temperament. It is certainly true that Agamben prefers Bartleby to Spartacus, while Badiou finds more to admire in the Great Proletarian Cultural Revolution than in the Tiananmen Square protests. Yet, these preferences do not efface the same ontopolitical tonality in the work of the two authors, which is at the same time extremely affirmative and highly minimalist, affirming in forms of life nothing but their facticity, their sheer being-thus, which becomes the condition of possibility of radical political transformation.

Whatever being and the problem of universalism

The first area of disagreement between Agamben and Badiou pertains to the interpretation of St Paul and the question of universalism. Badiou's 1997 book *Saint Paul: The Foundation of Universalism* marked the beginning of what might be called a new 'universalist turn' in continental philosophy after decades of discredit in poststructuralist philosophies of difference. In his book Badiou offered a stinging critique of particularistic 'identity politics', which he viewed as a necessary complement of the pseudo-universality of capitalism. He ventured to overcome this rampant particularism with a universalist politics of truth, the paradigm of which he found in Pauline epistles. Badiou reinterprets Pauline texts from his own ontological perspective, finding in Paul the examples of his categories of the event, intervention, fidelity and truth. Brusquely bracketing off the narrowly religious content of Paul's epistles as a 'fable',[3] Badiou reconstructs the formal model of Pauline universalism, arising from the event of Christ's resurrection, which is important solely as a starting point for the procedure that it launches:

Paul's general procedure is the following: if there has been an event, and if truth consists in declaring it and then in being faithful to this declaration, two consequences ensue. First, since truth is eventual, it is singular. It is neither structural, nor axiomatic, nor legal. No available generality can account for it, nor structure the subject who claims to follow in its wake. Consequently, there cannot be a law of truth. Second, truth being inscribed on the basis of a declaration that is in essence subjective, no preconstituted subset can support it; nothing communitarian or historically established can lead its substance to the process of truth. Truth is diagonal relative to every subset; it neither claims authority from, nor constitutes any identity. It is offered to all, or addressed to everyone, without a condition of belonging being able to limit their offer or this address.[4]

Thus, the truth that Paul affirms is a *singular universality*, an effect of the rupture of the event in a given world that carries universally valid consequences that cannot be restricted by any conditions of belonging. The Christian subject is constituted by one's intervention into the situation that declares the occurrence of the event and one's subsequent fidelity to it. The subject of truth does not, in Paul's famous words, discern between Jews and Greeks, men and women, free persons and slaves, and is generally indifferent to the particular words or situations, in which the process of truth unfolds, remaining 'subtracted from the organization of subsets prescribed by the State'.[5]

In his *Time That Remains*, published in Italian three years after the publication of Badiou's book, Agamben explicitly rejects Badiou's designation of Pauline messianism as universalist. In Agamben's reading, rather than offer a truth 'for all' (the conventional understanding of universalism), Paul affirms the non-coincidence of 'all' with themselves, whereby the particularistic division into Jews and Greeks, men and women, etc., is divided once more according to a new criterion, the distinction between 'flesh' (apparent, superficial belonging valid only in the eyes of the law) and 'breath' (genuine belonging on the basis of fidelity). We thus end up with a figure of the 'remnant' that does not fit in the opposition of Jews and non-Jews – a 'non-non-Jew' who is not under the positive law of a particular community but rather under the law of the Messiah:

> At this point one can measure the distance that separates the Pauline operation from modern universalism – when something like the

humanity of man is taken as the principle that abolishes all difference or as the ultimate difference beyond which further division is impossible.[6]

While Badiou's reading of Paul emphasises his indifference to differences, whereby particularities become tolerated as the sites traversed by universality, which must always be affirmed locally within a situation,[7] Agamben goes beyond what appears to him to be a mere benevolent or condescending 'tolerance'. What the Pauline double division does is render the operations of the law and other apparatuses that establish and sustain difference inoperative so that

> [all] that is left is a remnant and the impossibility of the Jew or the Greek to coincide with himself, without ever providing [one] with some other identity. You see why it makes no sense to speak of universalism with regard to Paul, at least when the universal is thought of as a principle above cuts and divisions and the individual as the ultimate limit of each division.[8]

The problem, nonetheless, is that the universal is *not* thought that way by Badiou. As a singularity that is not anticipated, prescribed by or subsumed under any law, it is clearly not 'above' cuts and divisions, but rather itself *consists* in the subtractive cut that separates one from the identities prescribed by the positive order that Badiou terms 'the state of the situation'. Secondly, as a subjective process that does not pre-exist the declaration of the event, universality cannot be localised within any particular subset, be it a group or an individual. Badiou's 'for all' is not identical to what Agamben terms 'modern universalism', which posits a difference (for example, humanity) that abolishes all differences, but rather consists in the subtraction *from* all differences that resembles the messianic division that produces the figure of the remnant. Badiou's political subject, subtracted from its 'intraworldly' determinations, is best grasped precisely as a 'non-non-Jew' (Greek, man, woman, etc.), the second negation negating the first and making it irrelevant.

In fact, in his earlier writings on language and community Agamben himself affirmed a conception of universality that resonates strongly with Badiou's subtractive universalism. These works are particularly influenced by Walter Benjamin's essay 'On

Language as Such and on the Language of Man',[9] where Benjamin addressed the idea of a pure language irreducible to any actually existing particular languages. While the latter remain subjected to the communicative function and hence reducible to mere signs, pure language would be strictly self-referential, no longer mediated by meaning, a language 'that does not mean anything but simply speaks'.[10] It would therefore signify nothing but its own existence and refer only to its own communicability, which Benjamin terms 'the expressionless word'.[11] For both Benjamin and Agamben, *all* languages express this communicability, yet in every particular language it remains crowded out by particular signified content:

> All historical languages, Benjamin writes, mean pure language. It is what is meant in every language, what every language means to say. On the other hand, however, it itself does not mean anything; it does not want to say anything, and all meaning and all intention come to a halt in it. We may thus say that all languages mean to say the word that does not mean anything.[12]

Agamben's later reinterpretation of political community is based on the transfer of this logic of universal language to the political realm. Bracketing off both particular languages and particular communities, he instead focuses on two elementary 'facts', *factum loquendi* and *factum pluralitatis*, the fact of language as pure communicability and the fact of multiplicity or plurality, that the respective sciences of language and politics both presuppose and efface.[13] For Agamben, all particular human communities (nations, states, cultures) seek to express the sheer *factum pluralitatis* of human multiplicity, which nonetheless remains ineffable in them, concealed by particular positive contents of these communities that serve as conditions of belonging to them and exclusion from them. Yet, the universal community that the *factum pluralitatis* affirms does not itself express anything, has no determining predicate or positive content, but simply exposes the being-in-common of all beings. Just as the universal language extinguishes all linguistic meaning but simply speaks, the universal community subtracts itself from every determinate aspect of belonging and simply exists as neither this nor that (Jew or Greek, male or female), but solely as 'thus' or 'whatever'.[14]

This understanding of the universality of language and community is clearly distinct from a simple reaffirmation of familiar liberal (Rawlsian or Habermasian) or Marxist universalisms, which explains Agamben's consistent refusal of the very label of universalism.[15] While, as we have seen, Badiou's version of universalism is just as far from the traditional notion of universalism, his terminological strategy is strictly the opposite of Agamben's and consists in enthusiastically adopting the term while radically transforming its content. In fact, these different choices characterise the two authors' approaches more generally. Throughout his work Agamben has been wary of any positive identification with many of the key terms of the Western ontopolitical tradition, which for him are hopelessly compromised by its biopolitical inflection:

> terms such as sovereignty, right, nation, people, democracy and general will by now refer to a reality that no longer has anything to do with what these concepts used to designate – and those who continue to use these concepts uncritically literally do not know what they are talking about.[16]

In contrast, Badiou has proceeded by reappropriating and transforming such key terms of the Western tradition as the subject, truth and equality.[17] Important as it is, this difference should not obscure the fact that the two authors' interpretations of Pauline messianism remain structurally similar, highlighting the subtractive character of messianic politics. This is in fact also the view of Badiou himself, who, as we shall see below, is otherwise quite explicit about his disagreements with Agamben:

> [I] know that Agamben's reading of Paul is very different from mine, but is this difference really a contradiction? In Paul there is an interplay between separation and universalism. For Paul, there is certainly a kind of separation necessary for his universalism because we have separated ourselves from the old man. We have, out of this separation, a newness of life. But it remains a universalism because there is no limit to this separation, there is no closure. Instead, [Paul] proposes something that is open to everybody, a collective determination, the realization of a separation in a universal field. So, naturally, there is, for Paul, in the process of universalism, something like division but this is a division internal to the subject itself. So I perfectly understand that universalism can take the form of a separation. There is always something like an intimate division when universalism takes the form of a separation. But there is never the pure opposition of universalism

and separation because there is something like the becoming-separate of a universalism.[18]

For Agamben, the separation within the subject leaves the remnant of 'whatever being' or 'being thus' that cannot constitute any overarching or hegemonic identity but only refers to the sheer *factum pluralitatis* of being-in-common, to *beings* taken up solely in their *being*. Yet, Badiou's universalism is constituted by the very same movement of separation or subtraction. Badiou's technical term for Agamben's 'remnant' is the 'generic' subset of the situation, which Badiou identifies with its truth. The generic subset that comprises the elements of the situation connected with the event is *indiscernible* within this situation, that is, it cannot be individualised by any of its positive predicates:

> [it] contains a little bit of everything [but] *only* possesses the properties necessary to its existence as multiple in its material. It does not possess any particular, discerning, separative property. At base, its sole property is that of consisting as pure multiple, of being. Subtracted from language, it makes do with its being.[19]

It is this indiscernible, non-identitarian mode of being that both Agamben and Badiou find in Paul and make the basis of their political philosophies. For both authors, whatever being, subtracted from every positive determination, serves as the basis for subverting and transforming the particular orders of 'worlds' (Badiou) or 'apparatuses' (Agamben) that themselves have no ontological foundation.[20] While the two differ on whether this mode of being should be termed universal, it is clear that both of them critically target the more familiar hegemonic or imperialist forms of universalism. Just as universal language was not intended as a forcible reorganisation of the myriad ways in which people communicate, that would make them speak a new language, so the universal political community is never attained by unification or integration of particular communities but rather by subtraction, separation and division that traverse every subject, be it an individual or a group. This approach does not merely *not* contradict pluralism but rather proceeds through a thoroughgoing pluralisation that leaves nothing identical with itself.

Bartleby and the problem of bare life

The second instance of disagreement between Agamben and Badiou that we shall address pertains to the attributes of the politics based on this generic mode of being. Whereas Badiou has famously sought to rehabilitate the politics of militant activism in the affirmation of political truths, Agamben's writings have been characterised by a focus on situations of extreme disempowerment, deprivation and dehumanisation, in which political activism appears impossible. Particularly emblematic in this respect is Agamben's reading of Melville's Bartleby, which was interpreted by critics as an indication of his excessive pessimism, which only finds an elusive spark of redemption in utter abjection and suffering, with which it is preoccupied to such an extent that some observers termed his approach 'pornographic'.[21] According to these accounts, if there is such a thing as 'Bartleby-politics',[22] it must be a politics that is from the outset resigned to failure.[23]

In an extended note in his *Logics of Worlds* Badiou has similarly contrasted his own affirmative project with Agamben's valorisation of weakness:

> [Agamben's] recurrent theme is being as weakness, its presentational poverty, power preserved from the glory of its act. Likewise, in politics, the hero is the one brought back to its pure being as a transitory living being, the one who may be killed without judgment, the *homo sacer* of the Romans, the *muselmann* of the extermination camp. Agamben, this Franciscan of ontology, prefers, to the affirmative becoming of truths, the delicate, almost secret persistence of life, what remains to one who no longer has anything; this forever sacrificed 'bare life', both humble and essential, which conveys everything of which we – crushed by the crass commotion of powers – are capable of in terms of sense.[24]

At first glance, the difference between the two authors is clear. Badiou's political subject actively struggles to pursue the truth of the event in the world, putting its life at risk, and is often defeated, only to be 'resurrected' in a new vehicle of the truth. In contrast, Agamben's political subject is always already defeated, if not outright destroyed, by the power it confronts, and the sole truth it 'delicately' or 'secretly' affirms is that of its own bare life devoid of any property. Badiou's difference from Agamben is well illustrated by his hasty dismissal of Bartleby, whose famous 'I would prefer not to' is perhaps the best example of Agamben's notion of inoperativity. In *Logics of Worlds* Badiou picks Bartleby as an example of the negation of a truth by its subject in the form of betrayal: 'One can, like the office clerk Bartleby in Melville's eponymous novella, "prefer not to". But then a truth will be sacrificed by its very subject. Betrayal.'[25] This reading is quite staggering, since Bartleby never betrayed anything or anyone, let alone the truth. On the contrary, his 'preference not to' arguably *was* his truth that he actually upheld faithfully until his death. Moreover, in its very lack of positive content this truth is not so far from Badiou's own presentation of truth as indiscernible, generic and universal.[26] Bartleby is a personification of a singular life subtracted from all particular predicates and is therefore closest to the model of universalism described above.[27]

Of course, Badiou's own favourite examples of political subjects are a world away from Bartleby: Spartacus, the French Communards, Mao, etc.[28] Throughout his works Badiou offers grand examples from the history of emancipatory and revolutionary politics (slave uprisings, peasant revolts, proletarian revolutions), which are all based on the transhistorical invariant that he terms 'the communist hypothesis' of radical equality.[29] In contrast, Agamben's political subjects tend to be rather less than heroic, even as they might also traverse some of these grand-political sequences as survivors or witnesses: Bartleby, Kafka's Joseph K and K the land surveyor,[30] Tiananmen protesters,[31] Anna Akhmatova,[32] etc. Yet, we cannot help but notice that for all the heroism of their protagonists, *all* of Badiou's grand-political sequences have ended in failure, be it in the form of defeat, retreat, betrayal or the perversion of original goals. Of course, these failures were often highly instructive, for example, demonstrating the direction that would be fatal for the truth procedure and thus serving to sustain it within history.[33] Yet, while Badiou succeeds in incorporating failure within the positivity of the truth procedure, this very incorporation ensures that the 'affirmative becoming of truths' is not without its own immanent negativity.

Moreover, some of the episodes in the unfolding of Badiou's politics of truth, for example, twentieth-century revolutionary movements, have brought to the forefront of politics the very bare life that Badiou wishes to dismiss as politically irrelevant: any serious engagement with twentieth-century socialism cannot ignore the facts of terror, famine and the Gulag.[34] This link between grand revolutionary politics and the inclusive exclusion of bare life supports Agamben's argument in Homo Sacer about the belonging of the revolutionary tradition of constituent power to the overall biopolitical constellation of Western politics.[35] Agamben has opposed the attempts of radical-democratic and communist thought to overcome the logic of sovereignty by the valorisation of constituent power as potentiality inexhaustible in any actual form of constituted structure of authority. Instead, he demonstrates that the opposition between constituent and constituted power is only apparent, since both dimensions are at work in the logic of sovereignty that includes its own suspension in its operations. Sovereignty is not (merely) the force of actualisation that exhausts all potentiality but also the force of potentiality that manifests itself in actuality in the form of the state of exception, whose paradigmatic nomos is the camp. The appearance of bare life as the product of twentieth-century revolutionary regimes is by no means coincidental or attributable to some deviation or perversion of the revolutionary intention. As long as revolution is conceived in terms of constituent power, bare life, the camps and other unsavoury aspects of sovereignty can never be left behind.

There is, however, an important exception to Badiou's commitment to grand politics, which is none other than Badiou himself as a political subject. Badiou's own micro-political engagement in the now-defunct Organisation Politique (OP)[36] was characterised by action at a distance from the state, the refusal to take part in elections and the renunciation of all figures of political representation. Badiou's Organisation was completely uninterested in instituting a new political system but was solely concerned with undermining the existing order on the basis of the axiomatic affirmation of equality. This approach is quite different from those of Spartacus, Mao and other heroic leaders of popular rebellions and revolutions that Badiou discusses in his works on politics. Indeed, in its combination of utter radicalism and practical modesty, axiomatic tone and strategic ineffectiveness, Badiou's own politics is, dare we say, somewhat Agambenian. While as a philosopher of politics Badiou prefers grand examples of revolutionary politics, in his own activity as a political subject *he is a lot like Bartleby*, repeatedly 'preferring not to' run in elections, read mainstream press, act in accordance with any managerial rationality or the imperative of profit, etc.[37]

Once again, the disagreement between the two authors is rather less pronounced than it at first appeared. Yet, does not Badiou's critique actually point to the ultimately irreducible difference between him and Agamben, the one pertaining to the political status of bare life or life as such? While Agamben has painstakingly pursued the possibility of an affirmative biopolitics, in which the living being would be the subject and not the object of power, Badiou has derisively dismissed the biopolitical problematic as one more illustration of the contemporary nihilism and has instead affirmed the politics of truth irreducible to the vital interests of the human animal. Even if it is granted that Badiou's generic universality is close to Agamben's non-identitarian remnant or that Bartlebyan inoperativity is not that far from Badiou's own version of militancy, the fact remains that Agamben finds the true locus of politics in the same terrain that for Badiou a genuine politics necessarily transcends. In the final section we shall contest such an interpretation, arguing that it is precisely on the terrain of biopolitics that the affinity of Agamben and Badiou becomes fully intelligible.

Form-of-life and the body of truth

Badiou has long been a principled opponent of biopolitics.[38] His writings since the 1980s have featured passionate polemics against the reduction of politics to the management of the bare existence of human beings. For Badiou, biopolitics, which he discusses in his *Logics of Worlds* under the rubric of 'democratic materialism', has become a spontaneous ideology of late-modern Western societies:

> [There] are only bodies and languages. Human rights are the same as the rights of the living. The humanist protection of all living bodies: this is the norm of contemporary materialism. Today, this norm has a scientific name: 'bioethics', whose progressive reverse borrows its name from Foucault: 'biopolitics'. Our materialism is therefore a materialism of life. It is a bio-materialism.[39]

This characterisation of contemporary politics goes back to Badiou's *Ethics*, whose key target was the reduction of the human being to the 'living animal', a 'biped without feathers whose charms are not obvious'.[40] Similarly, in *The Century*[41] Badiou scorned the 'animal humanism', promoted by contemporary liberal democracies, in which man figures only as a potential object of suffering, oppression, torture or genocide – in short, a 'pitiable animal'.

To these ethico-political discourses Badiou opposes a militant politics of truth, which consists in the affirmation of radical equality of all beings, hence his identification of this politics with the 'communist hypothesis'. Notwithstanding this opposition, the two key terms of biopolitics, the *body* and *life*, reappear in Badiou's politics of truth. Firstly, a politics concerned with the needs and desires of individual bodies is overcome through the constitution of a new, subjectivised *body of truth*, into which individual bodies are incorporated and become vehicles of universal, infinite and immortal truth.[42] Secondly, while Badiou is scornful about the use of life in its biological sense as the sole object of politics, his politics is oriented towards attaining a 'true life', defined as the participation in the subjective body of truth.[43]

In fact, Badiou's attempt to overcome biopolitics by overcoming biological life in favour of some other form of life follows almost to the letter the logic of biopolitics as presented by Agamben, that is, the 'inclusive exclusion' of *zoē* from *bios*. Agamben starts from the distinction between two terms for 'life' in Ancient Greek: '*zoē*, which expressed the simple fact of living common to all living beings (animals, men or gods) and *bios*, which indicated the form or way of living proper to an individual or a group'.[44] While *zoē* is sometimes interpreted as natural or even biological life, what Agamben emphasises is not any specific 'natural' qualification, but, on the contrary, the absence of any qualifications, which makes *zoē* common for humans, animals and gods. In the argument of *Homo Sacer*, the constitution of *bios* as the political form of life presupposes the entry of *zoē* into this realm in the marginalised, subordinated or suppressed position: it is included in the *polis*, but solely in the mode of its exclusion from it, as a negative foundation, 'as if politics were the place in which life had to transform itself into good life and in which what had to be politicised were always already bare life'.[45] It is this negative foundation that Agamben terms 'bare life'. While *zoē* is originally unqualified, bare life is qualified negatively by the fact of its exclusion, reduced to the sheer facticity of living. There is therefore nothing natural about it; on the contrary, as Agamben's examples of *homo sacer* and the *muselmann* suggest, this life stripped of all protections and exposed to violence might well be the most unnatural thing of all. Perhaps, a 'bared' or 'stripped' life would be a better term, highlighting the violence involved in the process of the constitution of a political form of life on the basis of the negative foundation of the simple fact of living.

It is easy to observe the parallels between this logic and Badiou's 'body of truth'. As Agamben himself argued, '[Badiou] still conceives of the subject on the basis of a contingent encounter with truth, leaving aside the living being as the "animal of the human species" as a mere support for this encounter.'[46] The true life of the 'superhuman' subject is obtained by the isolation of the physical life of the subhuman 'mortal animal' as its material support.[47] If that was all there was to Badiou's politics of truth, then it would amount to little more than a replication of the disavowal of the 'merely human' in modern biopolitics.[48] The question of biopolitics would then indeed divide Agamben and Badiou insofar as the latter would remain stuck in the same biopolitical paradigm, whose liberal version he so vehemently criticises. Yet, such a conclusion would be rather uncharitable since it would ignore the *content* of Badiou's truths. While no variation in content could admittedly change the formal belonging of his politics of truth to the biopolitical logic, it might produce a different *kind* of biopolitics, that is, an affirmative biopolitics long debated on in Italian political thought.[49]

At the end of *Homo Sacer* Agamben defined such a biopolitics in the following manner:

> This biopolitical body that is bare life must itself instead be transformed into the site for the constitution and installation of a form of life that is wholly exhausted in bare life and a *bios* that is only its own *zoē*.[50]

If biopolitics includes *zoē* into *bios* in the destitute mode of bare life, whose negation founds the political form of life, then the only possibility for biopolitics to refrain from this negation and begin to affirm life requires that *bios* and *zoē* become entirely indistinct. In this manner, life and its form would become inseparable, *bios* being only its own *zoē*, so that it is 'no longer possible to isolate anything like a bare life'.[51] The sheer facticity of *zoē*, 'the simple fact of living', will then no longer be negated as a foundation of *bios* but will rather define its entire content, there being no other form, essence, task or identity imposed on it. What Agamben calls *form-of-life*, the hyphens emphasising the integrity of life and its form,

Agamben, Badiou and Affirmative Biopolitics 179

may then be understood as 'a being that is its own bare existence, [a] life that, being its own form, remains inseparable from it'.[52]

Agamben's concept of form-of-life is certainly easy to misunderstand. After all, does not a '*bios* that is only its own *zoē*' correspond precisely to the structure of the sovereign state of exception, in which bare life is exposed to death? What is then the difference of form-of-life from bare life as the negative foundation of the political order? While sovereignty operates by capturing and *separating* bare life from the positive forms of *bios* or, in what amounts to the same thing, crushing these forms down to the level of pure survival, Agamben makes the opposite move of articulating *zoē* and *bios* into a new figure, in which fact and form, the unqualified and its qualification, are no longer separable and neither can dominate the other. In contrast to bare life inclusively excluded in the sovereign state of exception, this life is not de-formed but rather appropriates its simple facticity as the sole form proper to it. It is as if bare life, negated as the foundation of *bios*, reclaims itself for itself by taking up the space of *bios* entirely, voiding it of all determinate content. This life, while still in some sense 'bare', is no longer stripped of every possible qualification but rather demonstrates the irreducibility of its being to any such qualification:

> [The] only thing that the beautiful face can say, exhibiting its nudity with a smile, is 'You wanted to see my secret? Then look right at it if you can. Look at this absolute, unforgivable absence of secrets!' The matheme of nudity is, in this sense, simply this: *haecce*! There is nothing other than this. This simple dwelling of appearance in the absence of secrets is its special trembling – it is the nudity that signifies nothing and, precisely for this reason, manages to penetrate us.[53]

We encounter this figure of an integral form-of-life in the most diverse contexts of Agamben's work: the 'coming community' of whatever singularities devoid of identities and vocations,[54] the *experimentum linguae* that communicates the sheer existence of language and not its signified contents,[55] the 'glorious body' that is nothing but the earthly body divested of its functions and open to a new use,[56] the objects of profanation and play that are removed from the 'sacred spheres' regulating their existence and rendered available to free experimentation[57] and, most recently, the attempts of Franciscan monasticism to arrive at a form of life that would not simply apply any existing rules or laws to life or establish alternatives to them, but rather be 'completely extraneous to both civil and canon law', having its entire content in the life of Christ alone.[58] What unites all of these diverse figures is their subtraction from every particular predicate and their exposure in the bare facticity of their existence or 'being-thus', the mode of being that we have identified as the source of Badiou's and Agamben's convergent conceptions of the universal. It is important to recall that while this mode of being retains the particular predicates of whatever beings, their very retention makes it impossible for them to function as determinative predicates: being-thus is 'neither this nor that, neither thus nor thus, but *thus*, as it is, with all its predicates (all its predicates is not a predicate)'.[59] Form-of-life does not deform let alone destroy the particular forms of life, but suspends the determinative function of these forms and instead exposes them solely in the aspect of their being. In other words, whatever beings undergo neither a deprivation (of the old identity) nor a transformation (into a new one), but solely the exposure of the sheer fact *that* they are in the absence of any identification of *what* they are. Form-of-life is not some particular *bios*, but whatever *bios* grasped solely in the facticity and thusness of its *zoē*, akin to the language that speaks its own communicability or the community that lives its own existence. In other words, form-of-life is not constituted by any predication of *what* it is but solely by the exposure of the fact *that* it is. Would it then be possible that notwithstanding his explicit polemics against bare, biological or animal existence as the object of politics, Badiou's biopolitics has a similarly affirmative orientation?

At first glance, Badiou's polemic against Agamben's valorisation of bare life precludes this possibility. Badiou's reading of Agamben presents bare life as what remains of the living being after all positive forms of life are stripped away from it, a remainder that is without any truth of its own. Yet, as we have seen, Agamben's notion of the form-of-life actually performs the reverse gesture of *elevating* this unqualified remainder to the status of a positive form by erasing any difference between *bios* and *zoē*. While Badiou's account of his politics of truth polemically opposes *zoē* and *bios*, a more attentive reading of the process of the generation of truths in Badiou's meta-ontology demonstrates that his notion of the body of truth is strictly correlative to Agamben's form-of-life. Let us briefly revisit Badiou's account of this process in *Being and Event*.

The event which initiates the truth procedure is composed of the elements of the evental site and itself. The evental site is a set that is absolutely singular, that is, it *belongs* to the situation but is not *included* in it. The operation of inclusion proceeds by recomposing the elements of the original set into subsets. Since an absolutely singular set is present in the situation as undecomposable, 'all of a piece', it obviously cannot be counted in terms of its parts and thus remains without representation in the metastructure that Badiou terms the 'state of the situation': 'Such a multiple is solely presented as the multiple-that-it-is. None of its terms are counted-for-one as such; only the multiple of these terms forms a one.'[60]

The other component of the event is, paradoxically and from a strictly ontological perspective impossibly, the event *itself*.[61] Since the ontological axioms of set theory prohibit self-belonging, the belonging of the event to the situation can never be objectively inferred from the situation but must rather be decided upon or 'wagered' in the procedure of *intervention*. This procedure 'names' the unpresented elements that belong to the evental site, affirming the existence of a set without being able to designate it as *a* being and determine how it differs from other sets. The second procedure called *fidelity* then groups together the elements of the situation, whose existence is dependent on the event in question, resulting in the formation of that indiscernible subset that Badiou terms the truth and whose universality we have discussed above. Thus, the 'presentational poverty' that Badiou finds in Agamben actually characterises the entire process of the emergence of the truth, from its origin in the unpresented elements of the situation to its own status as indiscernible in it.

In fact, it is the presentational poverty of the event and the ensuing truth procedure that differentiate Badiou's event from the structure of the state of exception as described by Agamben, despite Agamben's somewhat awkward attempt to demonstrate otherwise.[62] While the event is by definition an exception in relation to the situation, its ontological undecidability and the indiscernibility of the truth unfolding from it ensure that it can never be incorporated into the state of the situation as its own, immanent exception that defines Agamben's sovereign ban. 'Ontology has nothing to say about the event', hence the situation cannot even register it, let alone make use of it in the manner the sovereign makes use of the anomie that it appropriates.[63] Insofar as the event and its consequences are not appropriable by the existing order of the situation, its exceptionality is, in the Benjaminian terms deployed by Agamben, 'real' rather than 'sovereign', that is, severed from all relation to the law and state and incapable of functioning as their negative foundation.[64]

If the truth makes do with its being without being discernible in language, if it does not possess any particular properties, its content must be exhausted in what pertains to the situation's very being prior to its internal structuration. This is what makes the truth universal, '[the] truth of the entire situation, of the being of the situation'.[65] If the truth had some positive content of its own, it could never have universal consequences for the situation but would merely produce an extraneous addition to it. Yet, as we have seen, the event does not produce any new content, but rather presents what was always in the situation to begin with but was not presented therein. What the truth manifests is nothing more (and nothing less) than the being of the situation or world as inconsistent multiplicity,[66] ordinarily concealed either by the structure of the situation (in the ontological terms of *Being and Event*) or the transcendental order of the world (in the phenomenological terms of *Logics of Worlds*).

Equality of things as they are

It is now easy to see that the truth that brings to appearance the being of the situation itself is strictly identical to Agamben's form-of-life exhausted in bare life or a *bios* that is its own *zoē*: both figures render form and content indistinct by exposing one as the other: 'it is the content but nothing contains it; it is form but it no longer forms anything, exposing, thereby, itself'.[67] The 'body of truth' manages not to negate the living body of the human animal through its inclusive exclusion only because what is 'excluded' in it (bare life as pure being) is *exactly the same* as what it is 'included' into (the truth as pure being). The body of truth is quite literally the same as the body of the living animal, but it is not *only* that. As we have seen, the truth does not produce any new content of the situation but it nonetheless adds to it something that would have remained unpresentable, had the event not occurred. What the truth procedure adds to the facticity of living bodies is the affirmation of their equality.[68] Yet, it is important to note that this 'new' content of the truth is not extrinsic to the original situation. Badiou's equality is not defined in programmatic terms as a future condition to be attained in a political project (of recognition, protection, redistribution, etc.), but is rather 'immediately prescriptive' since it *always already* characterises the being of every world, however unequally it is ordered in its appearance.[69]

> [The] word 'equality' must be secured in the absence of any economic connotations (equality of objective conditions, of status, of opportunity). Its subjective trenchancy must be restored: equality is something that opens onto a strict logic of the Same. Its advantage, then, lies in its abstraction. Equality here is a purely philosophical name. It is unhitched from every *programme*. [It means] that no lone singularity can have an entitlement that would render it unequal to any other. This can also be said: the essence of a truth is generic, that is, is without any differential trait that would allow it to be placed in a hierarchy on the basis of a predicate. And again: equality signifies that, from the vantage point of politics, what is presented has no need of being interpreted. What presents itself must be received in the nondescript nature and the egalitarian anonymity of its presentation as such.[70]

This notion of equality is simply a logical consequence of the genericity of the truth itself and not some extraneous principle or value. It arises out of the very character of the truth procedure as the ascent to appearance of the unpresented elements in the form of the indiscernible subset, which does not possess any 'differential trait' that would allow any unequal relation to be constituted. Badiou's equality is never economic, legal, cultural or any other specific equality, but the equality of beings *in their being*, whatever these beings are in their worldly appearance, identity or role. Equality is not a positive principle defining a certain *bios*, yet neither is it immediately given in the simple fact of *zoē*: were it not for the event, the unpresented elements of the situation would have remained such and the worldly hierarchies would have been maintained. Equality as truth is rather the result of the raising of the ontological attributes of *zoē* to the status of *bios*, the affirmation of unqualified and indeterminate life as the sole content of politics.

While Agamben hardly ever uses the concept of equality, due to the above-discussed wariness of relying on the key terms of the Western tradition, axiomatic or immediately prescriptive equality follows logically from his concepts of whatever being and being-thus: beings subtracted from every possible qualification, determination or predicate cannot but be equal. The same applies to the notion of communism: while Badiou has enthusiastically reaffirmed the idea of communism in the post-Cold War context, unhesitantly dehistoricising it as an eternal truth or at least a 'hypothesis', Agamben has been rather reticent about it, addressing the idea of communism only rarely and in a somewhat esoteric manner, for example, in the context of the discussion of pornography or monastic life.[71] There are evident advantages and drawbacks to both strategies. Rather than try to adjudicate between the two, we must recognise that despite their different terminological choices Agamben and Badiou have developed two versions of the same political logic that constitutes a positive form of life out of the condition proper to the unqualified being of any being whatsoever. The opposition between the 'secret persistence of bare life' and the 'affirmative becoming of truths' is therefore undone or at least relocated to the more superficial level of aesthetic preference. It is *out of* bare life that truths become and throughout their becoming, be it faint or bombastic, they remain the truths *of* bare life, which alone warrants an affirmation of equality that is not positive, programmatic or normative, but rather ontological.

In 2002 Agamben ended his lecture on the concept of the paradigm at the European Graduate School on a quote from Wallace Stevens, just like Badiou had done a few days earlier: 'Following Badiou's example, I propose to inaugurate a tradition here in Saas-Fee: every lecture must end with a quotation from Wallace Stevens'.[72] As Simon Critchley has demonstrated in his book on Stevens, the latter was the paradigmatic poet of the 'sheer "there is" of things'[73] that are indifferent to human attempts to grasp them and make them meaningful. Agamben and Badiou are certainly not alone among contemporary philosophers in affirming this persistent facticity of being, but they have arguably gone farthest in making this facticity a counter-intuitive source of radical political affirmation, whereby the being of things 'as they are' authorises the overcoming of the present order of things. It would therefore be appropriate to conclude by suggesting that both Agamben and Badiou respond, in their own ways, to the demand of the audience to Stevens's 'man with the blue guitar' to '[play] a tune beyond us, yet ourselves, a tune upon the blue guitar of things exactly as they are'.[74]

Notes

1. Paul Livingston, 'Agamben, Badiou and Russell', *Continental Philosophy Review*, vol. 42 (2009), pp. 297–325; Justin Clemens, 'The Role of the Shifter and the Problem of Reference in Giorgio Agamben', in Justin Clemens, Nicholas Heron and Alex Murray (eds), *The Work of Giorgio Agamben: Law, Literature, Life* (Edinburgh: Edinburgh University Press, 2008), pp. 43–65.
2. Eleanor Kaufman, 'The Saturday of Messianic Time: Agamben and Badiou on the Apostle Paul', *South Atlantic Quarterly*, vol. 107, no. 1 (2008), pp. 37–54; Gideon Baker, 'The Revolution Is Dissent: Reconciling Agamben and Badiou on Paul', *Political Theory*, vol. 41, no. 2 (2013), pp. 312–35.
3. Alain Badiou, *Saint Paul: The Foundation of Universalism* (Stanford: Stanford University Press, 2001), p. 4.
4. Badiou, *Saint Paul*, p. 14.
5. Badiou, *Saint Paul*, p. 15.
6. Giorgio Agamben, *The Time That Remains: A Commentary on the Letter to the Romans*, trans. Patricia Dailey (Stanford: Stanford University Press, 2005), p. 52.
7. Badiou, *Saint Paul*, pp. 98–9.
8. Agamben, *The Time That Remains*, p. 53.
9. Walter Benjamin, 'On Language as Such and on the Language of Man', in *Reflections*, trans. Edmund Jephcott (New York: Schocken Books, 1978), pp. 314–32.
10. Giorgio Agamben, *Potentialities: Selected Essays in Philosophy*, trans. Daniel Heller-Roazen (Stanford: Stanford University Press, 1999), p. 54.
11. Quoted in Agamben, *Potentialities*, p. 53.
12. Agamben, *Potentialities*, p. 53.
13. Giorgio Agamben, *Means without End: Notes on Politics*, trans. Vincenzo Binetti and Cesare Casarino (Minneapolis: University of Minnesota Press, 2000), p. 66.
14. Giorgio Agamben, *The Coming Community*, trans. Michael Hardt (Minneapolis: University of Minnesota Press, 1993), pp. 1–3, 17–21.
15. Agamben, *The Coming Community*, p. 9.
16. Agamben, *Means without End*, p. 110.
17. Alain Badiou, *Conditions* (London: Continuum, 2008), pp. 147–76.
18. Alain Badiou, 'Universal Truths and the Question of Religion', *Journal of Philosophy and Scripture*, vol. 3, no. 1 (2005), pp. 39–40.
19. Alain Badiou, *Being and Event* (London: Continuum, 2005), p. 371.

20. Alain Badiou, *Logics of Worlds* (London: Continuum, 2009), pp. 75, 357–80; Giorgio Agamben, *The Kingdom and the Glory: For a Theological Genealogy of Economy and Government*, trans. Lorenzo Chiesa with Matteo Mandarini (Stanford: Stanford University Press, 2011), pp. 53–66.
21. Jay M. Bernstein, 'Bare Life, Bearing Witness: Auschwitz and the Pornography of Horror', *Parallax*, vol. 10, no. 1 (2004), pp. 2–16; cf. Sergei Prozorov, 'Pornography and Profanation in the Political Philosophy of Giorgio Agamben', *Theory, Culture & Society*, vol. 28, no. 4 (2011), pp. 71–95.
22. Cf. Slavoj Žižek, *The Parallax View* (Cambridge: The MIT Press, 2006), pp. 342–3, 381.
23. Jessica Whyte, '"I Would Prefer Not To": Giorgio Agamben, Bartleby and the Potentiality of the Law', *Law and Critique*, vol. 20 (2009), pp. 309–24; Lorenzo Chiesa, 'Giorgio Agamben's Franciscan Ontology', *Cosmos and History*, vol. 5, no. 1 (2009), available at <http://cosmosandhistory.org/index.php/journal/article/view/130/239> (last accessed 20 April 2013).
24. Badiou, *Logics of Worlds*, pp. 558–9.
25. Badiou, *Logics of Worlds*, p. 400.
26. Badiou, *Being and Event*, pp. 327–54.
27. See Gilles Deleuze, 'Bartleby; or, The Formula', in *Essays Critical and Clinical*, trans. Michael A. Greco and Daniel W. Smith (Minneapolis: University of Minnesota Press, 1997), pp. 68–90, p. 74.
28. Badiou, *Logics of Worlds*, pp. 24–7, 51–7, 64–5, 493–503.
29. Alain Badiou, *The Communist Hypothesis* (London: Verso, 2010).
30. Giorgio Agamben, *Nudities*, trans. David Kishik and Stefan Pedatella (Stanford: Stanford University Press, 2010), pp. 20–35.
31. Agamben, *The Coming Community*, pp. 85–6.
32. Agamben, *Potentialities*, pp. 177–8.
33. Cf. Badiou, *The Communist Hypothesis*, pp. 1–40.
34. See Sergei Prozorov, 'Living Ideas and Dead Bodies: The Biopolitics of Stalinism', *Alternatives*, vol. 38, no. 3 (2013), pp. 208–27 for a detailed discussion.
35. Giorgio Agamben, *Homo Sacer: Sovereign Power and Bare Life*, trans. Daniel Heller-Roazen (Stanford: Stanford University Press, 1998), pp. 46–7.
36. Alain Badiou, *Ethics: An Essay on the Understanding of Evil* (London: Verso, 2001), pp. 95–119; Peter Hallward, *Badiou: A Subject to Truth* (Minneapolis: University of Minnesota Press, 2003), pp. 43–5, 227–42.

37. Badiou, *Conditions*, pp. 43–50.
38. Tyson Lewis, 'Philosophy – Aesthetics – Education: Reflections on Dance', *The Journal of Aesthetic Education*, vol. 41, no. 4 (2007), pp. 55–8; Livingston, 'Agamben, Badiou and Russell', p. 240; Adrian Johnston, *Prolegomena to any Future Materialism, Volume One: The Outcome of Contemporary French Philosophy* (Chicago: Northwestern University Press, 2013), pp. 89–91.
39. Badiou, *Logics of Worlds*, p. 2.
40. Badiou, *Ethics*, p. 12.
41. Alain Badiou, *The Century* (London: Polity, 2007), pp. 175–7.
42. Badiou, *Logics of Worlds*, pp. 33–4.
43. Badiou, *Logics of Worlds*, p. 507.
44. Agamben, *Homo Sacer*, p. 1.
45. Agamben, *Homo Sacer*, p. 7.
46. Giorgio Agamben, *Potentialities*, p. 221.
47. Badiou, *Ethics*, pp. 12–13.
48. Badiou, *The Century*, p. 178; Cary Wolfe, *Before the Law: Humans and Other Animals in a Biopolitical Frame* (Chicago: The University of Chicago Press, 2013), pp. 28–30.
49. Roberto Esposito, *Bios: Biopolitics and Philosophy*, trans. Timothy Campbell (Minneapolis: University of Minnesota Press, 2008).
50. Agamben, *Homo Sacer*, p. 188.
51. Agamben, *Means without End*, p. 9.
52. Agamben, *Homo Sacer*, p. 188.
53. Agamben, *Nudities*, p. 91.
54. Agamben, *The Coming Community*.
55. Giorgio Agamben, *Infancy and History: On the Destruction of Experience*, trans. Liz Heron (London: Verso, 2007), pp. 5–6.
56. Agamben, *Nudities*, pp. 91–103.
57. Giorgio Agamben, *Profanations*, trans. Jeff Fort (New York: Zone Books, 2007), pp. 73–91.
58. Giorgio Agamben, *The Highest Poverty: Monastic Rules and Form-of-Life*, trans. Adam Kotsko (Stanford: Stanford University Press, 2013), p. 122.
59. Agamben, *The Coming Community*, p. 93.
60. Badiou, *Being and Event*, p. 175.
61. Badiou, *Being and Event*, p. 190.
62. Agamben, *Homo Sacer*, pp. 24–5; cf. Clemens, 'The Role of the Shifter and the Problem of Reference in Giorgio Agamben', pp. 56–7.
63. Badiou, *Being and Event*, p. 190.

64. Walter Benjamin, *Illuminations*, trans. Harry Zohn (New York: Schocken Books, 1969), p. 257.
65. Badiou, *Being and Event*, p. 525.
66. Badiou, *Being and Event*, pp. 23–30.
67. Giorgio Agamben, *The Unspeakable Girl*, trans. Leland de la Durantaye (New York: Seagull, 2014), p. 38.
68. Badiou, *The Communist Hypothesis*, pp. 229–59.
69. Badiou, *Conditions*, p. 171.
70. Badiou, *Conditions*, p. 174.
71. Giorgio Agamben, *Idea of Prose*, trans. Michael Sullivan and Sam Whitsitt (Albany: State University of New York Press, 1995), pp. 73–4; Agamben, *The Highest Poverty*, p. 10.
72. Giorgio Agamben, '"What Is a Paradigm?" Lecture at the European Graduate School' (2002), available at <http://www.egs.edu/faculty/giorgio-agamben/articles/what-is-a-paradigm/> (last accessed 21 February 2015).
73. Agamben, *The Time That Remains*, p. 86.
74. Wallace Stevens, *The Collected Poems of Wallace Stevens* (New York: Vintage, 1990), p. 164.

9

Form-of-Life and Antagonism: On *Homo Sacer* and *Operaismo*
Jason E. Smith

Before the publication in 2011 of his *Altissima povertà. Regole monastiche e forme di vita*, perhaps the most important concept in the work of Giorgio Agamben remained an enigma.[1] The notion of a 'form-of-life' has been crucial for the conceptual system Agamben has slowly articulated since the first volume of his long-running *Homo Sacer* project appeared in 1995. This concept, however, was nowhere developed in a thematic way, referred to only rarely and seemingly in passing. Yet a detailed examination of those instances where this term does appear would show that they are always placed at crucial sites, as if a final elucidation of the concept of form-of-life would resolve any lingering problems or questions that have emerged in the course of Agamben's politico-philosophical reflections on sovereignty and biopolitics.

The preface to *The Highest Poverty* underlines the central place of 'form-of-life' and its proximity to practice of 'use' and specifically a 'use of bodies': 'to think a form-of-life, a human life entirely removed from the grasp of the law and a use of bodies and of the world that would never be substantiated into an appropriation'.[2] The Franciscan conceptual strategy set out to define the possibility of a life or human activity emancipated from the structure and pressures of property and juridical title; a strategy that has, as its final horizon, a conception of *usus pauper*, 'poor use' – a technical term bringing together use and poverty – that would not be normed by a notion of law at all. Such a strategy, which was developed in a polemic against the Catholic curia, emphasised not only the distinction between use and law, but more specifically between use and usufruct, between a 'free' use of the world without law and a juridically ratified right to use this or that object, space, body or structure.

The crucial notion of 'form-of-life' returns once again in

189

Agamben's most recent book, *L'uso dei corpi* (*The Use of Bodies*).³ While the book's 'Prologue' suggests that it will treat an entire series of concepts that have oriented the *Homo Sacer* project from the beginning – concepts such 'use, exigency, mode, form-of-life, inoperativity, destituent power'⁴ – it quickly becomes clear that 'form-of-life' has a privileged place in the book's conceptual architecture. And since the book is characterised by Agamben in the same 'Prologue' as the 'final [*ultimo*]' volume of the *Homo Sacer* sequence, the fact that the third and last section of this final instalment of the project is called simply 'Form-of-Life' further cements the central position of the concept. Already, at the conclusion of the preface to his 2007 book *The Kingdom and the Glory*, Agamben had spoken of the 'fourth part of the [*Homo Sacer*] investigation, dedicated to the form-of-life and use',⁵ as a terminal point that, once arrived at, would alone allow the full and complete sense of 'inoperativity' to be clarified.⁶

The Use of Bodies can, then, be seen as an attempt to resolve the impasses or aporias that *The Highest Poverty* locates in the attempts, by the Franciscan order, to theorise and practise a 'form-of-life'. What is curious about his approach to this long-awaited elucidation is that the second section of this third part is in fact a revised version of an essay that Agamben published *at least two years before* the first instalment of the *Homo Sacer* project. Here published in modified form and with a new title – now called 'A Life Inseparable from Its Form' – is a short essay from 1993 originally called, simply, 'Form-of-Life'.

I will not, in the short space of this chapter, be able to offer a reading of *The Use of Bodies*. What I would like to do, instead, is argue for the importance of this particular short essay in Agamben's *Homo Sacer* project, and the centrality of the concept of 'form-of-life' for Agamben's work in general. My ambition is not only to examine once again Agamben's initial sketch of this concept, but to demonstrate the extent to which the development of the notion of form-of-life was conditioned by his engagement with the legacy of *operaismo*, the Italian strain of Marxism developed in the 1960s and 1970s. Agamben's 'Form-of-Life' is significant then, in at least two ways. First, it is one of the few texts by Agamben to explicitly if discretely engage with this theoretical current and some of its most important representatives (Mario Tronti, Antonio Negri and Paolo Virno). And then, secondly, an analysis of this short text allows us to demonstrate how the concept 'form-of-life' is initially developed specifically through the mobilisation and displacement of three key concepts appropriated from this current: general intellect, multitude and antagonism.

Form-of-life

Agamben's 'Form-of-Life' originally appeared in both Italian and French in 1993. The French variant appeared in the journal *Futur Antérieur*, a Parisian review that in the 1990s brought together various tendencies within Italian post-*operaismo*, Michel Foucault's late work on biopower and the thought of Gilles Deleuze.[7] The essay can be situated at the switching point between the political and ethical reflections developed in *The Coming Community*, first published in 1990, and the appearance of the first volume of the *Homo Sacer* suite in 1995. *The Coming Community*, it will be recalled, proposed a novel articulation of three registers or levels of analysis. First, an ontological reflection on Being determined not as substance, predicate or whatness, but as thusness, as what is its mode, manner or how. Then, an ethical reflection that located the possibility of ethics in the acting of one's own inactuality or potentiality. And, finally, a political projection characterising the 'coming politics' as a struggle between a community of 'whatever singularities' who appropriate their own-non-belonging, their own lack of proper identity or properties, and 'State organization'.[8] This attention to the revolutionary political horizon, formalised in the image of coming *struggle* – a term that rarely appears in Agamben's work – between a certain figure of community or being-in-common and the state sets this particular work apart in Agamben's project. It is an aspect of his thought, moreover, which rarely appears within the framework developed beginning with 1995's *Homo Sacer*.

What is at stake in the early books of the *Homo Sacer* series is the topological relation between sovereign or state power, defined as the capacity to decide on a state of exception, and the extraction or production of so-called 'naked life', that is, a life extracted or separated from its 'form' and exposed or abandoned to sovereign power over life and death. But for the moment I simply want to note that in the short, transitional text on 'Form-of-Life', where this topological structure of internal exclusion between sovereign power and naked life is first proposed if not formalised, what is at stake is first and foremost the nature not of sovereign power and its obscure 'bearer', but of what Agamben calls a *'unitary power that constitutes the multiple forms of life as form-of-life'*, that is, an *'antagonistic* power [*puissance*]' that should be, he counsels, the 'unitary center of the coming politics'.[9] In this short text, then, Agamben projects two lines of inquiry, centred on two antagonistic poles in contemporary politics: the operations of sovereign power and the production of naked life, on the one hand, and the constitution, on the other, of a form-of-life that unifies or 'gathers' together what Agamben here calls the 'multiple forms of life' into a singular 'form-of-life'. Importantly, elsewhere in the text he qualifies multiple forms of life as 'forms of *social* life'.[10] In this essay, then, society, a term that rarely receives a specific treatment by Agamben, can be defined as an array of differing forms of life, all of them articulated in a totality defined by more or less conflictual relations.

Agamben's development of the concept of 'form-of-life' hinges in large part on the largely implicit distinction between a form of life, on the one hand, and form-of-life on the other. This distinction is clarified in part by Agamben's emphasis on the multiplicity of forms of life, and by the specifically 'social' character of this proliferation of forms. A form of life can be defined as an identity that is determined socially, that is, as a moment within a social totality. If forms of life are defined as social roles or functions, we can then argue – in a way that Agamben leaves underdeveloped in his account – that the relations between these roles are founded on a set of divisions that structure the social whole.[11] In Marx, for example, to speak of society is to speak of social divisions: specifically, a division of labour between classes. But where Marx emphasises, in the capitalist mode of production, a tendency toward a single division between classes, and a 'struggle' between these two classes, Agamben's analysis emphasises a plurality of what he calls 'social-juridical identities': 'the voter, the worker, the journalist, the student, but also the HIV-positive, the transvestite, the porno star, the elderly, the parent, the woman'.[12]

This list of 'identities' raises more questions than it answers. It is clear that a single individual could easily inhabit a number of these roles: one could very easily be at the same time a voter, a journalist, HIV-positive and a parent. What defines this list is the absence of any conflict or tension, any 'antagonism' between these identities. Moreover, two of the roles or functions invoked can be said to be defined, however, solely through an antagonistic relation to an opposed pole: 'worker' and 'woman'. That Agamben simply assimilates these terms as identities among others, with no indication of their singularity, is strange. To be sure, the name 'worker' can be framed as a sociological category – for example, all those in a given society who receive a wage in compensation for their labour – rather than as an antagonistic pole in the dynamic relation between capital and labour. By the same token, the category woman can name an anthropological division of sexual characteristics. But in contemporary capitalist societies the name is inseparable from the sexual division of labour; in this way, the name 'woman' is not one identity among others, but the name given to a fraction of society who are said to be suited to particular types of activity, and find themselves consequently subject to specific forms of domination. It is, therefore, a term constituted within an antagonistic relationship with the category of 'man'. Agamben's assimilation of these particular categories to the series he enumerates appears to ignore where these terms denote identities that are constituted through forms of antagonism; in this way, they can be said to have special status with regard to the series of 'juridico-social' identities to which they are assimilated. I will return to this important point in my conclusion.

If we return to Agamben's *Homo Sacer* project, we find that its infamous doubling between *zoē* and *bios*, that is, between the life that is indifferently distributed among animals, humans and gods, and the way a mode or manner of life individuates either an individual or a group, obscures the triangulation of *three* terms in Agamben's 1993 text. In 'Form-of-Life', what is emphasised in the relationship between naked life – here identified with *zoē* – and two other concepts, the multiplicity of 'forms of life' that have been identified as 'social', on the one hand, and on the other hand the 'form-of-life' that emerges as a power, a *potenza* and not a *potere*, antagonistic to sovereign power insofar as it is capable of *resisting* the sovereign operation of isolating naked life from its form. Three terms, and two operations: starting from multiple forms of life, we witness the confrontation between the separation of a life from its form on the part of sovereign power; and on the other hand we are told of a coming 'anti-state' politics that will be constituted through a practice that transforms the multiplicity of forms of social life into a single form-of-life (that is, as we will see, nevertheless traversed by a certain '*multitude*'). Finally, Agamben's analysis allows us to describe three separate 'situations', to use his term: the 'normal situations' in which naked life remains 'tied' to forms of life in their social articulation; states of exception in which naked life is extracted from, or separated from, any 'form' or mode of being by state or sovereign power; and finally, what we could call a revolutionary situation, in which a certain traversal of the multiplicity of forms of life occurs through a negation that is in no way symmetrical to that performed by sovereign power, a process that we must be reminded is both political and ontological in nature.

There is an image of Agamben, encouraged by certain passages from his work over the past twenty years, which contends that what is at stake in his political and historical thought is a variant of the Hölderlinian formula according to which, 'where danger is, grows the saving power also'.[13] Whatever the actual meaning of this formula in Hölderlin's poetic work, the reading given to this phrase is always a catastrophic, that is, dialectical one: salvation is nothing more than the appropriation, conversion or assumption of the danger itself, as if the content of catastrophe and salvation were the same, and what must be produced is a new form of appearing of this content, that is, a new subjective relation to it. And yet it is precisely this logic that Agamben swears off or disqualifies, when he explicitly cites Bataille's 'mistake' of elevating naked life, in its very abjection, to the level of a superior principle, 'sovereignty' or the sacred itself.[14] In Agamben's work, by contrast, there is an absolutely asymmetrical relation between naked life, as the effect of sovereign power's decision, and the practice that constitutes a form-of-life, even as both of these operations perform different forms of negation of the predicates and differential markers that structure forms of life in normal situations. For Agamben, 'a political life [. . .] oriented toward the idea of happiness and gathered up in a form-of-life' involves a 'non-state politics' or even an anti-state politics whose sole possibility consists in 'an irrevocable exodus from any and all sovereignty'.[15]

In another short text originally published three years before his 'Form-of-Life', Agamben offers a slightly different version of this 'non-state politics'. Where in 'Form-of-Life' he describes the constitution of a form-of-life as predicated on – and here Agamben strategically adopts a term from Paolo Virno – an 'exodus' from the space of sovereignty and its production of 'bare life', in this earlier essay he speaks instead of 'struggle' between two antagonistic poles. 'The coming politics', he writes, will no longer be a struggle to conquer or to control the state on the part of either new or old social subjects, but rather a struggle between the state and the nonstate (humanity), that is, an irresolvable disjunction between whatever singularities and the state organization.[16]

In the gap between 1990 and 1993 we can, moreover, see another important shift in Agamben's thought. Where in 1993 the conflict envisioned is between a 'life of potential' that must struggle to separate itself from the space of sovereignty, in 1990 he foresees a conflict instead between 'singularities' and the 'State' power. In the case of 'whatever singularities', neither the figure of life nor the category of potentiality is explicitly in play; in the case of the state, the specific relationship between sovereign power and naked life is not yet fully developed. What remains constant across these distinctions, however, is the bracketing of the figure of society. For Agamben, in a departure from classical Marxism, the struggle against the state is not assigned to a particular fraction or class of society, nor is this struggle assigned the objective of seizing and dissolving state or sovereign power. Its horizon is, instead, an enigmatic separation or exodus from the territory or spatiality characteristic of those particular forms of power.

Potentiality and multitude

In the final sections of 'Form-of-Life', Agamben develops his own concept of *form* – a term that, it should be noted, is quickly identified with manner or mode, that is, not with what 'life' is but how it is what it is – through the figure of 'thought'. The 'life of potentiality' is first of all determined by the activity of thought – thought being understood in the terms Aristotle famously develops in *De Anima*. Thought is a sense among others; but it is an exception to the activity of sensation insofar as, unlike touch, taste, sign or audition, it is a 'being', Aristotle asserts, 'whose nature is to be *en puissance*'.[17] That is, thought is a being whose being is to remain inactual in the very movement of its actualisation; or, better, the capacity that, in each determined act, with each determined content of thought, also experiences or feels its own capacity to be affected as such, its own potentiality. Now, importantly, Agamben quickly grafts this experience on to another, post-Aristotelian conception of thought or the intellect, namely, the Averroian affirmation of the 'one and only possible intellect accessible to all human beings'[18] – that is, the very potentiality of thought experienced in each determined act is identified with the universality, the pre-individual or diffuse nature of the intellect itself. Thought is a sense; thought senses its own potentiality in exercising itself; this potentiality is precisely the common or diffuse nature of the intellect, what exceeds any process of individuation.

This conception of the intellect as a common power is, according to Agamben, what marks the threshold of modern political thought, a rupture first formulated in the fourteenth century by Marsilius of Padua and, importantly, Dante Alighieri's *De Monarchia*. The decisive term in Dante's account of what we can call, for convenience's sake, the general intellect is a term that will be familiar to us all: *multitudo*. In a passage from the third section of the first book of *De Monarchia*, Dante underlines that what constitutes the 'mode of existence' specific to the human is exercise of the 'potential intellect'.[19] Lowlier creatures are capable solely of sensation; angels are endowed with an intellect. But the intelligence proper to these beings is completely deprived of all potentiality – that is, in a certain sense, deprived of the privation, the lack, potentiality is supposed to be. Since 'such beings exist only as intelligences and nothing else', their 'being is very simply the act of understanding that their own nature exists'.[20] Now, the human intellect is, as already mentioned, singular. And yet this singularity exists in the form of a potentiality that, according to Dante, 'cannot be fully actualized all at once [*tota simul*] in any one individual or in any one of the particular social groupings enumerated above ["single household", "small community", "city" or "individual community"]', there must be, then, 'a *multitudo* in the human race, through whom the whole of this potentiality can be actualized'.[21]

These lines constitute the most widely cited passage in *De Monarchia*, and there are libraries full of commentaries meant to clarify the content of this *multitudo*. For my purposes, though, what is at stake in this passage is Agamben's use of it, allowing him to complete, in a very abbreviated manner to be sure, his figure of thought, which we will recall is identified with the 'unitary power that constitutes the multiple forms of life into form-of-life'.[22] Once again: thought is that sense which, in sensing this or that, senses its own capacity to be affected, its pure potentiality. And: thought, as a singular power, is necessarily a common power which can never be exhausted by singular acts of thought or, to use the language of

Dante, any individual person, community, city or kingdom – that is, by any form of life. The term multitude, in this instance, therefore names that through which the whole of this potentiality can 'be actualised'; such a multitude can, however, neither be a singular individual or social grouping, nor can it be a single 'time' or instance, since the potentiality of the intellect can never be realised all at once. Multitude, then, is the condition for the actualisation of the potential intellect, as well as the name for an irreducibility of that potentiality itself.

This is all relatively schematic. But these propositions are the condition for understanding Agamben's intervention in this text. The final paragraph is quite clear: it is only when we conceive of the multitude as a common power of the intellect, as that thought which traverses the multiplicity of forms of life in order to constitute a form-of-life as multitude, that the nature of 'Marxist general intellect' takes on its full significance. Multitude, general intellect: it is to the tradition of post-workerism, such as it is developed in the work of Paolo Virno in particular, that these lines are addressed. In the final section of this chapter, then, I turn to the stakes of this engagement with *operaismo* and post-workism, and ask what it tells us about Agamben's notion of form-of-life.

Agamben and *operaismo*

Mapping out Agamben's relation to the Italian strain of Marxism known as *operaismo* is a tall order. On the one hand, it would be easy enough to assert that Agamben's work, with a few notable exceptions, makes little reference to the authors most recognised (in particular outside of Italy) as constituting the theoretical backbone of that tradition: Mario Tronti, Antonio Negri and Paolo Virno. If many of the conceptual foundations for this tradition were produced in close connection to the worker militancy of the 1960s and 1970s, Agamben has noted time and again that his own philosophical preoccupations were tied to his encounter with Heidegger in 1966, and his subsequent discovery of the works of Walter Benjamin. Moreover, in a 1985 interview with Adriano Sofri, a former leader of the militant organisation *Lotta Continua*, Agamben underlines his distance from, and even antipathy for, the wave of struggles that washed over Italy in 1968 and after.[23] Around 1986, however, it is possible to note a rapprochement with the legacy of *operaismo* and, indeed, with the struggles of the

1970s. It is through a friendship and philosophico-political alliance with Paolo Virno in particular that this increasing proximity to Italian workerism crystallises.

In his foreword to Paolo Virno's first published book of philosophy, written in the aftermath of Virno's arrest and imprisonment during the wave of repression following Aldo Moro's kidnapping and murder, Agamben spells out what he considers to be the key lessons of the struggles of the previous period:

> During the 1970s, in Europe, a disenchanted but not hopeless generation came to the fore to lay claim to the political not as an autonomous and totalitarian sphere, but as an ethical community of singularities; history not as linear continuity, but a history whose realization has been deferred too long; not work as economically finalized toward the production of commodities, but an inoperativity deprived of end [*priva di scopi*] and yet not unproductive.[24]

This passage would require a long commentary that I cannot develop here. I want only to emphasise that the beginnings of Agamben's engagement with this legacy of militancy and the workerism so closely tied to it lie in the mid-1980s: that is, at a moment in which many of the key figures associated with this historical experience were either in jail or in exile.

Before outlining the nature of Agamben's engagement with *operaismo*, it is useful to set out the basic concepts and theoretical framework we have come to identify with that tradition. In particular, it is important to stress the key role played by Mario Tronti in formulating the specific approaching to reading Marx and analysing contemporary forms of class struggle that will later be taken up and developed by Antonio Negri and Paolo Virno. For Tronti, the 'Copernican revolution' represented by *operaismo*'s method of reading Marx meant that the history of capitalism or of the capital relation was neither simply a certain phase in the development of productive forces nor a system of logical categories – from absolute to relative surplus value, say, or formal to real subsumption of labour by capital – developing according to their own internal necessity, as if the history of capital were nothing more than its becoming increasingly adequate to its own concept. To the contrary, the wager or axiom articulated by Tronti was that capital has no history of its own, and that its mutations are compelled by pressures exerted by proletarian aggression and conflict, a proletariat that is defined not by its capacity to produce surplus-value but by its refusal of its own identity as a class and a class defined by work. This refusal of work, this struggle against work, this relentless sabotage of its own identity as a commodity – labour-power – that is sold in exchange for wages, cannot be reduced to a simple 'resistance' on the part of a living, labouring humanity to its domination by capital; its definition, if this word even applies, is articulated in its active destruction or sabotage of its own objective existence as labour-power, its own identity as a category of capital and as an objective component in the organic and technical composition of capital (as 'variable capital'). In this way, the building or construction of a worker power, to use the name of an organisation that emerged in the wake of Tronti's work, and which included among its founders Antonio Negri, requires the destruction of worker identity and the abolition of the objective existence of the working class – as a class, as a productive force.

The figure of the worker, then, should not be situated at some point exterior to the capital relation and imaged as a 'living' labour or as a creative force crushed by the dead weight of the past (dead labour), as a productive energy that is siphoned off by an undead vampire whose days are, all the same, numbered. The proletariat is not one pole of a relation from which it might withdraw in order to come into its own, being nothing more than what Benjamin Noys refers to as a 'relation of rupture', an activity of sabotage or undermining the relation that is the whole of its existence. The proletariat is, for Tronti, neither an ontological given (a human essence, a productive substance) that alienates itself in the form of capital, nor is it a historical force that might survive its own mutual implication in the capital relation, organising itself into socialist or communist relations that would be still governed by the categories of capital: value, production, work.

Marx's so-called 'Fragment on Machines' from the *Grundrisse* was crucial to the *operaismo* tendency of Italian Marxism, which emphasised and articulated together two decisive yet enigmatic threads in these notebooks: the themes of the general intellect and living labour. The general intellect refers to the moment, in the development of the productive forces, when scientific knowledge and the accumulation of knowledge produced collectively by society over the course of centuries comes to be an immediate and dominant force in the production process. This knowledge, this 'common power' to use Agamben's term, assumes material form in increasingly complex machines and systems of automation, which replace both the physical exertion characteristic of previous figures of labour-power and the quantity of labour-time necessary for the production of social wealth. For the *operaisti*, the importance of the analysis proposed in the 'Fragment on Machines' was that its emphasis on the role of scientific knowledge in the production process seemed to anticipate the transformations of the capitalist production process that they felt the classical organisations of the worker's movement did not have the means to analyse. This lack of analysis of the transformations of the capitalist production process resulted, in turn, in an inability to understand changes in class composition, on the one hand, and mutations in the forms of struggle, on the other.

In the 1980s, Paolo Virno took up this analysis in a very different historical moment. Virno's strategy is nevertheless a classical workerist one: a strategy of inversion. Reading Marx, with Tronti and in his wake, meant the wilful transpositions of his categories: the construction of their 'subjective' counterparts. Marx, the scientist, concerned himself with the 'self-valorisation' of capital, the objective process of capital accumulation. The workerists, taking Marx's analysis as their starting point, but with close attention to contemporary worker militancy, transpose these concepts; they speak, in their turn, of worker self-valorisation, and the accumulation of worker struggles. Virno arrives at his theory of mass intellectuality by applying Tronti's 'method' to the 'Fragment on Machines' and then drawing upon this to analyse contemporary capitalism. Contemporary production is, Virno argues, characterised by an 'immaterial labor' that involves linguistic competence, the circulation of affects, ethical tendencies. And insofar as these forces accumulate around the figure of the general intellect, the contemporary form of production necessarily announces not simply a disproportion between labour-time and social wealth, but a bifurcation – not necessarily *antagonistic*, but more of a separation, even an exodus – between productive forces and the general intellect.

Agamben's 'Form-of-Life' concludes with a decisive intervention with respect to the Marxist and workerist theses about the development of the general intellect. For Marx, what is important about the moment when the general intellect – again, scientific, abstract knowledge – comes to dominate the production process is that, at a certain point, with the proportional diminution of labour-time in the production process, labour-time itself can no longer function as the measure of value, so 'monstrous' – this is Marx's word – is the disproportion between labour-time and produced wealth. For Marx, this is a breaking point: a mode of production founded in the production of exchange-value, that is, on the extraction of surplus labour, literally has no sense if the quantity of surplus labour-time is reduced to an absolute minimum, to next to nothing. Agamben, however, argues that for the Marxist thesis to 'acquire its sense', it must be understood not in terms of the objectification of scientific knowledge in the form of fixed capital, but only from the perspective of the figure of thought he has outlined. By which is meant: the concept of the general intellect only assumes its properly antagonistic character when it is no longer understood, as Marx himself does, as the 'mere, massive inscription of social knowledge in the production process'.[25] What Marx, in 1858, projected as a crisis for capitalism, that is, like all crises, an objective disproportion (here, between labour-time and social wealth) that transcodes a subjective antagonism, is quite simply the 'current phase of capitalism', that is, the 'society of the spectacle'.[26]

Where the workerist tradition sees the general intellect, as the contemporary form that living labour assumes, as an antagonism internal to the capital relation, Agamben asserts that this reading of general intellect reduces it to a form of life among others – that is, the contemporary form of capitalism itself, in which life as a power is objectified in fixed capital, in machines, in systems of automation, in the spectacle. But what is crucial to the workerist reading of the general intellect is its assertion that what Marx calls the general intellect is not simply the accumulation of abstract, scientific knowledge in the form of fixed capital – that is, the articulation of life and social production, of life as capital – but a set of capacities that are social in nature, yet cannot be objectified in the form of machinery and, more generally, cannot be appropriated as capital.

Agamben appears to appropriate most directly from Virno's critical variation on the notion of the general intellect – namely, mass intellectuality – the contention that intellectuality is the name for a host of capacities and practices that are irreducible to, and resist, incorporation within the capitalist production process. More specifically, these capacities and 'potentialities' take on an irreducibly subjective dimension insofar as they are cannot be completely captured by capitalist accumulation in the objective form of machines. But, where Virno outlines a kind of division internal to the general intellect, between the knowledge objectified in fixed capital as 'dead labour' and the diffuse, mass intellectuality of living labour, Agamben drops any reference to labour at all, and transforms the qualifier 'living' into the substantive 'life'.

This is, however, only the starting point of his own transformation of the concepts we owe to Marx and to *operaismo*. In these elusive passages at the end of 'Form-of-Life', Agamben establishes a series of equivalents: community, *multitudo*, form-of-life. What is crucial in his speculative construction is, we will recall, the opposition between multiple 'forms of life' and a 'unitary form-of-life': intellectuality is *'the unitary power that constitutes the multiple forms of life into form-of-life'*.[27] This established, Agamben then reintroduces a multiplicity within this unity: a unitary form-of-life is necessarily a multitude (a 'dissolute' multitude, if we are to believe Hobbes, who explicitly opposes multitude to people in these terms).[28] Community is therefore the name of the peculiar unity of a 'diffuse' intellectuality that is also a dissolute multitude.

In Agamben's conceptuality, form-of-life is not only opposed to the state and its sovereign operations; it is, as community, just as emphatically opposed to, and in antagonistic relation with, *society*. Since at the very least Ferdinand Tönnies's *Community and Society*, the *opposition* between community and society has become a cliché. This opposition is defined by the forms of relation characteristic of collective life: the immanent or substantial ties of community, the dissolution of those same ties in the icy waters of society, understood as a 'system of needs' or as a pure and simple 'cash nexus'. In society, one only ever encounters, Agamben writes, 'multiple forms of life' which are 'abstractly recodified into juridico-social identities'. Such forms of life, insofar as they are 'always already in act' and take the form of 'such and such identity', cannot constitute a community, in Agamben's sense of the term: among them one finds only 'coincidences and factual partitions'.[29] These factual partitions are equally objective divisions, not only among the vast array of 'identities' ('the journalist, the student, but also the HIV-positive') that crystallise in capitalist social formations, but among objectively determined *classes* as well. Such classes are not, moreover, neutral distributions of bodies, activities and wealth: they are formed through struggle and are mutually defined through their antagonistic relation to one another.

Agamben's intervention in the workerist development of Marx's concept of the 'general intellect' therefore involves a tactical alliance or convergence with certain aspects of the post-workerist Italian tradition. The surest sign of this rapprochement is not his deployment of key concepts from that tradition – in particular that of general intellect and its 'political' supplement, *multitude* – but the rare and perhaps unique appearance within his work of another term dear to classical *operaismo*: *antagonism*. The workerist and post-workerist traditions understand the concept of antagonism in terms of the dynamic of capitalist social relations. This conflictual and asymmetrical relation between living and dead labour is one in which living labour is always 'primary', at once the source of the capitalist valorisation process within which it is caught up, yet whose resistance to that form of capture drives capitalist development itself: a development that will eventually free human activity from the dynamics of value production altogether. Agamben's rewriting of this scenario situates the antagonism less within the dynamics of capitalist production than within the relation between 'massive inscription of social knowledge in productive processes', on the one hand, and 'intellectuality as antagonistic potentiality and form-of-life' on the other. To speak of this form-of-life as 'antagonistic' is to emphasise that community can constitute itself only through an antagonistic relationship to society: that each term implies the disappearance of the other.[30] Community is the enemy of the social, that is, the objective or factual partitioning of society into classes (even if the dominant class takes the form, for example, of fixed capital, that is, as dead labour). To the divisions of society Agamben opposes the multitude of community. The overcoming of capitalist society assumes the name not of socialism but of community: communism.

Agamben's concept of 'form-of-life' can be said to represent his own contribution to the revolutionary and communist tradition with which he has, in his own terms, often felt 'ill at ease'.[31] It is a concept that, as I have hoped to show, was initially forged in relation to three other concepts that have their origins within the Italian 'workerist' strain of Marxism: general intellect, multitude and antagonism. While Agamben never formulates his own departure from this tradition explicitly in these terms, we might wager that what sets his own approach apart is his deployment of the classical opposition between community and society, and by the more ambiguous distinction – and even opposition – between communism and socialism. In *The Coming Community* Agamben speaks of a coming 'struggle' between an emergent community of 'whatever singularities' and what he calls simple 'State power'; in the *Homo Sacer* project, the notion of state power will be supplemented largely by a more refined analytic of power, weaving together a problematic of sovereignty on the one hand, and biopower on the other. The intervening 'Form-of-Life', however, seems to situate the site of struggle between community and 'society', rather than the state; that is, between what it calls 'form-of-life' and 'forms of life'.

The idea of a form-of-life is necessarily predicated on the suppression of the divisions represented by the multiplicity of forms of life, that is, what Agamben calls 'juridico-social' identities. This emphasis on the unitary aspect of a form-of-life signifies that communism entails first and foremost the overcoming of social divisions and the social distribution of functions, roles, activities. But as I have already underlined, the reduction of society to a mere collection of such identities reduces two 'identities' and two divisions in particular to mere juridico-social sites: the worker, on the one hand; woman, on the other. Moreover, Agamben's articulation of the notion of community with the figure of the multitude reintroduces differentiations and tensions into this unitary power, without offering a theory of how these potentially conflictual differences relate to the concept of antagonism. With the publication of Agamben's final instalment of the *Homo Sacer* project, *The Use of Bodies*, his readers can begin to more adequately assess the extent to which his deployment of the concept of form-of-life offers renewed prospects for radical politics. Such an evaluation, however, will have to contend with whether Agamben's treatment of the notion of 'society' as a mere collection of identities and roles does not neglect two key sites of antagonism, two identities produced through forms of conflict specific to the capitalist mode of production: class and gender. The lasting contribution of that 'generation' of the 1970s is, arguably, its confrontation with these two sites and its recognition that class antagonism was inseparable from the sexual division of society, and its overcoming. The great failures of that generation are, most likely, attributable to its inability to develop forms of struggle adequate to this reality.

Notes

1. Giorgio Agamben, *Altissima povertà. Regole monastiche e forme di vita* (Vicenza: Neri Pozza, 2011). The English translation of the title, *The Highest Poverty: Monastic Rules and Form-of-Life*, trans. Adam Kotsko (Stanford: Stanford University Press, 2013), is incorrect: it transforms the plural '*forme di vita*' into the singular 'form-of-life', adding hyphens that do not exist in the Italian. As I will attempt to demonstrate, understanding Agamben's *Homo Sacer* project hinges, in large part, on the distinction between forms of life and a singular form-of-life.
2. Agamben, *The Highest Poverty*, p. xiii.
3. Giorgio Agamben, *L'uso dei corpi* (Vicenza: Neri Pozza, 2014).
4. Agamben, *L'uso dei corpi*, p. 9.
5. Giorgio Agamben, *The Kingdom and the Glory: For a Theological Genealogy of Economy and Government*, trans. Lorenzo Chiesa with Matteo Mandarini (Stanford: Stanford University Press, 2011), p. xiii.
6. Relying on Agamben's peculiar ordering system – the order in which the volumes appear do not coincide with their place in the *Homo Sacer* sequence – we find two volumes, *The Highest Poverty* and *The Use of Bodies*, together making up the fourth part of the project (indexed as *Homo Sacer* 'IV,1' and 'IV,2', respectively).
7. Giorgio Agamben, 'Forma-di-vita', in *Politica* (Napoli: Cronopia, 1993), pp. 105–14; Giorgio Agamben, 'Forme-de-vie', *Futur Antérieur*, vol. 15, no. 1 (January 1993), pp. 81–6; Giorgio Agamben, 'Form-of-Life', in *Means without End: Notes on Politics*, trans. Vincenzo Binetti and Cesare Casarino (Minneapolis: University of Minnesota Press, 2000), pp. 3–14.
8. Giorgio Agamben, *The Coming Community*, trans. Michael Hardt (Minneapolis: University of Minnesota Press, 1993), p. 85.
9. Agamben, 'Form-of-Life', pp. 11, 12 (original emphasis; my emphasis on 'antagonistic').
10. Agamben, 'Form-of-Life', p. 5 (trans. slightly modified; my emphasis).
11. On these questions, see Daniel McLoughlin, 'The Politics of Caesura: Giorgio Agamben on Language and the Law', *Law and Critique*, vol. 20, no. 2 (2009), pp. 163–76.
12. Agamben, 'Form-of-Life', pp. 6–7.
13. Frederich Hölderlin, 'Patmos', in *Frederich Hölderlin Poems and Lectures*, trans. Michael Hamburger (Ann Arbor: University of Michigan Press, 1968), pp. 462–3.

14. Agamben writes that 'to have mistaken such a naked life separate from its form, in its abjection, for a superior principle of sovereignty or the sacred – is the limit of Bataille's thought, which makes it useless to us' (Agamben, *Means without End*, p. 7). In her *Catastrophe and Redemption: The Political Thought of Giorgio Agamben* (Albany: State University of New York Press, 2013), Jessica Whyte deals with the ambiguous theme or operation of 'redemption' or 'salvation' in Agamben's thought, though this particular reference to Bataille is not addressed.
15. Agamben, *Means without End*, p. 8.
16. Giorgio Agamben, 'Marginal Notes on Commentaries on the Society of the Spectacle', in *Means without End*, p. 88. It is not insignificant that these lines were written as a purported response, as the title indicates, to the Italian translation of Guy Debord's 1988 book *Commentaries on the Society of the Spectacle*.
17. Aristotle, *De Anima*, trans. W. D. Ross (Oxford: Clarendon Press, 1961), 429a–b.
18. Agamben, 'Form-of-Life', p. 9.
19. Dante, *Monarchy*, trans. and ed. Prue Shaw (Cambridge: Cambridge University Press, 1996), p. 7.
20. Dante, *Monarchy*, p. 7.
21. Dante, *Monarchy*, pp. 6–7.
22. Agamben, 'Form-of-Life', p. 11.
23. Giorgio Agamben with Adriano Sofri, 'Un'idea di Giorgio Agamben', *Reporter* (9–10 November 1985), pp. 32–3.
24. Giorgio Agamben, 'Nota alla prima edizione', in Paolo Virno, *Convenzione e materialismo: L'unicità senza aura* (Rome: DeriveApprodi, 2011), p. 9.
25. Agamben, 'Form-of-Life', p. 10.
26. Agamben, 'Form-of-Life', p. 10.
27. Agamben, 'Form-of-Life', p. 10 (original emphasis).
28. Hobbes, *De Cive*, XII, 'Speaking as in a dissolute multitude, and yet not fashioned Government, they destroy the frame.' 'Leviantano e Behemoth', the second chapter in Agamben's recent *Stasis. La guerra civile come paradigma politico* (Torino: Boallati Boringhieri, 2015), treats this figure of the 'dissolute multitude' at length.
29. Agamben, 'Form-of-Life', p. 9.
30. In *L'Uso dei corpi*, the term antagonism, so rare in Agamben's work – and tied entirely to his engagement with Virno and workerism – is replaced with the idea of 'destitution'.
31. Agamben and Sofri, 'Un'idea di Giorgio Agamben'.

10

What Is a Form-of-Life?: Giorgio Agamben and the Practice of Poverty

Steven DeCaroli

> What is your aim in philosophy?
> To show the fly the way out of the fly-bottle.
>   Ludwig Wittgenstein, *Philosophical Investigations*, I, 309

What I would like to attempt in this chapter, which at first might seem a simple matter, is to determine the meaning of what Giorgio Agamben calls a 'form-of-life' and to make clear how its technical sense differs from the term 'form of life', which bears a slightly different inscription, and in relation to which form-of-life remains in continual tension.[1] Although both terms have been part of Agamben's lexicon for over two decades,[2] the manner in which they have been discussed in the secondary literature remains unconvincing – in part because these considerations are often limited to simple repetitions of Agamben's sparse formulation. But this is not entirely the fault of Agamben's readership. There is a great deal of ambiguity, if not outright inconsistency, in the manner in which Agamben deploys the terms and, until quite recently, their presentation has been, somewhat notoriously, uncertain.

In order to comprehend the strategic function these terms play in Agamben's thought we must, however, approach them obliquely because it is not possible to adequately understand what is meant by form-of-life unless we first come to terms with the role that the concept of necessity plays in Agamben's analysis of juridical power. As will become clear in what follows, Agamben's investigation into the limits of legal authority is guided by his treatment of necessity, a concept that plays a central role in two pivotal texts, *State of Exception* and *The Highest Poverty*, which, despite their evident differences, in fact mirror each other quite closely.[3] Since it is within the pages of the more recent of these two books, *The Highest Poverty*, that Agamben provides his fullest treatment to date of the positive content of form-of-life – an undertaking announced in the book's subtitle – it will serve as the focus of this study.[4]

Two necessities

The Greeks gave the name *Ananke* to the personification of necessity and in Orphic theology she appears as the wife of *Demiurgus* and as the mother of both the *Moerae* (the fates) and *Heimarmenē* (destiny). In her lap rests a spindle around which the world revolves and we are told that her power was irresistible, even to gods – a view corroborated by Simonides of Ceos who, in a passage cited by Plato in the *Protagoras*, tells us that 'against necessity [*ananke*] not even the gods make war'.[5] But if necessity forces the hand of both mortals and gods, she does not do so alone. For according to Pausanias' *Descriptio Graeciae*, there was a sanctuary on the north slope of the Acrocorinth dedicated not only to *Ananke* but also to *Bia* (violence), where the two goddesses were worshipped together in the same shrine – a shrine, he adds, which it was 'not customary to enter'.[6]

The proximity of necessity and violence arises, of course, in the context of biological survival where, in accordance with natural law (*ius naturale*), the use of force to secure basic necessities is justified. It is, however, in the domain of politics that this relation has proven most consequential. When Aristotle turns his attention to the topic of the *polis*, for instance, he begins not with politics itself but with a discussion of the *oikos*, the private realm of the household, which, in addition to being responsible for procuring the biological necessities of daily living, serves both as the backdrop against which the *polis* will be defined and as the domain of necessity from which the political order will continually seek to distance itself. Likewise, when, in a brief essay from 1993, Agamben states that 'Political power as we know it . . . always founds itself – in the last instance – on the separation of a sphere of naked life [*nuda vita*] from the context of the forms of life',[7] it is to this primary political division of *oikos* from *polis* that he refers. What we have is an attempt to exclude from the realm of political life both the constraints of necessity that oblige human action to conform to the requirements of survival and the violence that accompanies this pursuit, not only because every necessity conceals the potential for an emergency, but because there is simply no necessity that law can hope to command.

But despite every effort, the absolute separation of *polis* from *oikos* has never held fast. The necessity that politics seeks to exclude finds its way back into the *polis*, and it does so for two reasons – first, because the *polis* cannot exist without the necessary work of the *oikos* and, second, because the logic of political life generates formidable necessities of its own. As we will see, these two reasons correspond not only with two distinct types of necessity, but also designate two points at which the rule of law reaches its operational limit.

The demands of biological life have always, from time to time, erupted within the *polis* and when raw necessity confronts the juridical order, when the need for survival impinges upon the aims of politics, the force of law begins to deteriorate. It is well known that, for Aristotle, membership in the *polis* was possible only through the strict exclusion of those (women, slaves, etc.) whose lives remained tethered to the labour required for survival, and therefore to the *oikos*, and so it is not surprising that it is from out of their ranks that the *polis* first encounters its antithesis, that is to say, *the poor* – the name we give to the appearance of biological necessity within the borders of the state. It is with this in mind that Aristotle tells us, 'poverty is the parent of revolution and crime',[8] for under conditions of material scarcity the legal order gives way to the demands of biological need, giving full meaning to the Latin adage, often repeated in medieval legal literature, 'necessity knows no law' (*necessitas dat legem non ipsa accipit*).[9]

But the appearance of poverty is not the only manner in which the separation of the *oikos* from the *polis* reveals its fragility, for the state is concerned with its own survival as well. The violence that political life sought to avoid by excluding necessity from its domain reappears in the form of necessities born within the political order itself – a purely political form of survival, which concerns not the ability to live but the capacity to rule. When, in his seminar of 1977–8, Michel Foucault introduces the notion of necessity in relation to what the seventeenth century knew as *coup d'État*, it is this second form of necessity to which he refers. Following Giovanni Palazzo's early definition, *coup d'État* refers not to the seizure of state power by outside forces, but to the state 'acting of itself on itself' in response to a necessity that is 'above the law', and it is 'in the name of the state's salvation', that is to say, its survival, that the state undertakes the suspension of law and legality.[10] Politics, Foucault concludes, is therefore, 'not something that has to fall within a form of legality or a system of laws. Politics is concerned with something else, although at times, when it needs them, it uses laws as an instrument. Politics is concerned with necessity.'[11] What we encounter here is necessity born of the state itself, emerging from the need to preserve legitimacy so as to retain the authority to rule. When political life appears on the verge of collapse, when the ability to extend force to law is placed in jeopardy, the political order begins to mirror the biological order by turning not to law, because the law's viability is precisely what is in question, but to extra-legal forms of legitimacy and to violence: 'When necessity demands it,' Foucault writes, '*raison d'État* becomes *coup d'État*, and then it is violent.'[12] At this point, however, the parallel between the biological order and the political order comes to an end because, whereas life encounters biological necessity whenever objective conditions give rise to the risk of death, the state confronts political necessity strictly by way of a decision – thereby disclosing the essential meaning of Carl Schmitt's famous definition of sovereignty, according to which the 'sovereign is he who decides on the exception'.[13]

Two investigations

Any interpretation of the political meaning of necessity, then, must begin with the peculiar fact that necessity stands on opposite ends of the law, positioned, as it were, at the two poles where law reaches its operational limit. On one side there is biological necessity, the point at which law must abdicate its authority in favour of biological survival, and it is in this sense that the law is constrained by biological necessity. And on the other side there is the loss of political legitimacy, the point at which law is stripped of its general capacity to command, and it is in this sense that law is constrained by the requirements of political necessity. On the one hand, we encounter conditions leading to necessary use (*usus necessitatis*), and on the other we encounter conditions that give rise to a state of necessity (*status necessitatis*). Although there is a risk of oversimplification, Agamben's ongoing investigations into the limits of juridical power can be understood as proceeding down both these lines of inquiry.

The first investigation leads us to *State of Exception*, which, as the title indicates, concerns *status necessitatis* or, more specifically, the nature of authority (*auctoritas*) insofar as it retains the power to suspend law. Agamben's analysis demonstrates that authority is not only a power that persists in the absence of the law, but coincides with the life of the sovereign in whose person life and law are made indistinguishable. Authority is 'what remains of law if law is wholly suspended', and in this sense authority is 'not law but life', a 'law that blurs at every point with life'.[14] Being a living law, the sovereign, the *auctor*, makes the political emergency possible by making political necessity intelligible, that is, by entangling the survival of the state with the survival of the ruler. And insofar as a political emergency is possible, authority is revealed to be a dependent power not only because political life depends upon *material* necessities provided by the private domain of the household, but because authority depends also on *cognitive* necessities (belief and obedience) furnished by a population.

And the second investigation leads us, of course, to *The Highest Poverty*, which considers *usus necessitatis* and the role it plays in monastic communities that sought, through the practice of poverty, to live life beyond law. In this text Agamben asks: to what extent is it possible to envision a viable community premised neither on sovereignty nor on the juridical allocation of rights? Are there historical precedents for this type of community? And, if so, what type of life – what form of life – characterises this community and makes extra-legal existence possible? If strength of authority is directly proportional to the way of living (form of life) that sustains it, then the aim of Agamben's most recent work is to formulate a way of life (form-of-life) wherein authority is rendered *un*sustainable.

Monastic rule

In the opening pages of *The Highest Poverty*, which are devoted to a discussion of the birth of monastic rule during the fourth and fifth centuries, Agamben explains that his investigation will be an attempt, by means of a study of monasticism, 'to construct a form-of-life', a life 'that is linked so closely to its form that it proves to be inseparable from it'.[15] Although, according to Agamben's analysis, monastic communities ultimately fail to achieve this inseparability, the persistence with which they repeatedly approach its realisation is nonetheless instructive. Of paramount importance is the novel manner in which later forms of monasticism, and in particular the Franciscan Order, confronted the problem of the relationship between rule and life, collapsing the distinction in a way that was decidedly *not* achieved through either perfect obedience under law or strict conformity to the duties of office – subjects Agamben explores in a subsidiary text on liturgy and divine office, *Opus Dei*.[16] As we will see, what makes the Franciscan Order significant is the manner in which it bridged the disconnection between, on the one hand, the demands spelled out in the rules and, on the other hand, the imperfect ability of the monastic community to comply with those demands. Whereas other monastic communities accomplished this reconciliation between rule and life through an extreme intensification of monastic discipline, the Franciscans did very much the reverse. As Agamben explains:

> The traditional juridical idea of the observance of a precept is here reversed. Not only is it the case that the Friar Minor does not obey the rule, but live it – with an even more extreme reversal, it is life that is to be applied to the norm and not the norm to life.[17]

Consequently, the 'most precious legacy' of Franciscanism is, as will become clear in what follows, precisely 'how to think a form-of-life, a human life entirely removed from the grasp of the law' and therefore how to establish a community 'no longer on the level of doctrine and law, but on the level of life'.[18]

According to Agamben's presentation, the earliest monastic rules were not juridical texts but rather codes of conduct, which, by being something other than law, reconfigured the relation between norm and life. 'What is a rule, if it seems to be mixed up with life without remainder? And what is a human life, if it can no longer be distinguished from the rule?'[19] The manner in which Agamben formulates these questions is undoubtedly intended to invite a comparison with the special relationship that the sovereign maintains with the law, thereby invoking the central theme of *State of Exception*, namely, the sovereign whose authority makes his life indistinguishable from law. Likewise, quoting Cándido Mazón's *Las reglas de los religiosos*, Agamben explains that the rules of monastic orders 'are not truly laws or precepts in the strict sense of the term', but neither are they reducible to 'mere advice that leaves the monks at liberty to follow it or not'.[20] Here too we find a conspicuous parallel with *State of Exception* insofar as *auctoritas*, according to Theodor Mommsen's definition, which Agamben cites, is 'more than advice and less than command, an advice which one may not safely ignore'.[21]

Roughly speaking, then, there is an inverse parallel between monastic rule and sovereign authority, between *regula* and *auctoritas*. While monastic rules guided the lives of monks who lived outside the law and who refused every right furnished by the juridical order, sovereign authority grounds the force of law insofar as it survives in the person of the sovereign who exists beyond it. Monastic rules, like authority, were not laws and did not attain their efficacy by juridical means, yet they functioned very differently from sovereign authority insofar as they did not serve as the foundation for a legal system. Instead of joining the obligated to an elevated source of power, as in the case of law, monastic rules bonded together (each-to-each) those who had given themselves over to this obligation, thereby creating a common life over which rules had no binding claim. The form of life (*forma vitae*) invoked by the rule, then, is a common life constituted absent the imposition of law, and all monastic *regula* must be understood in these terms. 'Common life', Agamben maintains, 'is not the object that the rule must constitute and govern. On the contrary ... it is the rule that seems to be born from "cenoby" [common life].'[22]

The notion of a *forma vitae* championed by the Franciscans is, however, considerably older than Franciscanism itself and can be found as far back as Cicero, Seneca and Quintilian – a lineage that brings with it synonymous meanings that accompany *forma*: *imago*, *exemplar*, *exemplum*. The sense of a model or an example that characterised these earlier traditions carried over into the Franciscan *forma vitae*, and understood in these terms the phrase 'form of life' may also be rendered 'example of life' or 'paradigm of life' since a form of life is that type (*typos*) of life that can serve as an example of a way of living – which is precisely how we ought to understand the monastic rule, especially when we recall that the supreme rule for Francis was not a code but the concrete, exemplary life of Christ. 'One could not say more clearly that if a life (the life of Christ) is to furnish the paradigm of the rule, then the rule is transformed into life, becomes *forma vivendi et regula vivifica*.'[23]

'Living according to a form', Agamben tells us, 'undoubtedly implies, according to a frequent meaning of the term *forma* in medieval Latin, an exemplary relation with others',[24] but, he reminds us, 'the logic of the example is anything but simple and does not coincide with the application of a general law'.[25] The peculiar logic of the example, about which Agamben has said a great deal, fits nicely here for there is, after all, no separation between the example and the thing it exemplifies. The example is always already an instance of its exemplarity and so it is impossible to cleanly distinguish between the example as a rule and the example as instance of adherence to that rule. The example exercises a normative force without relying on law and so Sulpicius Severus can write, regarding the embodiment of monastic regulation, 'Be a form of living for all, be an example.'[26]

The great insight of the monastics, then, was to refuse to produce on top of common life, which is by its nature precarious, a legal framework that purports to protect, stabilise and defend it, because the cost of this stabilisation is a legal logic that permits the type of exclusion that political order seems to require and which Agamben's famous figure of *Homo sacer* exemplifies. Ironically perhaps, and despite its religious nature, Agamben finds in monasticism a community characterised by a *refusal of authority*, a refusal to recognise and thereby make operative the work of law and sovereignty. The monks' refusal to employ legal codes as a mechanism for binding community was therefore neither the result of de facto illegality, nor of a rebellious refusal to obey, but of a form of life that rendered juridical authority inoperative, a life characterised by a type of poverty which was not only material but juridical.

Abdicatio iuris

It is no surprise that when Agamben takes up the question of the relation between *forma vitae* and the law, he begins with poverty, and specifically the *altissima paupertas* (highest poverty) of Francis. From the beginning, the Friars Minor stressed not merely the embrace of material poverty but, in a move that produced tension with the Papacy, the abdication of every right (*abdicatio omnis iuris*), which is to say, the adoption of *juridical poverty*. 'What the Franciscans never tire of confirming', we are told, 'is the lawfulness for the brothers of making use of goods without having any right to them (neither of property nor of use).'[27] Bonagratia, who is among the first to develop the notion of use without right by placing the Franciscan vow of poverty in the context of necessity, argues that, 'as the horse has de facto use but not property rights over the oats that it eats, so the religious who has abdicated all property has the simple de facto use [*usum simplicem facti*] of bread, wine, and clothes'.[28] While Francis's devotion to animals is undoubtedly implied in this formulation, as Agamben points out, animals are not here brought into the human fold; rather, the brothers are 'equated with animals from the point of view of the law'.[29] Just as in the state of innocence, 'human beings had the use of things but not ownership, so also the Franciscans . . . can renounce all property rights while maintaining, however, the de facto use of things'.[30] The separation of ownership from use, implicit in the *abdicatio iuris*, therefore constituted 'the essential apparatus that the Franciscans use to technically define the peculiar condition that they call "poverty"'.[31]

Under the papacy of John XXII, however, the possibility of separating ownership and use is called into question and the Pontiff's pronouncements on the subject, put forth in the bull *Ad conditorem canonum*, marks a critical moment in the history of Franciscanism. The Curia's argument hinged on isolating a sphere of conduct wherein the separation of use from ownership is impossible. This was accomplished by claiming, in the case of consumable goods such as food or water, that use entails the necessary destruction of the thing consumed. Therefore, '[t]he purely ontological problem is whether a use that consists only in abuse (that is, in destruction) can exist and be possessed other than by right of ownership.'[32] Whereas the Friars wished to preserve a right of usage in the absence of ownership, and so claimed to use out of necessity, the Curia argued that necessary use and, indeed, all forms of use that involve consumption imply a de facto right of ownership.

The Franciscans, of course, responded to this critique and Agamben articulates the monastic position by citing both Hugh of Digne and Ockham. According to Hugh's *De finibus paupertatis*, natural law 'prescribes that everyone have use of the things necessary to their conservation, but does not obligate them in any way to ownership'.[33] Hugh's strategy for distinguishing use from ownership rested, therefore, on the distinction between natural law and positive law, between *quid facti* and *quid iuris*. He tells us, for instance, that conserving one's life through the use of food and clothing does not constitute ownership but rather simple use, because the right of ownership can be renounced, whereas the right to use in the interest of survival cannot be. The problem with this formulation, however, is that by defining simple use in opposition to ownership, Hugh defines it in entirely legal terms. Necessary use is anchored in the theory of natural law which positive law recognises, thereby tethering it to a legal logic and placing Hugh's presentation in the awkward position of having to present in juridical terms the right to have no rights.

Ockham defended the Franciscan position in a similar fashion by distinguishing between the natural right of use (which appears when one enters a state of necessity measured against the needs of survival) and the positive right of use (which is entirely the result of law and legal dispensation). Though they retained no positive right to the things they used, the Friars nevertheless claimed a natural right limited to cases of extreme necessity:

> Brothers have permission to use things for a time other than a time of extreme necessity [*pro alio tempore quam pro tempore necessitatis extremae*], but they do not have any right of using at all except for the time of extreme necessity.[34]

Whereas monks had *permission* to use things when it was not necessary to do so, they did not have a *right* to use those things unless they did so under conditions of necessity, because in such cases their actions assumed a legal status (via natural law), thereby becoming a matter of right. As Agamben puts it, 'They have renounced all property and every faculty of appropriating, but not the natural right of use, which is, insofar as it is a natural right, unrenounceable.'[35] Thus,

> [i]t is not the rule so much as the state of necessity that is the apparatus through which they seek to neutralise law and at the same time to assure themselves an extreme relationship with it (in the form of *ius naturale*).[36]

Although Ockham strayed into the same trap as Hugh, justifying the Franciscan notion of use in terms that are entirely juridical, he had, in a sense, flipped the relation between law and necessity that characterised monastic life.[37] Under normal conditions, where positive law is generally applied, the Friars Minor had no legally enforceable right to use, but in cases of extreme necessity, as Ockham argues, the brothers 'recover a relationship with law'[38]

– but in this case it is natural law, not positive law. 'Necessity, which gives the Friars Minor a dispensation from the rule, restores (natural) law to them; outside the state of necessity, they have no relationship with the law.'[39] Thus, what for others is the normal condition of living under rights extended by law became for the monastics an exceptional state. Monastic life was lived outside of the law, coming into contact with the law only when conditions were necessary for survival, whereas others live continually under the law and begin to exit the law only in an emergency – 'what for others is an exception becomes for them a form of life'.[40] Monastic use and legal use overlap or come into contact only in this very narrow condition known as necessary use – *usus necessitatis* – and so, Agamben concludes, '[u]se and the state of necessity are the two extremes that define the Franciscan form of life.'[41]

Abdicatio officium

But since, as we saw above, use and necessity are not limited to material or biological existence, but appear also in the more circumscribed context of political life, Agamben turns next to a consideration of office (*officium*). What is important to understand here is that office is also a kind of property and therefore not only is it something that can be put to use, it is also something in relation to which one can be poor. Office is a type of status and, as with all status, what distinguishes it ontologically is a capacity to bring into existence, within a social domain, real powers and real effects. To hold an office, in other words, is to possess the power to transform some portion of social reality, which in the case of clerical office is best exemplified by the priestly power to perform the sacraments.

A key procedural question arising from the power of religious office was whether sacraments performed by an unworthy priest were still valid. Holding firm to the integrity of the institution of offices, which was its prerogative to dispense, the Church answered the question affirmatively, claiming that a priest is merely the instrument of God. Monastics, however, held an entirely different view, claiming that monks are not given rights according to status, but in accordance with the life they lead. It was not, therefore, a matter of a person empowered by his office, the efficacy of which would thereby ultimately lie in an authority located external to the officeholder, transferred through *officium*, but of a person whose meritorious disposition and spiritual attitude instantiated its own efficacy. 'To a life that receives its sense and its standing from the Office', Agamben explains, 'monasticism opposes the idea of an *officium* that has sense only if it becomes life.'[42]

As was mentioned above regarding monastic rule, with which office is closely connected, earlier forms of monasticism attempted to solve the general problem arising from the disconnect between ideal conduct presented in the rule and actual monastic behaviour by creating a *regula vitae*, 'an unprecedented intensification of prayer and *officium*'[43] in which the rules of devotion were so completely absorbed into their way of life that there was not a moment which was not given over to their fulfilment. Franciscanism, however, took a different path, substituting for *regula vitae* the idea of *forma vitae*; and this is 'not because it is constituted as an *officium* and a liturgy, nor because the law has for its object the relation between a life and its form, but precisely by virtue of its radical extraneousness to law and liturgy'.[44] Indeed, it stands to reason that a movement dedicated to living a life beyond the privileges of right and ownership would shed any pretence to office which, insofar as it gains its effectiveness through legal status, is a species of property that the practice of poverty disables. Since divine office never came to define Franciscan identity, the Order stood in an extraneous relation to the Church and for this reason the development of the Order exhibited none of the anticlericalism common to other monastic movements of the same period. 'Life according to the form of the holy Gospel is situated on a level that is so distinct from that of the life according to the form of the holy Roman Church that it cannot enter into conflict with it',[45] and consequently Francis could 'always give to the Church what is the Church's without polemic'.[46]

To walk this road, to establish a community without law, property or office, is to confront the question of what a law is in its most general sense: to live outside of law is not to repeal this or that statute or decree, but to dismantle the peculiar idea that life is something to which a rule or status of any sort might be 'applied'. As we will see, the means of accomplishing this task is to reveal the artifice of authority upon which law and office depend. But this is no easy task. Indeed, as Agamben makes clear, the real temptation that confronted monastic life was not the enticements of greed and lust, but the tendency to slip into strict codes of conduct and to police communal life in a mistaken attempt to preserve it:

The great temptation of the monks was not that which paintings of the Quattrocento have fixed in the seminude female figure and in the shapeless monsters that assail Antony in his hermitage, but the will to construct their life as a total and unceasing liturgy or Divine Office.[47]

Olivi and Paul

In the final pages of the book, Agamben turns his attention to the work of the thirteenth-century Franciscan theologian, Pierre Jean Olivi, who brought the Franciscan way of life closest to its full conceptual manifestation. What surfaces in Agamben's analysis is not only a testimony to the radicalism of Olivi's understanding of use, but a segue to a positive definition of form-of-life, which, up until this point in Agamben's own writings, in proximity with figures such as the *homo sacer* and the *Muselmann*, has been presented in a predominantly negative fashion. In other words, while figures such as the *homo sacer* introduce us to lives removed from the normal legal order, the manner of their exclusion is conditioned negatively in relation to the law's withdrawal, not positively in the absence of *any* relation to law. In the pages of *The Highest Poverty*, and especially in its final section, Agamben shifts the direction of his political intervention, taking us down a more prescriptive path, and Olivi marks one interlocutor who aids in this movement.

What is at stake for Olivi in the texts Agamben cites is nothing short of an ontology of signs. Does a sign, or a status, or a right add something essential to the thing or person to whom it is applied? In Olivi's analysis of these questions, Agamben contends, 'we see articulated, according to an intention that undoubtedly characterised Franciscan thought, an ontology that is so to speak existentialist and not essentialist'.[48] But what does an existentialist ontology mean in this context? Olivi's inquiry concerns the degree of reality contained in socially constituted phenomena such as sacraments, offices and rights. Speaking generally of signs, Olivi writes:

> Insofar as you can consider them with subtlety and clarity, you will find that signification does not add to the real essence of the thing that is used as a sign anything other than the mental intention of those who have instituted it and accepted its validity and of those who accept it in action in order to signify and of those who hear it or receive it as a sign.[49]

All socially constituted phenomena exist, therefore, only within the domain of 'mental intentions', in the form of collective intentionality, and never at the level of essences. An essentialist understanding of social phenomena, which, for instance, might attribute reality to the power of an office, is therefore simply the effect of having misperceived as real what is in fact only a sign. By contrast, an existential understanding follows from the ability to perceive within social phenomena the un-mystified, un-glorified, perceiver-dependent process whereby humanity manufactures significance in the world.[50]

The conflict that Olivi and the Franciscans have with the law (or rather, their attempt to render the law inoperative) thus takes place on the level of the law's operational existence. And therefore, '[t]he conflict with law – or rather, the attempt to deactivate it and render it inoperative through use – is situated on the same purely existential level on which the operativity of law and liturgy acts.'[51] What Olivi suggests is, in fact, a profane ontology – an awareness of the mundane operation that lies behind all that operates *as if* sacred.[52] 'The sphere of human practice, with its rights and its signs, is real and efficacious', Agamben explains, 'but it produces nothing essential, nor does it generate any new essence beyond its own effects. The ontology that is in question here is thus purely operative and effectual.' And so, he concludes, '[f]orm of life is the purely existential reality that must be liberated from the signature of law and office or duty (*ufficio*).'[53] If one is able to genuinely understand how, through the projection of status, we come to create things like kings or gods – if one sees how this works – then the risk of attributing to a king or a god an essence lying beyond the social mechanics of their construction is greatly reduced. Practically speaking, this entails an ongoing practice of exposing the immanent work of thought that is involved in producing something that functions *as if* it had an essence.

However, rather than follow Olivi, who lays bare the nature of office and ownership by revealing them to 'have a reality that is only psychological . . . and procedural',[54] the Franciscan polemicists chose, as we have seen, to mobilise their claim along the more cautious juridical path separating use from ownership. This tactic undercut the profound novelty of their position and ultimately caused Franciscanism to become fixed within the order of the Church and canon law. Thus, '[w]hat is lacking in the Franciscan literature', Agamben laments, 'is a definition of use in itself and not only in opposition to law.'[55]

In pursuit of such a definition, Agamben invokes Saint Paul. Drawing from the extensive analysis he has undertaken of the Pauline literature, especially in *The Time That Remains*, Agamben sees in Paul's writings a strategic resource, certainly available to the Friars, which could have enabled them to break free from the purely negative and ultimately juridical defence of their ostensibly non-juridical way of life and manner of using. Paul's attempt to deactivate the law and to render the law inoperative through use is, Agamben explains (thereby bringing Paul into direct conversation with Olivi), 'situated on the same purely existential level on which the operativity of law and liturgy acts'.[56] By constructing a defence of use in exclusively juridical terms the Franciscans were prevented from discovering in Paul's writings, especially in the verses of 1 Cor. 7: 20–31, a theory of use which entails 'using the world as not using it or not abusing it (*et qui utuntur hoc mundo, tamquam non utantur*)', and which could have furnished a powerful argument against John XXII's theses on the use of consumable things as *abusus*.[57]

What we learn from Olivi is that the ontology of social categories is fundamentally a theory of use, which has the potential to remind us that we are always 'using' our social perception. It is for this reason, Agamben argues, that the Friars should have turned to Paul and to his notion of using 'as if not' using (*hōs mē*) to recover a theory of use designed to expose the purely functional, that is to say, existential, utility of social status. As we will see shortly, it is precisely this manner of awareness that I take to be the foundation of Agamben's notion of form-of-life. In its full and proper sense, form-of-life names the habit of putting into practice the Pauline *hōs mē* as a means of making visible what Olivi called our 'mental intentions' so as to deactivate the social status and privilege it sustains.

The Capuchin Constitution

The Highest Poverty concludes with a two-paragraph chapter that begins with the following observation:

> What was lacking in the Franciscan doctrine of use is precisely the connection with the idea of form of life that Olivi's text seems to implicitly demand. It is as if the *altissima paupertas*, which according

to the founder was to define the Franciscan form of life as a perfect life (and that in other texts, like the *Sacrum commercium Sancti Francisci cum Domina Paupertate*, effectively has this function), lost its centrality once it was linked to the concept of *usus facti* [necessary use] and ended up being characterised only negatively with respect to the law.[58]

As we have seen, life defined by the practice of *altissima paupertas* is a life lived outside the law and in accordance with a way of living for which the law has no terminology. Poverty, of both property and right, disarms law not by breaking it, but by refusing it – in the manner of a gift respectfully declined, or in the style of Bartleby's courteous refrain, 'I would prefer not to.'

Although Agamben claims that the Franciscans failed to articulate this type of use, due to their 'preoccupation with constructing a justification of use in juridical terms',[59] there is at least one place within the Franciscan literature where the Friars seem to be saying something very close to what Agamben denies of them. In the 1536 *Capuchin Constitution* (*Le Constitutioni de' Frati Minori Cappuccini di San Francesco*, corrected and revised in 1577), a text Agamben does not cite but which is absolutely central to the development and historical expansion of the Franciscan ideal, not only is *all use* understood in terms of necessary use precisely so that the legal bond between usage and ownership can be rendered inoperative, but the manner in which use is separated from the law appears to employ the strategy implicit in the Pauline *hōs mē*. 'Let every Friar remember', the *Constitution* reads, 'that evangelical poverty consists in the firm resolution of not becoming attached to any earthly thing, of using the things of the world most sparingly *as if* compelled by necessity.'[60]

Not *by* necessity, but *as if by* necessity. Recall that, according to Agamben, the fatal error made by the Franciscan polemicists in response to the Papacy was to turn to necessity and the natural law that it invokes. But the passage from the *Constitution* says something quite different. It does not instruct the monks to use only when their survival is at risk, but rather to use as they would *as if* their survival was at risk. In other words, use as if you were in a state of necessity, even though you are not. But, of course, under such conditions positive law does not formally recognise natural law at work. These are entirely different claims. From the point of view of the law the consumption of bread that is not one's own is justified due to need, but in a different situation where one consumes bread as if by necessity, no court would rule this justified. To put it simply, the law recognises *by* but not *as if by*.[61]

But there is more. A few lines later we encounter a statement that expresses the Franciscan position in all its sophistication. '[W]e wish it to be understood', the *Constitution* continues, 'that we have in fact no jurisdiction, ownership, juridical possession or usufruct or legal use of anything, *even of the things* we use through necessity [*ne anco di quelle, che per necessita usiamo*].'[62] Here it is stated with perfect clarity that *even in those instances when the Friars do use by necessity* (which natural law *does* justify), all claims to right of use granted under natural law are rejected. With these words, the drafters of the *Constitution* demonstrate a full awareness of the need to eliminate every connection to the law, including natural law, and explicitly adopt a means of achieving this that is strikingly similar to the Pauline *hōs mē*. In doing so, they skilfully avoid, by means of a uniquely juridical form of poverty, the negative definition of use that Agamben identifies in other Franciscan documents. By rejecting outright the legal status of natural necessity, these passages appear to speak directly to what Agamben wants the Franciscans to say but yet seems to suggest that they have not said. Agamben's intuition that the Franciscans were doing genuinely radical and sophisticated work in conceiving a form of life beyond legality is correct, but the Friars seem to have taken this task further than Agamben either is aware of or is prepared to admit.

Form-of-life

In his opening lecture of 1978–9, Foucault includes a discussion of his method:

> What I would like to show is not how an error ... or how an illusion could be born, but how a particular regime of truth, and therefore not an error, makes something that does not exist able to become something. It is not an illusion since it is precisely a set of practices, real practices, which established it and thus imperiously marks it out in reality.[63]

Then, in the final lecture of the year, Foucault returns to the theme with which he began, this time supplying terminology designed to name it. Speaking of the nature of civil society, Foucault cautions that 'we should be very prudent regarding the degree of reality we accord to this civil society', not because it is not real, but because it is real in a way that is difficult to grasp and which can very easily slip through our fingers. 'Civil society', he writes, 'is like madness and sexuality, what I call transactional realities [*réalités de transaction*].'[64] What Foucault describes in these passages regarding his own research into the nature of madness and sexuality offers an apt depiction of Agamben's methodological intention as well and can be extended to his study of law and office. Law and office, together with the authority associated with each, are themselves *réalités de transaction*, powers made manifest at the moment their status as effects of social perception disappears, replaced by an assumed natural order; and so to study them historically is not merely to depict them or to narrate them, but rather by accounting for their existence, is to thereby embark on the work of dismantling them.

The deactivation of our transactional realities requires not a seizure of state power or the establishment of a radically new order, but the exposure of a reality that has always been at work. Ludwig Wittgenstein's *Philosophical Investigations* is a uniquely instructive resource in this regard, especially because its pages contain perhaps the best-known appearance of the term 'form of life'.[65] Although Wittgenstein is speaking here specifically about language, his words are applicable to all forms of signification:

> We must do away with all *explanation*, and description alone must take its place. And this description gets its light, that is to say its purpose, from the philosophical problems. These are, of course, not empirical problems; they are solved, rather, by looking into the workings of our language, and that in such a way as to make us recognise those workings: *in despite of* an urge to misunderstand them. The problems are solved, not by giving new information, but by arranging what we have always known. Philosophy is a battle against the bewitchment of our intelligence by means of language.[66]

The problem Wittgenstein outlines is solved not by finding new ideas or by discovering superior content for thought, but by attending to the operation of thinking itself, that is, by observing thought at work. Philosophy, Wittgenstein shows us, is attention paid to the mind so as to reveal the process whereby we create a perceiver-dependent world, and in becoming aware of this work of creation, we begin to loosen the grip that categories of thought have on judgement. In order to achieve this insight, however, philosophy must overcome not only the human inclination to misunderstand how thought works, but also the deceptively natural manner in which this misunderstanding appears to us, which is to say, in the form of *understanding* itself. When we become aware of this, and if this awareness can be sustained, form of life becomes form-of-life, thereby ushering in a way of living that no longer projects onto the world an ontology of essence and transcendence, along with the privileges that these empower.

In his early essay 'Form-of-Life', Agamben addresses the subject of thought in a manner reminiscent of Wittgenstein, giving to thought a technical sense that places it in close proximity to form-of-life.

> I call *thought* the nexus that constitutes the forms of life in an inseparable context as form-of-life. I do not mean by this the individual exercise of an organ or of a psychic faculty, but rather an experience, an *experimentum* that has as its object the potential character of life and of human intelligence.[67]

For Agamben, thought names not the exercise of the brain or a general faculty of mind, but rather the experience of cognition itself. 'To think', he continues,

> does not mean merely to be affected by this or that thing, by this or that content of enacted thought [i.e., to think is not simply to think within the constraints of the customs or forms of life we encounter], but rather at once to be affected by one's own receptiveness and experience in each and every thing that is thought.[68]

To think, in other words, is to be and to remain aware of our own receptiveness and to be cognisant of the tendency to lock ourselves into modes of truth:

> only if living and intending and apprehending themselves are at stake each time in what I live and intend and apprehend – only if, in other words, there is thought – only then can a form of life become, in its own factness and thingness, *form-of-life*.[69]

This also explains the lexical distinction Agamben draws between form of life and form-of-life. The hyphens do not erase form of life, destroy it or replace it, but make us aware of its being used, and in doing so render its most virulent force inoperative. When Saint Paul claims that during the time of the Messiah ordinary law will not be replaced by a new law but will instead be rendered inoperative, his understanding is akin to Agamben's notion of form-of-life. The law remains but now it is seen for the contingent set of beliefs it is. And in a recent impromptu discussion held at the Embros Theatre in Athens, Agamben seems to corroborate this interpretation:

> We have to stop thinking of any revolutionary action as directed toward the constitution of a new juridical order. Benjamin calls this pure violence, which is a violence that will never constitute a new juridical order. You depose without restoring another. If you are really, strongly and clearly able to demonstrate the illegitimacy of the political order, in a way you are deposing it.[70]

Likewise, we are told in a passage from Benjamin, which Agamben often cites, the messianic world to come will be no different than the world as it is now. Rather, it is the way we comport ourselves toward this world that will change, and this is precisely the double vision that form-of-life aims to express.

In his first book, *The Man without Content*, there is a short passage that seems to elegantly capture the problem that Agamben confronts with the notion of a form-of-life. He speaks of the principle whereby 'it is only in the burning house that the fundamental architectural problem becomes visible for the first time'.[71] The general problem expressed in this analogy is, of course, how one reveals the constructed nature of those things that, for one reason or another, are taken as given. But the analogy also raises the more practical question of how we might observe the architecture of our house without having to burn it entirely to the ground. It is here that we encounter perhaps the greatest obstacle confronting Agamben's programme, namely, the risk that in dismantling our house we will introduce a profound ontological disorientation, drawing us to the brink of the vertigo we know as nihilism. While I do not have the space to fully engage this issue here – I have done so elsewhere[72] – this represents a key juncture in Agamben's work. Herein we grasp the task of Agamben's project, namely, to openly face the groundlessness of nihilism and to discover in it not a road to despondency but a path to happiness. In the past, Agamben has located this sentiment in Benjamin's short 'Theologico-Political Fragment' where the notion of happiness is linked not to permanence, nor to perfection, but to transience ('The rhythm of this eternally transient worldly existence, transient in its totality, in its spatial but also in its temporal totality . . . is happiness'[73]). Now, in *The Highest Poverty*, impermanence and contingency appear once again, extended to monastic life where the outcome of Franciscan poverty is neither resignation nor loss, but the achievement of a happy life, an '"apostolic" or "holy" life, which they profess to practice in perfect joy'.[74]

What Franciscan life offers, although in an incomplete fashion, is an encounter with the problem of translating the contingencies of non-appropriative use into an ethos or way of living that claims no social or juridical foundation – a way of life to which Francis bestows the name poverty. Not poverty regarding material things, although the Friars certainly lived modestly, but rather poverty regarding those less tangible things, such as possession and privilege, that mark out for us, today as well as in the past, the contours of our shared social reality – the real operation of which we are, in most circumstances, not even dimly aware. We are speaking here of a socio-political form of poverty and therefore its realisation cannot be accomplished independently. Just as the exercise of authority cannot be accomplished by a king in isolation from the obedience of those who bow before him, so too the realisation of poverty in the juridical sense cannot truly materialise in the absence of a community of practitioners. Which is why the common life of the monastics, and cenobitic life in general, is central to the possibility of Agamben's project: 'there where I am capable we are always already many (just as when, if there is a language, that is, a power of speech, there cannot then be one and only one being who speaks it.)'[75]

Form-of-life, then, is a *kind* of form of life. It is a life that remains aware of its way of living *as* a way of living. And unlike all other forms of life, form-of-life takes as its principle stance an explicit awareness of the manner in which it functions or operates as a form of life. This is the particular ontological consciousness that form-of-life asks us to adopt and to retain. The habit of being aware of the contingency of our cognitive orientation is precisely what distinguishes form-of-life from any other form of life and, of course, necessarily lurks within every form of life because *every* worldview is capable of bearing witness to its own profane construction. In his use of hyphens, Agamben attempts to indicate lexically the notion that, although we cannot entirely escape our conventional worldview – our various forms of life that structure the social world and give it meaning – we can nevertheless recognise its absolute conventionality and thereby operate differently with respect to the world we already have.

Agamben's form-of-life urges us to never let rules become transparent to their use, to never let use become dogmatic or proper, to never let laws disappear into operational neutrality, or lose a sense of their practical character and their instrumentality. What Agamben seeks in a form-of-life is a continual awareness of the forces that ceaselessly entice us to naturalise our use of things – be they words or laws, gods or kings – and he asks whether it is possible to conceive of a way of living that disarms these concepts not simply by replacing them, but by patiently exposing the machinery of their operation. In the final instance, *politics is a type of awareness*, not of the minor and mundane adjustments that comprise juridical existence, but of the largely hidden attitudes that sustain that existence and determine the scope of what is valid within it. Our task, and the task of any politics understood as a form-of-life, is the sustained practice of exposing the effects of this awareness. I believe Giorgio Agamben's positive project rests on this insight.

Postscript

In the single paragraph that comprises the entire preface to *Toilers of the Sea*, Victor Hugo speaks of necessity, binding the yield of his pen to the pursuit of its understanding. Dividing necessity in three, he refers to a triple *ananke*, placing before us a preface that could very easily stand in as Agamben's own:

> Religion, society, nature; these are the three struggles of man. These three conflicts are, at the same time, his three needs: it is necessary for him to believe, hence the temple; it is necessary for him to create, hence the city; it is necessary for him to live, hence the plow and the ship. But these three solutions contain three conflicts. The mysterious difficulty of life springs from all three. Man has to deal with obstacles under the form of superstition, under the form of prejudice, and under the form

of the elements. A triple *ananke* (necessity) weighs upon us, the *ananke* of dogmas, the *ananke* of laws, the *ananke* of things.[76]

Notes

1. Many of the ideas presented in this chapter were developed in the context of a graduate seminar on Agamben that I taught at National Taiwan Normal University in Taipei during the spring of 2014. I would like to extend my warm appreciation to the students and faculty of NTNU who participated in that seminar and who were a constant source of inspiration to me. My appreciation also extends to Taiwan's National Science Council (NSC) for generously funding my year in Taipei and to my marvellous colleagues at NTNU who invited me to join them.
2. See, for instance, Agamben's brief essay from 1993 entitled 'Form-of-Life', in *Means without End: Notes on Politics*, trans. Vincenzo Binetti and Cesare Casarino (Minneapolis: University of Minnesota Press, 2000).
3. Giorgio Agamben, *State of Exception*, trans. Kevin Attell (Chicago: The University of Chicago Press, 2005); Giorgio Agamben, *The Highest Poverty: Monastic Rules and Form-of-Life*, trans. Adam Kotsko (Stanford: Stanford University Press, 2013).
4. The opening section of this chapter draws from work that I have previously published. In the earlier publication I discuss necessity in relation to Agamben's *State of Exception*, whereas in the current chapter I follow the theme of necessity as it appears in *The Highest Poverty*. Most of the material contained here is new, but in a few places I have chosen to retain the language found in the previous publication. See Steven DeCaroli, 'Political Life: Giorgio Agamben and the Idea of Authority', *Research in Phenomenology*, vol. 43, no. 2 (2013), pp. 220–42.
5. Plato, *Plato in Twelve Volumes*, vol. 3, trans. W. R. M. Lamb (Cambridge, MA: Harvard University Press, 1967), 345d.
6. Pausanias, *Description of Greece*, vol. 1, trans. W. H. S. Jones (New York: G. P. Putnam's Sons, 1918), ii. 4.6.
7. Agamben, 'Form-of-Life', p. 4.
8. Aristotle, *Politics*, in *The Complete Works of Aristotle*, vol. 2, ed. Jonathan Barnes (Princeton: Princeton University Press, 1984), 1265b13.
9. Francis Bacon once warned, in the pages of his essay, 'Of Seditions and Troubles', 'the rebellions of the belly are the worst' (Francis

Bacon, 'Of Seditions and Troubles', in *Essays, Civil and Moral* (New York: P. F. Collier & Son, 1909–14).
10. Giovanni Antonio Palazzo, *Discorso del governo e della ragion vera di Stato* (Naples: G. B. Sottile, 1604).
11. Michel Foucault, *Security, Territory, Population: Lectures at the Collège de France, 1977–1978*, ed. Michel Senellart, trans. Graham Burchell (New York: Palgrave Macmillan, 2007), p. 263.
12. Foucault, *Security, Territory, Population*, p. 345.
13. Carl Schmitt, *Political Theology: Four Chapters on the Concept of Sovereignty*, trans. George Schwab (Cambridge, MA: The MIT Press, 1985), p. 5.
14. Agamben, *State of Exception*, p. 80.
15. Agamben, *The Highest Poverty*, p. xi.
16. Giorgio Agamben, *Opus Dei: An Archaeology of Duty*, trans. Adam Kotsko (Stanford: Stanford University Press, 2013).
17. Agamben, *The Highest Poverty*, p. 61.
18. Agamben, *The Highest Poverty*, p. xiii.
19. Agamben, *The Highest Poverty*, pp. 4–5.
20. Cándido Mazón, *Las reglas de los religiosos: Su obligación y naturaleza juridical* (Rome: Pontifica Università Gregoriana, 1940), p. 171, quoted in Agamben, *The Highest Poverty*, p. 34.
21. Theodor Mommsen, *Römisches Staatsrecht*, vol. III, 1034, quoted in Agamben, *State of Exception*, p. 78.
22. Agamben, *The Highest Poverty*, p. 58.
23. Agamben, *The Highest Poverty*, p. 107.
24. Agamben, *The Highest Poverty*, p. 105.
25. Agamben, *The Highest Poverty*, p. 95.
26. Sulpicius Severus, *Epistolae*, 2.19, quoted in Agamben, *The Highest Poverty*, p. 95.
27. Agamben, *The Highest Poverty*, p. 110.
28. Bonagratia of Bergamo, 'Tractus de Christi et apostolorum paupertate', ed. L. Oliger, *Archivum Franciscanum Historicum*, vol. 22 (1929), p. 511, quoted in Agamben, *The Highest Poverty*, p. 110.
29. Agamben, *The Highest Poverty*, p. 111.
30. Agamben, *The Highest Poverty*, p. 113.
31. Agamben, *The Highest Poverty*, p. 113.
32. Agamben, *The Highest Poverty*, p. 130.
33. Agamben, *The Highest Poverty*, p. 123.
34. Agamben, *The Highest Poverty*, p. 114.
35. Agamben, *The Highest Poverty*, pp. 114–15.
36. Agamben, *The Highest Poverty*, p. 116.

37. Agamben observes, '[a]long with the *abdicatio iuris*, the other argument the Franciscans used in the polemic with the Curia is an ingenious generalization and at the same time inversion of the paradigm of the state of necessity' (Agamben, *The Highest Poverty*, p. 114).
38. Agamben, *The Highest Poverty*, p. 115.
39. Agamben, *The Highest Poverty*, p. 115.
40. Agamben, *The Highest Poverty*, p. 115.
41. Agamben, *The Highest Poverty*, p. 116.
42. Agamben, *The Highest Poverty*, p. 117.
43. Agamben, *The Highest Poverty*, p. 121.
44. Agamben, *The Highest Poverty*, p. 121.
45. Agamben, *The Highest Poverty*, p. 122.
46. Agamben, *The Highest Poverty*, p. 120.
47. Agamben, *The Highest Poverty*, p. xii.
48. Agamben, *The Highest Poverty*, p. 135.
49. Ferdinand Delorme, 'Question de P. J. Olivi "Quid ponant ius vel dominium" ou encore "De signis voluntariis"', *Antonianum*, vol. 20 (1945), pp. 309–30, p. 324, quoted in Agamben, *The Highest Poverty*, p. 136.
50. In *The Kingdom and the Glory*, through an investigation of glorification and acclamation, Agamben explores humanity's tendency to attribute essences to political and religious authority.
51. Agamben, *The Highest Poverty*, p. 136.
52. I do not have the space to expand on this here, but those familiar with Agamben's work will immediately recognise the technical use of profanation in Agamben's thought.
53. Agamben, *The Highest Poverty*, p. 136.
54. Agamben, *The Highest Poverty*, p. 138.
55. Agamben, *The Highest Poverty*, p. 139.
56. Agamben, *The Highest Poverty*, p. 136.
57. Agamben, *The Highest Poverty*, p. 139.
58. Agamben, *The Highest Poverty*, p. 144.
59. Agamben, *The Highest Poverty*, p. 139.
60. *The Capuchin Constitution of 1536*, trans. Paul Hanbridge (Rome: Collegio San Lorenzo da Brindisi, 2007), pp. 22–3 (my emphasis). The original text reads: 'E guardinsi I Frati di non mettere il loro fine nel lauorare, pe in quello pore alcuno affetto, ne occuparuisi tanto, che estinguino, deminuischino, o ritardino lo spirit, al qual deueno servir tutte le cose, ma sempre havendo l'occhio aperto' (ch. 5). See *Le Constitutioni de' Frati Minori Cappuccini di San Francesco* (Appresso Gabriel, Giolito de' Ferrari, 1577), pp. 21–2.

61. The type of poverty expressed in the 1536 *Constitution* is a qualified poverty, not real poverty. By the time we arrive at the twelfth century, monastic poverty must no longer be equated with asceticism or the poverty of destitution, but rather with a commitment to live in the absence of ownership. Although Francis modelled his voluntary poverty on the poverty of the involuntary poor, it should not be understood as being the same thing. For the ordinary poor, poverty is an undeniable source of suffering which no theoretical overlay can, or should, glamorise. This is true of both Francis and Agamben. But thankfully both thinkers make clear that becoming poor in an ordinary sense is not their aim.
62. *The Capuchin Constitution of 1536*, p. 23 (my emphasis). The original text reads: 'Pero noi uolendo in cosi degno essempio, imitare Christo in verita, et realmente osservate il Serafico precetto della celeste pouerta; facciamo intendere come in effetto non habbiamo alcuna giuriditione, domino, propriera, giuridica possession, uso frutto, ne uso giuridico di alcuna cosa, ne anco di quelle, che per necessita usiamo' (ch. 6). See *Le Constitutioni de' Frati Minori Cappuccini di San Francesco*, p. 23.
63. Michel Foucault, *The Birth of Biopolitics: Lectures at the Collège de France, 1978–1979*, ed. Michel Senellart, trans. Graham Burchell (New York: Palgrave Macmillan, 2008), p. 19.
64. Foucault, *The Birth of Biopolitics*, p. 297.
65. Space does not permit me to expand on the connection with Wittgenstein, but Agamben's use of 'form of life' is inspired, at least in part, by Wittgenstein's use of the term in the *Philosophical Investigations*, where the enigmatic concept, which is mentioned only five times, is deployed to express the condition necessary for linguistic communication and the acquisition of meaning: 'To imagine a language means to imagine a form of life' (Ludwig Wittgenstein, *Philosophical Investigations*, trans. G. E. M. Anscombe (Oxford: Basil Blackwell Ltd. 1958), p. 8).
66. Wittgenstein, *Philosophical Investigations*, p. 47.
67. Agamben, 'Form-of-Life', p. 9.
68. Agamben, 'Form-of-Life', p. 9.
69. Agamben, 'Form-of-Life', p. 9.
70. Giorgio Agamben, informal discussion at the Embros Theatre in Athens, 18 November 2013, available at <https://vimeo.com/80059143> (last accessed 22 November 2014). The transcription is my own.
71. Giorgio Agamben, *The Man without Content*, trans.

Georgia Albert (Stanford: Stanford University Press, 1999), p. 115.
72. See Steven DeCaroli, 'The Idea of Awakening: Giorgio Agamben and the Nāgārjuna References', *Res Publica: Revista de Filosofía Política*, vol. 28 (2012), pp. 101–38.
73. Walter Benjamin, 'Theologico-Political Fragment', *Selected Writings, Volume 3: 1935–1938*, trans. Edmund Jephcott, Howard Eiland, et al., ed. Howard Eiland and Michael W. Jennings (Cambridge, MA: The Belknap Press of Harvard University Press, 2002), p. 306.
74. Giorgio Agamben, *The Highest Poverty*, p. 92. For a more sustained analysis of the relationship between impermanence and joy, see Steven DeCaroli, 'The Idea of Awakening', pp. 101–38.
75. Agamben, 'Form-of-Life', p. 10.
76. Victor Hugo, *Toilers of the Sea*, trans. Isabel F. Hapgood (T. Y. Crowell and Company, 1888), p. 5.

11

Law and Life beyond Incorporation: Agamben, Highest Poverty and the Papal Legal Revolution

Miguel Vatter

One of the central concerns of Agamben's *Homo Sacer* project is to identify the traits of a life that escapes being captured by law.[1] *The Highest Poverty: Monastic Rules and Form-of-Life* provides one of the most sustained treatments of this problem by arguing that the Franciscan movement offers the first exemplar of an extra-juridical 'form-of-life',[2] at once rejecting the connection between law and life that characterises sovereignty, and developing a radically anti-consumerist relation to the world. According to Agamben, the Franciscan ideal of giving up on all ownership (designated as 'highest poverty') radically calls into question the internal relation between having ownership over things (*dominium*) and being a subject of rights (*sui iuris*) in the tradition of Roman law. Against the background of this principle of Roman law, it becomes conceivable that a form of life in which individuals own nothing would be equivalent to a form-of-life that has escaped capture from law.

This chapter reconstructs and problematises Agamben's account of form-of-life and its emancipatory potential in *The Highest Poverty* by situating it within the context of the 'papal legal revolution' of the twelfth and thirteenth centuries.[3] The Franciscan movement coincides with a moment of profound jurisprudential innovation, when Roman law is recovered and reinterpreted in light of both of Trinitarian theology and Aristotelian naturalism, in order to serve as the ultimate weapon in the 'global civil war' of Western Christendom between the Papacy and the Holy Roman Empire. Recent research on the papal legal revolution indicates that this recovery of Roman law had the unintended consequence of establishing the conditions for the emergence of modern capitalism and of the modern nation-state that together would bring to an end both ecclesiastical and imperial claims to 'universal dominium'. The conflict between the Franciscan monastic order and the hierocratic designs of the Papacy gave a new form to Roman private law that sealed the connection between property and right by inventing the subjective and natural right to private property. Likewise, canon law and the civilian commentaries to the *Corpus Iuris Civilis* brought about fundamental innovations in public law, above all, by introducing the idea that groups and associations become capable of acting collectively by being incorporated through a fictional legal personality whose ultimate representative is the sovereign. In short, the papal legal revolution is a central moment in the development of both what Schmitt called 'political theology' and of what Agamben calls 'economic theology'.

However, Agamben's reconstruction of the juridical controversies around the Franciscan ideal of 'highest poverty' does not register the interesting coincidence of this spiritual movement with the emergence of the idea of corporate personality that stands at the origins of the development of the concept of sovereignty. By leaving underdeveloped the problem of incorporation, this chapter argues that Agamben not only leaves unthought the very legal *dispositif* that ultimately spelled the defeat of the Franciscan project to emancipate life from law, but also forecloses the possibility of establishing a different relation between law and life that escapes inscription within the Roman conception of law by rejecting the identity between association and incorporation.

The first part of the chapter discusses Agamben's understanding of the Franciscan ideal of a life beyond law within the context of the papal legal revolution. It begins by rehearsing Agamben's notion of sovereignty as the capture of life by law in his earlier works. Secondly, it discusses the idea of form-of-life as a life lived beyond law by reconstructing Agamben's account of the Franciscan jurisprudence that thinkers such as Ockham and Olivi developed through the notion of 'factual use' (*usus facti*). Thirdly, it introduces the concept of corporate personality or *persona ficta* and discusses the role it plays within the Franciscan controversy and in the new articulation of sovereignty and government within political theology. Lastly, it raises the concern that in Agamben's own thought, the possibility of a life beyond law has not entirely overcome a reliance on corporate personality and on the personalisation of law.

The second part of the chapter discusses the possibility that the failure to separate use from ownership in law may be due to the flattening of law onto sovereignty through reliance on the concept of corporate personality. Aside from the Franciscan movement, another rejection of corporate personality occurred, around the same time, in the common law traditions of Northern Europe and the development of the idea of a 'trust' which is opposed to that of 'corporation'. The second part of the chapter puts forward an interpretation of the 'trust' as a legal dispositif that allows for a non-messianic rejection of corporate personality by establishing a different relation between life, law and ownership which is irreducible to both political and economic theology.

From state of exception to form-of-life

In *Homo Sacer* and *State of Exception* Agamben radicalises Schmitt's famous claim that valid law is applicable only in a state of normalcy and not in chaos or anarchy.[4] For Schmitt, the function of the sovereign is to decide whether a normal state of affairs exists, or whether there is a state of exception. Agamben suggests that Schmitt's concept of sovereignty in turn presupposes a paradoxical 'logic' of the exception whose central axiom is that 'the rule applies to the exception in no longer applying, in withdrawing from it'.[5] What makes an exception something more than a punctual event that interrupts a continuum of normality, what turns it into a 'state' of exception, is the fact that an exception to the law can only come about through the sovereign self-suspension on the part of the law itself. For Agamben, the exception does not come from a 'reality' that lies outside the law, considered as a natural cause of the 'emergency', but it is the law that suspends itself and in so doing creates the exception.

For this reason, it is misleading to criticise Agamben as if he presupposes the exception prior to the rule. Such criticism argues that

> for an exception to be a meaningful concept, it has to be evaluated and understood against the background of an ordinary case. The very term 'exception' points to something that stands outside the normal rule or state of affairs, and does not conform to the ordinary case.[6]

Agamben agrees, except that for him it is the sovereign moment in every legal system that is prior to the exception, rather than a basic law, like a written constitution. In particular, the objection addressed by recent constitutional legal thinkers to Agamben and

Schmitt, according to which giving the power to declare what is an exception over to a sovereign is tantamount to making the distinction between normal and exceptional a matter of 'rhetoric', thereby making an exception into something 'exceptionless',[7] is already recognised by Agamben: for him, every state of exception declared by the juridical order is always a 'willed' state of exception, not a 'real' one, and partakes of the 'fictional'.[8] Where Agamben parts company with these critics of Schmitt is that for them, the law is thought to have an objective or independent existence apart from the decision on the exception, that is, they believe that law is enabled to exercise its rule (the 'rule of law') in a 'normal' way, without recourse to the logic of exception.[9] For Agamben, on the contrary, the law is through and through a matter of fiction, in the sense that, considered by itself, the law lacks any objective referent.[10]

Since the law has no objective referent, if it is going to enter into force, it must be given its referent from the outside. Agamben argues that what is given to law as reference is life itself. The manner in which law captures this life is through the declaration of the state of exception:

> The statement 'the rule lives off the exception alone' must therefore be taken to the letter. Law is made of nothing but what it manages to capture inside itself through the inclusive exclusion of the exception: it nourishes itself on this exception and is a dead letter without it. In this sense, the law truly 'has no existence in itself, but rather has its being in the very life of men'.[11]

The logic of the exception, therefore, is not simply a (paradoxical) piece of formal logic. It only makes sense within the larger claim that the law lacks all meaning unless it has life as its object, and that it can gain life as its object only through taking exception to itself in an internal moment of sovereignty.

But why it is that law 'must' be the capture of life is never fully accounted for in *Homo Sacer*. Agamben's biopolitical reading of Schmitt relies on a single line in Schmitt ('In the exception the power of real life breaks through the crust of a mechanism that has become torpid by repetition'),[12] where the German jurist states that in order for law to become something living, rather than merely mechanical, the exception is of more importance than the rule. In *State of Exception* this interpretative basis of Agamben's entire discourse undergoes a revision of sorts, in the sense that Agamben is now more concerned to clearly separate and oppose Benjamin's 'real' state of exception from Schmitt's 'virtual' state of exception. For this reason, Agamben states explicitly that the connection between law and life is not 'necessary' or 'internal' at all, but that a new conception of the political is possible on the basis of the separation between law and life, one that maintains both in a different 'use'.[13]

The Highest Poverty takes up this constellation of ideas (separation of law from life, real state of exception, factual use) by investigating the possibility of a particular conduct of life, a form-of-life, that stands entirely outside of law.[14] Agamben argues that St Francis took up the monastic idea of a 'rule' of life, a kind of spiritual 'office', and turned it upside down by claiming that the only 'rule' was to live in imitation of the life of Jesus, that is, to lead a life outside of all 'office'.[15] 'The form is not a norm imposed on life, but a living that in following the life of Christ gives itself and makes itself a form.'[16] Franciscanism gives rise to a fundamental tension between rule and life, 'not because life is absorbed into liturgy, but on the contrary, because life and Divine Office reach their maximum disjunction'.[17] According to Agamben, Franciscanism managed to avoid entering into direct conflict with the Church because its form of life 'was radically heterogeneous to institutions and law'[18] and thus it could always 'give to the Church what is the Church's without polemic, namely the administration of the *officium* that belongs to it'.[19] Thus, the apostolic life according to St Francis is a version of the messianic life, or form-of-life, that constitutes Agamben's affirmative answer to the problem of the capture of life by the form of law which he has thematised since *Homo Sacer*. On Agamben's reading, the Rule of St Francis turns the life of Jesus into the foundation for a form of 'bare life' that establishes a 'real' state of exception and thus manages to escape being captured by every form of sovereign power.

Franciscanism and the problem of ownership

Franciscans made a vow of 'highest poverty' which they understood in terms of the intention *to own nothing* and only *to make use* of necessary things. Highest poverty, in this sense, is the practice that corresponds to the principle of an *abdicatio omnis iuris*, that is, the possibility for human beings to exist outside of law and without rights (hence for Agamben 'highest poverty' corresponds to a form of 'bare life' that lies beyond the threshold of sovereignty). The ideal of highest poverty attempted to cut the knot tying ownership (*dominium*) and rights (*ius*) established by Roman law. Thus, the ideal of highest poverty required giving up not only the right to own something, but even the right to make use of anything. The only permissible thing, for the Franciscan friar, was to hold onto the 'natural' right to the actual use of things for the sake of preserving his 'bare' life on the pilgrimage here on earth towards Heaven. This 'natural' right the friar shared with all living creatures alike. The only acceptable relation to things is that of mere use, *usus facti*, analogous to what animals enjoy with respect to the products of the earth.

The Franciscan movement implicitly called on the Church, and on the Pope as its highest representative, to return to the original form of life of Jesus and the Apostles and thereby give up 'dominion' over all worldly things.[20] This was a radical, messianic demand to make on the Church since, at least after the so-called Donation of Constantine, the Holy Roman Church understood itself as the highest 'worldly power', holding the prerogatives previously exercised by the Roman Emperor as *dominus mundi* (owner of the world).[21] In fact, the lifespan of St Francis coincided both with the papacy of Innocent III and the reign of Frederick II, who between them, and with the help of canon and civilian lawyers, spearheaded the so-called papal legal revolution by separating the jurisdiction of the Church from that of secular kingdoms, starting off a process whereby the Church would come to resemble a sovereign state, and, conversely, the sovereign state would acquire the status of a Church. This process would eventually lead to the so-called Westphalian order, characterised by the maxim *cuius regio, eius religio* ('whose realm, their religion'). The confluence of these antithetical yet mutually imbricated constructions of sovereignty is the stuff out of which Schmitt theorised 'political theology'.

However, the defence of 'highest poverty' elaborated by Ockham (a member of the Franciscan Order) is widely seen as planting the seeds of the primacy of individual rights over the rights of sovereignty, thus anticipating the critique of sovereignty put forward by late modern liberalism.[22] Agamben's interpretation of the jurisprudential controversy surrounding Franciscanism centres on Ockham's development of natural right because of its apparent closeness to the question of property and use. Since the internal relation between ownership and being a subject of rights was central to Roman law, the Franciscan apologists appealed to a Christian conception of a pre-lapsarian state of nature, in which there was neither empire nor law and where everything belonged to all in common. On this Augustinian view, both the state and private property were the result of the Fall of human beings into sin. Thus, Franciscans could argue that the practice of using something without owning it is analogous to a return to the state of innocence: *abdicatio iuris* is a practice of returning to the state of nature from original sin.

Agamben rightly shows that Ockham's defence best articulates this application of the dispositif of the state of nature. Ockham argues that in a state of extreme necessity, everyone has the natural right to make use of things belonging to others.[23] He distinguishes between the natural right to use and the positive right to use, the latter alone depending upon a positive legal constitution or on man-made law. Thus, for Ockham the friars have no positive right to things but only a natural right to use them in a state of necessity. 'Highest poverty' indicates the abdication of all positive rights, but not of the primordial natural right. This means that in 'normal' conditions (that is, those established when a sovereign, jurisdictional authority exists), Franciscans live in a state of exception to (positive) right; whereas, in conditions of 'exception' or of extreme 'necessity', when there is no sovereign authority, Franciscans return to 'natural' right. Agamben concludes that 'what for others is normal thus becomes the exception for them; what for others is an exception becomes for them a form of life'.[24] In short, Franciscans use the state of exception in order to neutralise the grasp of (positive) law. This does not, however, mean that they enter into a zone of lawless violence: to the contrary, their form of life returns under the fold of law, if only the natural law. Here one finds an 'affirmative' understanding of the (real) state of exception which reverses the (virtual or fictional) state of exception that captures life in a place of anomie and leaves it open to violation and death. However, such a strategy still remains implicated in the very dispositif of the state of exception that belongs to an understanding of law beholden to sovereignty, and thus falls within the purview of political theology. As such, Agamben ultimately rejects Ockham's strategy.

In the controversy with the Franciscans, the appeal to *usus facti* was met with another critique on the part of the civilian lawyers employed by the Church to reassert the claims of Roman law on which rested their dominion, both secular and spiritual. The critique was simple: if the Franciscans gave up ownership of their possessions to the Pope, then they must have owned them before. What, indeed, is the point of the Papacy having dominion over something which the friars have already used up (for example, the food they eat, the clothes they wear, the buildings they inhabit, etc.)? For civilian lawyers, the fact that the Papacy cannot do what it wants with the property of Franciscans meant that real dominion remained with them, not with the Pope. In general, these lawyers asked: how can one consume a piece of bread without having absolute dominion over it? What is left over to the Church, who nominally owns the bread eaten by the friar, once it is digested by him? In using up, and thereby destroying, things such as edibles and clothing, the friars proved that they were the rightful owners, since only if something is yours can you destroy it. Thus, as Agamben notes, this papal rejection of *usus facti* presupposes the distinction between use and consumption: to consume something is just what it means to have ownership over it, not to have use of it.[25]

Once again, Ockham provides a rebuttal by distinguishing the *usus iuris* (the right to use) from the *usus facti* (the factual use) of something: I have the former when I rent a house; this gives me the right to live in it even though I do not actually need to live in it; I have the latter, when I simply live in the house (as a squatter, say), without having a right to do so. In discussing Ockham's response, Agamben polemicises against those interpreters like Villey and Grossi, who see in Ockham's concept of *usus iuris* the birth of a subjective right to property, as the power or potential of a subject to make use of something. For Agamben, instead, the subjectivisation of right in Ockham is ultimately only a legal strategy to defend *usus facti* outside of all law. However, Ockham's subtle reasoning cannot place factical use beyond the sphere of law in a real sense because the distinction between *factum* and *ius* is ultimately internal to the sphere of law, 'instituting between them a threshold of indifference, by means of which the fact is included in the law'.[26]

To explain this point, Agamben appeals to Savigny who offers an interpretation of *res nullius*, that class of things which become the property of whoever first finds them. For Savigny, *res nullius* shows that possession is a kind of facticity that gives rise to a right: possession is the factual side of ownership whereas property is its legal side. Now, Savigny was a historian of Roman law, and in this argument he probably presupposed the de jure/de facto analysis pioneered by Baldus to legitimise the claims of sovereign authority of inferior corporations. Baldus argued that, despite the emperor being the de jure possessor of the entire world, de facto it was city-republics and monarchies that owned parts of this world and, on this factual basis, they could not-recognise the jurisdiction of the emperor and exercise it themselves by way of their corporate personalities.[27] The point being, as Agamben recognises, that the facticity of use is not sufficient to separate use from ownership and thus maintain life outside of law, because the law itself establishes the distinction de jure/de facto in order to capture what lies outside of it, according to the logic of the inclusive exception. But this point must be pressed further to understand that this very logic depends on the theory of corporate personality, the analysis of which is missing in *The Highest Poverty*.

Franciscanism and the problem of corporate personality

The Franciscan controversy not only had the unintended consequence of establishing a natural right to private property, it also sealed the hegemony of the papalist conception of a corporation as a 'fictional person', which lies at the basis of the modern conception of the sovereignty of the nation-state.[28] Canon law is generally acknowledged as the source of an important change in the Roman law of corporations. Whereas on the Roman law conception, a corporation or *universitas* is just the aggregate of the individual members of the group (a definition still held by Accursius and other Glossators), on the definition given by Innocent IV and also found in civilian lawyers like Bartolus and Baldus, instead, a corporation or *universitas* is 'a body composed of a plurality of human beings and an abstract unitary entity perceptible only by the intellect and thus distinct from its human members'.[29] On this conception, an association of individuals is a group of people who have been *incorporated* into a juridical personality which is distinct from the natural persons involved in the association. Each one of these natural persons has 'limited liability' with respect to this corporation. This aspect of the corporate form became fundamental for the development of the capitalist conception of the firm, and is intended to assure that the individuals who run the company, who invest in the company, and who work for the company are not personally liable to creditors of the company, or to legal prosecution in case the company incurs violations of the applicable legal, moral or other codes in the countries in which it operates.

On the traditional Roman conception of corporations, 'all power resided in the community and was delegated to an official who acted on behalf of the community'.[30] The model is that of a tutor representing a minor until the latter comes of age and becomes bearer of his rights in his own person (*sui iuris*). However, with the canon law conception of juridical personality, the group, so to speak, is never allowed to attain maturity: it is perpetually represented by a *persona ficta* with its own dignity, rights and special powers of legislation. Additionally, since the personality of the group is 'fictional' it needs to be embodied by a real person, who will be nothing short of 'the personification of the community in its head'.[31] On this canon law conception, once a group of people are 'incorporated', their association, their form of life in common, has a 'personality' by fiction, not in reality: the corporation is not a living thing because it does not have any volition or intention of its own. The corporation is intrinsically 'stupid', and therefore considered to be *irresponsible for its actions*. The theory of corporations thus makes groups or associations into permanent minors. This explains another important characteristic of incorporated bodies: that they exist only because they are recognised by a sovereign authority.[32]

The conception of the corporation as a fictional person was decisive in establishing the dualism between sovereign and law, between state and society, which lies at the heart of the concept of state sovereignty as it was later developed in the *ius publicum europeum*.[33] Schmitt's 'political theology' set out to defend this idea of *ius publicum* both against the rise of liberalism, and its culture of subjective rights, and against the emergence of pluralism, which conceived of the state merely as the 'community of all communities'.

Given the centrality of the corporation to modern sovereignty, it is strange that Agamben nowhere discusses the importance of the canon law theory of corporations for the Franciscan controversy. Indeed, it is arguable that the theory of corporations was also an unintended consequence of the Franciscan challenge. Jurist-popes like Innocent III and Innocent IV tried to make the Franciscan demand to give up all dominion over things compatible with the Church's worldly dominion by arguing that the Franciscan Order was a *corporation*. In Roman civil law, the use of anything required dominion over it. Conversely, to have dominion over an object meant that one could use it as one pleased or that one could alienate the object. The Popes argued as follows: if the Franciscan brothers relinquished ownership over all things, but still needed to make use of things (at least for purposes of eating, shelter, etc.), then the owner would have to be the company of the Franciscans, namely, their juridical personality, since outside of the state of nature (or the state at Creation), anything found in a civil condition must belong to someone: it must become the thing of someone if it is going to be used by anyone.

The decisive philosophical claim here depends on the ontological dualism of person and thing.[34] If anything is a thing, then it cannot be a person, because it is the thing of someone. To be a person (in law) means to become an owner.[35] Thus, if the Franciscan order wanted to have a personality (concretely, if the friars wanted to embody the personality of Saint Francis of Assisi), then they would have to admit that they owned something. But since by adopting the form of life of St Francis, no person of the Order could possess something, then it would have to be the Order as fictitious corporate personality that owned everything that the friars needed to use up. If interpreted along these lines, it can be said that the papal strategy in turning the Franciscan Order into a corporation was precisely to deprive this group as a group of its 'personality': as an order, it had a personality only 'as a fiction', and its representative or head or guardian was none other than the Pope, who in turn was the vicar of Jesus Christ. Thus, the Papacy took over dominion over all things of the Franciscan Order, like a father holds dominion over the things used by the son.

Unsurprisingly, one of the important arguments employed by the Franciscan movement to justify the separation of use from property was the claim that the friars had the status of *alieni iuris*, of minors under the tutelage of a person who is *sui iuris*, and so were like children and madmen (Agamben notes St Francis's self-designation as *parvulus* and *pazzus*) who are incapable of owning property.[36] Agamben mentions in this regard Gregory IX's *Elongati* bull, in which the Church, in its representative of the Pope, like a 'father' to the Franciscans, gets to own the property which they, like the 'sons' of the Pope, get to use. Here one can clearly see that these arguments presuppose not only a discourse on corporate personality, but also a Trinitarian development of the idea of representation, neither of which is thematised by Agamben. The papal solution to the Franciscan challenge played on all registers of the problem of the relation between person and thing. The Franciscans wanted to live like Jesus, and so give up the right to use things; the Papacy said that they could so live only by accepting to be incorporated into another person, a juridical person, that would own for all of them what none could possess individually: in this moment, the possibility of living in the form of life of Jesus was subsumed under the tutelage of the person of Christ (and its vicar, the Pope).

Agamben's return from jurisprudence to theology

The Highest Poverty concludes that the legal defence of 'highest poverty' mounted by the Franciscan movement with Ockham, a defence articulated in terms of the tradition of Roman law, was unable to break the connection between use and ownership that existed in Roman law. As discussed above, the inability to provide an alternative jurisprudence that would separate use from ownership not only turned out to be decisive in the establishment of the right to private property as the fundamental natural right in modernity, but also had the unintended consequence of strengthening the idea of sovereignty. For Agamben, the controversy between the Franciscan apologists and the lawyers and theologians of the Church illustrates the basic aporia of using legal devices to undo the capture of life by law itself. However, Agamben's own proposed solution to this aporia seems to be unaware of its reliance on the concept of corporate personality used by the Papacy to counteract the Franciscan challenge.

At the end of *The Highest Poverty* Agamben argues that Olivi, the most radical and messianic of the Franciscan apologists, tried to undo the papal subsumption of Jesus' life into Christ's person. For Olivi, the attempt to create a space outside of the law (*abdicatio iuris*) by separating use from ownership could not succeed if it remained articulated within a legal framework as, for example, in Ockham's employment of the idea of a state of exception. Olivi, instead, argued that the exodus from law and sovereignty depended on a new praxis of use, which he called *usus pauper*. By distinguishing and privileging the *usus pauper* from the *usus facti*,

Olivi was looking for a concept of use that is not just negatively related to law (as its mere abdication) but has its own self-standing ground and operation. For Agamben, the abdication of all rights is merely the 'matter' of form-of-life, whose true 'form' is poverty. Thus, on this reading, 'highest poverty' designates a form-of-life that is 'the purely existential reality that must be liberated from the signature of law and office or duty'.[37]

The Franciscan movement quickly divided itself into Conventuals, who argued that *usus facti* requires relinquishing ownership but does not entail *usus pauper*, and the Spirituals (the standpoint advocated by Olivi) who saw in the *usus pauper* the only way to live without rights. Agamben returns to his previous messianic reading of Paul in *The Time That Remains* in order to understand what *usus pauper* entails.[38] The concept of use divorced from the sphere of right relies on the Pauline idea of the *hōs mē* ('as not'): to make a use of worldly things 'as though' one did not own them. The premise of this argument is that 'a life' is not something that one can have under one's will (and that is why life falls outside of the purview of subjective rights).[39]

Already at the end of *The Kingdom and the Glory* Agamben had explained what is at stake in the 'life' of Jesus understood through the *hōs mē* of Paul:

> Under the 'as not', life cannot coincide with itself and is divided into a life that we can live (*vita quam vivimus*, the set of facts and events that define our biography) and a life for which and in which we live (*vita qua vivimus*, what renders life livable and gives it meaning and form). To live in the Messiah means precisely to revoke and render inoperative at each instant every aspect of the life that we live, and to make the life for which we live, which Paul calls the 'life of Jesus' (*zoē tou Iesou* – *zoē* not *bios*!) appear within it [. . .]. The messianic life is the impossibility that life might coincide with a predetermined form, the revoking of every *bios* in order to open it to the *zoē tou Iesou*.[40]

A messianic life in accordance with the 'life of Jesus' would mean, here, revoking all *bios* in order to eternalise the earthly *zoē* of 'bare life'. For Agamben, the Church invented saintliness as a way to represent a 'glorious life'. The life of saints is a glorification of a *bios* dedicated to following (divine) law to the point of martyrdom. But for that very reason, the 'glorious life' of the saints was entirely opposed to the real sense of a 'messianic life', which consists in the paradoxical glorification of an entirely earthly *zoē*. Saintliness separates eternal life from the inoperativity of life and is, as such, the highest expression of a life subsumed under form (life-in-form). Messianic life, by contrast, consists in seeing the coincidence of eternal life and animal life: it is the highest expression of form within life itself (form-of-life).

The last section of *The Highest Poverty* explicates this distinction between the glorious life of the saint and the messianic life of Francis. The Franciscan form-of-life in which *bios* emerges as fidelity to animal *zoē*, in which form is not imposed on life by law but comes from life itself, is articulated by Agamben (by way of Olivi) through the distinction between the 'life' of Jesus and the 'person' of Christ. Agamben suggests that Olivi's distinction between life and person relies on Joachim of Fiore's eschatological construal of divine providence,[41] which was entirely opposed to the 'economic theology' of previous Trinitarianism, described by Agamben in *The Kingdom and the Glory*. Joachim claimed that the Trinitarian 'Person' of Christ as Son of God merely brought to an end the Old Testament (Mosaic law), but that the age of the Second Person, represented on earth by the vicariate of both Pope and Emperor, was not the last age of history before the Second Coming. Instead, Joachim prophesised that an entirely separate 'Third Age' of history, which corresponded to the Third Person of the Trinity (the person of the Holy Spirit), was about to begin (circa 1260, on his calculations). This Third Age would bring to an end the New Testament, that is, the law of the Church, and inaugurate one last historical epoch of Spirit, characterised by those who follow the 'life of Jesus (Christ)'. What political form corresponded to this age of Spirit was the object of numerous speculations, but Joachim of Fiore was indeed credited in the late middle ages with having correctly prophesised the emergence of the new spiritual men, represented by the Franciscan and Dominican orders, as harbingers of the messianic age of peace.[42] Joachim's spiritual age was meant to occur after the coming of the Antichrist but before the Second Coming of the Redeemer: it consisted in a messianic 'end' of history, but achieved historically.

Agamben's reading of Olivi's messianic opposition between the Franciscan conception of the 'life' of Jesus and the ecclesiastical and political realisation of the 'person' of Christ in the priestly and political offices of government corresponds exactly to the above Joachimite interpretation of the 'life' of Jesus, which falls outside the Trinitarian construction of government described in *The Kingdom and the Glory*. This may also explain why Agamben explicitly recalls Olivi's belief that Francis, like John the Baptist, was another prophet 'and more than a prophet'.[43] What this 'more than a prophet' refers to is the fact that, on Agamben's reading, St Francis is the author of a Rule through which he does not merely de-sanctify himself *avant la lettre* (since following the Rule does not lead to a 'glorious life' but to a 'messianic life'), but also becomes the last legislator-prophet of the (bare) life of all men: 'the Franciscan form of life is, in this sense, the end of all lives [. . .] the form-of-life that begins when the West's forms of life have reached their historical consummation'.[44]

As is well known, in *Meaning in History*, Karl Löwith argued that the Joachimite prophecy lies at the basis of modern philosophy of history as a secularised *Heilsgeschichte*.[45] Agamben's employment of Joachim in *The Highest Poverty* rejects this theory of secularisation, which for Löwith climaxed with the divinisation of the state, and rather sees the political task in the deactivation of all ecclesiastical and political government, in the desanctification or profanation of all forms of life based on ownership and exercise of rights, and lastly in the paradoxical glorification of that most inglorious 'bare life' inclusively excluded by all governments.[46] All of Agamben's messianism thus remains dependent on a particular shift from 'person' (of Christ) to (a) 'life' (of Jesus) that is explicated through Joachim's Christology. Together, the ending of both *The Highest Poverty* and of *The Kingdom and the Glory* raise the question as to whether Agamben ultimately manages to escape from under the shadow of the political theology of representation and incorporation.

Of trusts and corporations: towards a jurisprudence of the common

While the doctrine of corporate personhood became central to the development of civil jurisprudence, the hold of the idea of the fictional person on the tradition of common law was weaker in regions far from the papal seat, like Germany and England.[47] One explanation for the resistance to imperial Roman law in these regions was advanced in the first decade of the twentieth century by F. W. Maitland, perhaps England's foremost historian of law, in a famous series of articles dedicated to the figure of the 'unincorporated body' in English jurisprudence.[48] Maitland argued that English common law, at the margins of Roman law, developed a kind of anti-corporation, a form of association that was called a 'trust' in England, and a *Genossenschaft* ('fellowship') in Germany. This term refers to a social reality, an association or community, without fictitious corporate personality, and thus without rector or guide, whose existence is directly the *unlimited* responsibility or liability of all members towards each other. Whereas all associations modelled after Roman law, that is, all corporations, are based on the idea of organisation, on a hierarchy of offices endowed with dignity and prerogatives, the existence of the unincorporated body is determined by the principle of solidarity.

On Maitland's reading of this legal-economical dispositif, the trust is a sort of political anti-body, an anti-corporation, that generates immunity against every form of sovereignty thanks to the solidarity and commonality of its members. Roberto Esposito has shown that Roman law, and by extension the concept of sovereignty which is based on it, is constituted in and through a mechanism of immunisation from the common.[49] Esposito suggests that today we need to offset our immunitary political communities, centred on the immunities (subjective rights) protecting the individual from the claims made on it by the common, and we stand in need of a form of communitarian auto-immunity, of social bonds that open each member to the other, rather than closing him or her from the other.[50] The trust is an excellent example of the kind of auto-immunitary resistance to an excess of immunities (an excess found in the non-recognition of superiority and limited liability in corporations as well as in subjective rights) developed in the tradition of Roman law.

The trust or 'unincorporated body' is an interesting innovation in social ontology because it appears to be the first time in modern legal history that a group is recognised as having a *real*, not a *fictional* personality. Maitland took over the idea that associations have a real personality from the German historian of law Otto von Gierke, the primary antagonist of the Romanist historian Savigny on whom Agamben relies. Gierke postulated the existence of 'group personality' in order to distinguish, in principle, a fellowship or trust from a corporation, an association based on solidarity ('fellowship') from one based on sovereignty (lordship or *Herrschaft*).[51] Gierke's legal theory has since fallen into disrepute not least because of the difficulty of making sense of his idea of 'group personality', and, in particular, of separating it from the conception of person, both real and fictional, received from Roman law.

Strictly speaking, this 'group personality' (*Gesamtpersönlichkeit* or *Gemeinwesen*) is best understood as 'im-personal': the group as such should be addressed always and only in the 'third person' and never as another 'I' or as a 'Thou'. The reason is that the group, as a being-in-common, cannot be represented by one person, contrary to what happens with the idea of a corporate personality.[52] This 'social body without corporation' or a 'community without society' should not be considered an immature collection of individuals, which is 'alive' only thanks to its representative 'head' or 'guardian', but as a social group that makes use of reason in common (a truly 'public' use of reason).[53]

The great advantage of this idea of the real personality of the group is that it requires *no concession by a sovereign* in order to bring it into existence.[54] In a trust it is the *forms of life-in-common* exhibited by these fellowships that generate the *rights and duties* of its members. These rights and duties are, strictly speaking, *neither private nor public*: they designate the space of what today Negri, Agamben and Esposito call the common. In the common, rights and duties are neither *the product of positive state legislation* nor are they held *individually in the state of nature*. Phrased affirmatively, in the common, rights are not protections or immunities of the individual against the common, but exist strictly in a *federal* context. Rights exist as the result of the power acquired by individuals in and through their alliances (*foedera*), which, in turn, are generated only thanks to the individual's participation in the common form of life. Conversely, duties towards the common do not weaken the individual's self-identity (and hence do not need to be coerced out of him or her through the threat of punishment, as occurs in corporations), but rather empower the individual's differentiation or distinction. With this federalist conception of rights and duties, one arrives at an idea of a social body that legislates *in and for itself*, without the intermediary of sovereignty or organisational forms of legitimate domination. Such an association is therefore 'free' with respect to the corporation of the state. Gierke and Maitland suggest that the state can legitimately exercise coercion only on condition that it 'acknowledges' (or gives 'positive legal form' to) society's autopoietic, 'natural' or 'living' legislation.[55]

Agamben, Poverty and Papal Legal Revolution 251

These rather brief comments may help to indicate in what sense the idea of 'group personality' is helpful in thinking an affirmative biopolitics.[56] For example, on the basis of this social ontology of group personality (whereby a group is no longer reducible to the tacit or explicit contracts between individuals underwritten by the sovereign power), one can easily make sense of the idea of a labour union that can legitimately resist the state, the Church, and a fortiori all corporations and companies, without having to appeal to the conception of law grounding these political bodies, because such a union, in virtue of expressing a form of life-in-common of workers, is *in itself* generative of rights and duties. In fact, as Runciman has explained, the theory of group personality developed by Maitland, Figgis, Cole and Laski was designed to justify not only the social struggles of unions against the state and against the class of owners, but also the struggles of churches against the hegemony of the Church of England.[57]

Apart from problematising the theory of corporate personality that lies at the basis of sovereignty, Maitland's account of trust also allows for an entirely different connection between use and ownership than the one established in Roman law, and thus lends itself to an interesting comparison with the promise and failures of the Franciscan project as outlined by Agamben. In his celebrated essay 'Trust and Corporation', Maitland argues that the concept of trust is born in the context of a struggle about property, much like its antonym, the idea of a corporation.[58] But whereas the corporation is a legal instrument that favours the class of owners (those who have *dominium*), the trust was a legal instrument that favoured those who had little or nothing other than their bare lives.[59] In medieval England most land belonged, by 'right of conquest', to the Norman kings and a few barons. This land was subdivided into many small plots of land given to the peasants so that they could work the land and, literally, feed the appetites of the nobility. What land the king and his court did not own was considered 'the commons': spaces where anyone could graze their domestic animals, gather wood, go hunting, etc. Around the fifteenth and sixteenth centuries, as Marx recounts in chapter 26 of *Capital*, smaller feudal lords began to expropriate (by means of 'enclosures') 'their' land from the peasants in order to give it over to sheep grazing, which produced wool, which gave way to the first industries in the cities, and with that to primitive forms of capitalist production. The expulsion of the peasantry from the commons 'freed' up labour-power for the first textile industries in the cities, and gave rise to the first 'industrial workers' who were 'free' to sell their labour-power for wages.[60]

During the thirteenth century, the problem facing the peasantry was that anything possessed by the tenant (for example, a house, a field, cattle, etc.) could not be given as inheritance to someone else in his or her family by means of a will (testament). With the death of the peasant, all goods of any value fell back in to the hands of the king or baron. So the question arose: how can the fruits of social labour be passed down to the next generation? Or, phrased somewhat differently, the question was: how can children be prevented from being born into a state of indebtedness, and thus, de facto, into slavery? The problem has a certain resemblance to the challenge faced during the same period by the absolute monarchs and addressed in Kantorowicz's discussion of the immortality of the Reign: how can the Crown itself be made immortal even though the physical king or queen may die? But whereas Kantorowicz claimed that this question was answered through the political theology of the 'corporation sole', Maitland, who first drew attention to this strange figure in the tradition of Roman law, seeks to dispel its illusion. If Kantorowicz pursues the idea of a corporation composed by all human beings (the 'Dignity of Man'), and represented by a new world empire, Maitland seeks in the idea of trusts something far closer to Agamben's problem of eternalising the species-life (*zoē*) of humanity.

According to Maitland, the legal dispositif of the trust was invented to address the sustainability of species-life as opposed to the immortality of the state. The idea is that anyone, as 'owner', can create a 'trust' which contains 'their' use-values and designate a group of friends or associates, the *trustees*, to administer 'their' property *for a third person*. Trustees are to look after this property *for the beneficiary* of the trust, namely, for the third person who is designated to inherit the use of the goods, and this third person can be anyone. These trustees can *own* the trust *without thereby making use of it for their own profit* (for example, trustees cannot 'sell' the property to someone else who is not the original beneficiary of the trust). In order to protect the beneficiary, the buyer of any property is supposed to ask for the title deeds, to ensure that they would not acquire a property sold by a trustee as if the latter were the beneficiary. In this way the trust, in principle, can be transmitted from generation to generation, incremented in time (if the trustees are not irresponsible), saved from creditors (if the trustees owe money to someone, they cannot take it from the trust), so that property may be used by a third person (the beneficiary) without being consumed by its owner (the trustees).

Maitland's description of the structure of the trust shows the high degree of impersonality that characterises this juridical dispositif: what is 'mine' becomes 'yours' (that is, it becomes the property of the trustees, who have the legal title of dominion over the goods), but 'you' (the trustees) 'own' the goods only in accordance with common law, and must hold these goods 'for the use [*a son oes*]' of a third person, namely, the beneficiary of the trust, and this in accordance to the law of equity.[61] One of the functions of the Courts of Equity was to give remedies for injustices occasioned by rulings of the common law courts: for instance, if by common law the wife of the peasant had no right to the separation of goods, by equity she could be the beneficiary of a trust that contained all these goods for her own use. In the trust, then, the third person becomes the subject of justice as equity, where in common law justice is purely distributive and commutative, ultimately a matter of guilt and punishment, of debtors and creditors, of first and second persons.

The dispositif of the trust offered a materialist and juridical basis for an idea of association that is alternative to that of the corporation: the idea of a union or 'club' headed by a board of trustees that is established in order to benefit third persons. These third persons can be one or more individuals grouped around any common purpose whatsoever, from a club dedicated to the preservation of endangered species to a union of workers intent on exercising their common labour-power under self-management. Club property is to be used by all members without any one person or group of persons actually owning the club.[62] If the trust gets taken to litigation by any external person, the trustees represent the association as if it were a person (an owner), but the personality of the group or club is not fictional or vicarious, as is the case with a corporation, but real.

Maitland's genealogy of the trust was an attempt to recover an alternative path to the one that led to the current omnipotence of the corporation. With the rise of the capitalist corporation and of the corporation of the modern state, however, this alternative jurisprudence gradually disappeared. By the end of the nineteenth century, trusts became indistinguishable from corporations while, conversely, corporations became trusts to better defend their capital. This move put an end to all 'justice' (that is, equity) in economics and gave rise to the sense in which today one speaks of wealth as creation of 'equity'. The same indistinction between trusts and corporations allowed for the rise of monopolies, and, eventually, led to the necessity for 'anti-trust' laws. The confusion of trust and corporation can be illustrated by the example of a company like Apple, a multinational corporation that looks and feels like a huge fan club for social media addicts.

Conclusion

Recent work by Agamben, Negri and others on the idea of common use has given new life to the antiquarian controversies between the Franciscan Order and the Papacy over 'highest poverty' and the right to property. Francis's call to renounce all ownership and restrict interaction with (living and non-living) things to mere use (*usus facti*) may have found its time of 'readability' in the age of the Anthropocene. Clean air, drinkable water, biodiversity, certain natural landscapes as well as cultural sites, the Internet: these are examples of goods that cannot be reduced to 'consumption' goods if their 'use' is to continue to 'sustain' all life on the planet. With respect to such goods, it is by definition necessary to separate use from ownership, and thus they need to be placed in a new common.[63] The urgent task nowadays concerns the development of a new juridical constitutionalism for the common, capable of getting us beyond the paradox of the Franciscan demand for a right not to have rights over worldly things, *Hoc ius: nullum in his que transeunt ius habere*. The genealogy of the parallel but opposed development of corporations and trusts may shed some further light on this challenge.

As Negri and others have argued, the new-found importance of sustainable forms of life corresponds to a major transformation of labour under current capitalist conditions of production from being the (material) activity of generating products (commodities) to being the ('immaterial') activity of providing 'services' (forms of life). In the idea of a 'service' one sees the alienated form in which someone makes use of something without having to own it. For example, a communications 'service' plan has attached to it the use of a certain device, but this is an object that the user will never properly 'own' because it is part of the 'plan' that he or she should continuously 'upgrade'. In reality, the contract signed with the communications company is not comprised of an exchange between the user's money and the company's commodity, but rather, as we have become more aware in the last years, it regulates a permanent exchange of information that 'feeds' a networked and 'connected' form of life in which the 'value' that users are after is what Benjamin called 'exhibition value' and, more recently, Agamben has thematised as 'glorification' (of which the demand to be 'liked' or 'followed' in social media is just one example among many).

Agamben's recent attempt in *The Kingdom and the Glory* to explore the fundamental role played by prayer in establishing the power of economic government may appear less arcane if one reflects for a moment on the fact that that the same word, 'service', is a synonym for 'liturgy' or public worship. *The Highest Poverty* has implications for our understanding of the political possibilities in the age of immaterial labour and the service economy insofar as it identifies, in St Francis's Rule, the revolutionary demand of turning the 'bare' fact of living (shared in common by all classes, estates and species, and lying beyond all conventional rules or norms) into the sole liturgy. On this reading, St Francis's 'highest poverty' constitutes a radical profanation of the path to salvation offered by the Church through the priesthood. Priesthood exemplifies the ideal of achieving the 'sanctity' of *bios* by turning life into a means for prayer and labour. 'Highest poverty', to the contrary, consists in a return to a condition of natural right where everything is held in common by all creatures, exemplified by St Francis's peculiar community with animals, which anticipates the Marxist messianic tenet of the 'naturalisation of man' and the 'humanisation of nature'.

However, Agamben's messianic formulations betray a continued reliance on the 'economic theology' of the Church, if only in the most extreme and antinomical form of the Trinitarianism advocated by Joachim of Fiore. By way of contrast, the analysis of trusts shows another possible path to profane what Benjamin called 'capitalism as religion'. In England, all churches except the Church of England, but including the Roman Catholic Church, were considered trusts whose beneficiary was not a person or group of persons but a purpose, namely, charity. Trusts allowed churches to be conceived as charities, rather than as 'worldly powers'. The significance of this move is visible if one recalls that

Spinoza, in the *Theologico-Political Treatise*, argues that the only legitimate purpose of religion is that of making possible works of charity.[64] In Spinoza, religion ceases being the figuration of the totality of society and becomes a name for what one does as part of a group or association of charity works. Thanks to the dispositif of the trust, every church, and in particular the Catholic Church, as regards its legal standing, became, so to speak, a labour union for believers that Jesus is the Christ, and had no more nor less significance, legally speaking, than a club of football supporters. In sum, if the invention of the corporation was thought up as a principle to organise a society in the form of a Church made up of different orders (angelical, sacerdotal, lay), then the invention of the trust, by way of contrast, had the effect of profaning society by making a club out of every religion: the idea of a hierarchical order of society is thereby shattered. On this view, the English monarchy, the Crown, is just one more trust, whose trustee is the king or queen, and whose 'beneficiary' is the British people. This also explains the paradox of the monarchy now understood as a one-person club discussed by Maitland only in order to reject it: 'sure proof that the idea was sterile and unprofitable'.[65] Kantorowicz thought otherwise. His famous problem, 'what happens to the club (the Crown) when its only member dies (the physical king)?', has become, after the most recent global financial crisis, once again today's urgent question: what happens to the state's debt when the only one who could redeem it, namely, the state as sovereign, is dead? Perhaps it is time to answer these questions by changing radically the terms of the debate, and begin by ridding ourselves of the long legacy of the jurisprudence of incorporation in order to develop a new jurisprudence of federation and of the common that would have as an important tool a renewed conception of the trust.

Notes

1. The second section of this article reprises the last part of Miguel Vatter, 'Il-limitato e s-corporato. Dalla corporazione al comune passando per il trust', *Filosofia Politica*, vol. 3 (2013), pp. 3–26.
2. On this technical term in Agamben, see Alex Murray, 'Form-of-Life', in Alex Murray and Jessica White (eds), *The Agamben Dictionary* (Edinburgh: Edinburgh University Press, 2011), pp. 71–3; Timothy Campbell, *Improper Life: Technology and Biopolitics from*

Agamben, Poverty and Papal Legal Revolution 257

Heidegger to Agamben (Minneapolis: University of Minnesota Press, 2011); David Kishik, *The Power of Life: Agamben and the Coming Politics* (Stanford: Stanford University Press, 2012); as well as Miguel Vatter, 'In Odradek's World: Bare Life and Historical Materialism in Agamben and Benjamin', *diacritics*, vol. 38, no. 3 (2008), pp. 45–70.

3. On the papal legal revolution, see Harold Berman, *Law and Revolution: The Formation of the Western Legal Tradition* (Cambridge, MA: Harvard University Press, 1983); Brian Tierney, *Religion, Law, and the Growth of Constitutional Thought 1150–1650* (Cambridge: Cambridge University Press, 1983); Hauke Brunkhorst, *Critical Theory of Legal Revolutions: Evolutionary Perspectives* (London: Bloomsbury, 2014).
4. Carl Schmitt, *Political Theology: Four Chapters on the Concept of Sovereignty*, trans. George Schwab (Cambridge, MA: The MIT Press, 1988), pp. 19–22; Carl Schmitt, *Legality and Legitimacy* (Durham, NC: Duke University Press, 2004).
5. Giorgio Agamben, *Homo Sacer: Sovereign Power and Bare Life*, trans. Daniel Heller-Roazen (Stanford: Stanford University Press, 1998), p. 18.
6. Oren Gross, 'The Normless and Exceptionless Exception: Carl Schmitt's Theory of Emergency Powers and the "Norm–Exception" Dichotomy', *Cardozo Law Review*, vol. 21, no. 5 (2000), pp. 1825–68, p. 1833.
7. Gross, 'The Normless and Exceptionless Exception', pp. 1848–50.
8. Giorgio Agamben, *State of Exception* (Chicago: The University of Chicago Press, 2005), pp. 57–64.
9. For further examples, see Andrew Arato, 'Their Creative Thinking and Ours: Ackerman's Emergency Constitution after Hamdan', *Constellations*, vol. 13, no. 4 (2006), pp. 546–72; Sanford Levinson, 'Preserving Constitutional Norms in Times of Permanent Emergencies', *Constellations*, vol. 13, no. 1 (2006), pp. 59–73.
10. For two recent approaches to the importance of fiction in the question of the state of exception, see Daniel McLoughlin, 'The Fiction of Sovereignty and the Real State of Exception: Giorgio Agamben's Critique of Carl Schmitt', *Law, Culture and the Humanities* (2013), pp. 1–20; Victoria Kahn, *The Future of Illusion: Political Theology and Early Modern Texts* (Chicago: The University of Chicago Press, 2014).
11. Agamben, *Homo Sacer*, p. 27. Only this explains the inordinate weight that Agamben assigns to the citation of the German historian

of Roman law, Savigny, in *Homo Sacer*: 'Das Recht hat kein Dasein für sich, sein Wesen vielmehr ist das Leben der Menschen selbst, von einer Seite angesehen.'
12. Carl Schmitt, *Political Theology*, p. 15.
13. On this motif, see Catherine Mills, 'Playing with Law: Agamben and Derrida on Postjuridical Justice', *South Atlantic Quarterly*, vol. 107, no. 1 (2008), pp. 15–36; Jessica Whyte, '"A New Use of the Self": Giorgio Agamben on the Coming Community', *Theory and Event*, vol. 13, no. 1 (2010); Jessica Whyte, *Catastrophe and Redemption: The Political Thought of Giorgio Agamben* (Albany: State University of New York Press, 2013).
14. Giorgio Agamben, *The Highest Poverty: Monastic Rules and Form-of-Life*, trans. Adam Kostko (Stanford: Stanford University Press, 2013), pp. 91–6.
15. Agamben, *The Highest Poverty*, pp. 116–22.
16. Agamben, *The Highest Poverty*, p. 105.
17. Agamben, *The Highest Poverty*, p. 119.
18. Agamben, *The Highest Poverty*, p. 121.
19. Agamben, *The Highest Poverty*, p. 120.
20. For the discussion of what Francis and the subsequent Franciscan movement and its inner sects intended by giving up all *dominium*, as well as for the messianic and eschatological interpretations of the doctrine, see Malcolm Lambert, *Franciscan Poverty: The Doctrine of the Absolute Poverty of Christ and the Apostles in the Franciscan Order 1210–1323* (London: S.P.C.K, 1961).
21. For discussions of this point, see Joseph Canning, *The Political Thought of Baldus de Ubaldis* (Cambridge: Cambridge University Press, 1987); Kenneth Pennington, *The Prince and the Law, 1200–1600* (Berkeley: University of California Press, 1993).
22. The story is recounted in Brian Tierney, *The Idea of Natural Rights* (Grand Rapids, MI: William B. Eerdmans Publishing, 1997).
23. Agamben, *The Highest Poverty*, p. 114.
24. Agamben, *The Highest Poverty*, p. 115.
25. Agamben, *The Highest Poverty*, pp. 129–31.
26. Agamben, *The Highest Poverty*, p. 138.
27. See the discussion in Canning, *The Political Thought of Baldus de Ubaldis*.
28. On the connection between corporate personality and modern state, see among many others Joseph Canning, 'Ideas of the State in Thirteenth and Fourteenth-Century Commentators on the Roman Law', *Transactions of the Royal Historical Society*, vol. 33

(1983), pp. 1–27; Quentin Skinner, 'A Genealogy of the Modern State', *Proceedings of the British Academy*, vol. 162 (2009), pp. 325–70.
29. Canning, *The Political Thought of Baldus de Ubaldis*, p. 186.
30. Brian Tierney, *Religion, Law, and the Growth of Constitutional Thought 1150–1650* (Cambridge: Cambridge University Press, 1983), p. 26.
31. Tierney, *Religion, Law, and the Growth of Constitutional Thought*, p. 26.
32. See the detailed discussion of this point found in David Runciman, *Pluralism and the Personality of the State* (Cambridge: Cambridge University Press, 2005).
33. I refer to my discussion of this point in Miguel Vatter, 'The Political Theology of Carl Schmitt', in Jens Meierhenrich and Oliver Simons (eds), *The Oxford Handbook of Carl Schmitt* (Oxford: Oxford University Press, 2014).
34. In this sense, I tend to agree with Esposito's argument according to which the problem of the person is the crucial dispositif of political theology. See Roberto Esposito, *The Third Person* (London: Polity, 2012); Roberto Esposito, *Due: La macchina della teologia politica e il posto del pensiero* (Turin: Einaudi, 2013).
35. On the distinction between medieval and modern subjective rights, see Janet Coleman, 'Pre-Modern Property and Self-Ownership Before and After Locke: Or, When Did Common Decency Become a Private rather than a Public Virtue?', *European Journal of Political Theory*, vol. 4, no. 2 (2005), pp. 125–45.
36. Agamben, *The Highest Poverty*, pp. 111–12.
37. Agamben, *The Highest Poverty*, p. 136.
38. Agamben, *The Highest Poverty*, pp. 139–40.
39. On the current post-Deleuzian debate on the idea of 'a life', see Federico Luisetti, *Una vita: Pensiero selvaggio e filosofia dell'intensità* (Milan: Mimesis, 2011).
40. Giorgio Agamben, *The Kingdom and the Glory: For a Theological Genealogy of Economy and Government*, trans. Lorenzo Chiesa with Matteo Mandarini (Stanford: Stanford University Press, 2011), pp. 248–9.
41. Agamben, *The Highest Poverty*, pp. 142–3.
42. However, on certain other variations of the theme, it is the lineage of Frederick II who is identified as the harbinger of the messianic age. On all these themes, see Marjorie Reeves, *The Influence of*

Prophecy in the Later Middle Ages: A Study of Joachimism (Oxford: Clarendon Press, 1969). The 'spiritualist' sect of Franciscanism followed Joachim's prophecy; their most important representative was Olivi.
43. Agamben, *The Highest Poverty*, p. 143.
44. Agamben, *The Highest Poverty*, p. 143.
45. Karl Löwith, *Meaning in History* (Chicago and London: The University of Chicago Press, 2006).
46. Here Agamben seems to follow the hypotheses on Joachim and Olivi found in Jacob Taubes, *Occidental Eschatology* (Stanford: Stanford University Press, 2009).
47. Interestingly, these were the regions that saw the early emergence of modern capitalism as well as the worker's movement.
48. I refer to the new edition, F. W. Maitland, *State, Trust and Corporation*, ed. David Runciman and Magnus Ryan (Cambridge: Cambridge University Press, 2003).
49. Roberto Esposito, *Immunitas* (Turin: Einaudi, 2002); Roberto Esposito, *Bios: Biopolitics and Philosophy*, trans. Timothy Campbell (Minneapolis: University of Minnesota Press, 2008); Roberto Esposito, *Communitas: The Origin and Destiny of Community* (Stanford: Stanford University Press, 2010).
50. On this motif in Esposito, see Vanessa Lemm, 'Nietzsche, *Einverleibung* and the Politics of Immunity', *International Journal of Philosophical Studies*, vol. 1 no. 21 (2013), pp. 3–19.
51. Otto von Gierke, *Community in Historical Perspective*, trans. Mary Fischer, ed. Antony Black (Cambridge: Cambridge University Press, 2002). This volume is a translation of selections from *Das deutsche Genossenschaftsrecht*, mainly coming from volume 1, *Rechtsgeschichte der deutschen Genossenschaft*. In the 'Editor's Introduction', Black gives the usual definition of group personality: 'Groups really have a personality, a mind and a will, and the state and the law ought to recognize this' (p. xvi). As I shall argue, the view that a group has a 'personality' analogous to that of an individual is misguided, and is not what Gierke meant.
52. On the logic of 'impersonality', see Esposito, *The Third Person*. In Maitland, the point that a trust is always made so as to give 'rights to a third person' is found in 'The Unincorporate Body', in *State, Trust and Corporation*, pp. 54–5.
53. For another argument that groups have minds of their own, see Phillip Pettit, 'Groups with Minds of their Own', in Frederick Schmitt (ed.), *Socializing Metaphysics* (New York: Rowman and Littlefield,

2003), pp. 167–93; Christian List and Phillip Pettit, 'Group Agency and Supervenience', *Southern Journal of Philosophy*, vol. 44 (2006), pp. 85–105. However, Pettit's reasoning remains indebted to the civilian assumption that groups can only be constituted through incorporation.
54. See Maitland's essay 'Moral Personality and Legal Personality', in *State, Trust and Corporation*, pp. 64–70.
55. See the discussion in Runciman, *Pluralism and the Personality of the State*, pp. 119–21.
56. But there are passages in Maitland in which both federalist and biopolitical language come together: Maitland, 'Moral Personality and Legal Personality', p. 66).
57. This point was already clear in Maitland: 'First and last the trust has been a most powerful instrument of social experimentation [. . .]. It (in effect) enabled a married woman to have property that was all her own until at length the legislature had to give way [. . .]. The case of the married woman is especially instructive. We see a prolonged experiment. It is deemed a great success. And at last it becomes impossible to maintain (in effect) one law for the poor and another for the rich, since, at least in the general estimation, the tried and well-known "separate use" has been working well' (Maitland, 'The Unincorporate Body', p. 56). The same process, I would argue, applies to the right to gay marriage in our present situation.
58. F. W. Maitland, 'Trust and Corporation', in *State, Trust and Corporation*, ed. David Runciman and Magnus Ryan (Cambridge: Cambridge University Press, 2003).
59. Indeed, in *Franciscan Poverty*, Lambert suggests that in England the Franciscan order, through the means of trusts, apparently had a much easier time in resisting the anti-Franciscan reaction coming from the Papacy.
60. Here I refer to the discussion of the commons and the common in Michael Hardt and Antonio Negri, *Commonwealth* (Cambridge, MA, and London: Harvard University Press, 2009); Michael Hardt and Antonio Negri, *Multitude: War and Democracy in the Age of Empire* (New York: Penguin Books, 2005).
61. See the discussion of 'use' in Maitland, *State, Trust and Corporation*, pp. 84–9.
62. See Maitland, *State, Trust and Corporation*, pp. 114–18.
63. See Hardt and Negri, *Commonwealth*; Jeremy Rifkin, *The Zero Marginal Cost Society* (New York: Palgrave Macmillan, 2014).
64. Benedict de Spinoza, *Theologico-Political Treatise*, ed. Jonathan

Israel and Michael Silverthorne (Cambridge: Cambridge University Press, 2007).
65. See Maitland, 'The Crown as Corporation', in *State, Trust and Corporation*, p. 46.

Notes on Contributors

Mathew Abbott is Lecturer in Philosophy at Federation University Australia, where he researches and teaches aesthetics, political philosophy and modern European thought. His book on Giorgio Agamben – *The Figure of This World: Agamben and the Question of Political Ontology* – was published in 2014 by Edinburgh University Press. Mathew's latest monograph is *Abbas Kiarostami and Film-Philosophy*, also published with Edinburgh University Press.

Giorgio Agamben is an Italian philosopher and one of the most renowned thinkers of our time. Most recently he has taught at the IUAV University in Venice, Italy, and he holds the Baruch Spinoza Chair at the European Graduate School in Saas-Fee, Wallis, Switzerland. He previously taught at the Collège International de Philosophie in Paris and at the University of Macerata in Italy. He is best known for the *Homo Sacer* project.

Simone Bignall is Senior Lecturer in Indigenous Strategy and Engagement at Flinders University in South Australia. She is the author of *Postcolonial Agency: Critique and Constructivism* (Edinburgh University Press, 2010). She is co-editor with Paul Patton of *Deleuze and the Postcolonial* (Edinburgh University Press, 2010); with Marcelo Svirsky of *Agamben and Colonialism* (Edinburgh University Press, 2012); and with Sean Bowden and Paul Patton of *Deleuze and Pragmatism* (Routledge, 2014). She is currently completing a book titled *Excolonialism: Ethics after Enjoyment*.

Justin Clemens is an Associate Professor at the University of Melbourne, Australia. His recent books include *Psychoanalysis Is* *an Antiphilosophy* (Edinburgh University Press, 2013) and, with A. J. Bartlett and Jon Roffe, *Lacan Deleuze Badiou* (Edinburgh University Press, 2014). He currently holds an Australian Research Council Future Fellowship, working on Australian poetry today.

Steven DeCaroli is Associate Professor of Philosophy at Goucher College in Baltimore, Maryland, USA and was recently a research fellow and visiting professor in the graduate school of National Taiwan Normal University in Taipei. He has published extensively on the work of Giorgio Agamben, including the co-edited volume, *Giorgio Agamben: Sovereignty and Life* (Stanford University Press, 2007).

Nicholas Heron is a Postdoctoral Research Fellow in the Institute for Advanced Studies in the Humanities at the University of Queensland, Australia. He is the translator of Giorgio Agamben's *Stasis: Civil War as a Political Paradigm* (Edinburgh University Press and Stanford University Press, 2015), and the author of a forthcoming book provisionally entitled *Liturgical Power: Between Economic and Political Theology*.

Daniel McLoughlin is Senior Lecturer in the Law School at the University of New South Wales, Australia. He has published extensively on Agamben's work, and contemporary continental political theory more broadly, in journals including *Theory & Event*, *Law and Critique*, *Law, Culture and the Humanities* and *Angelaki*.

Sergei Prozorov received his doctoral degree from the University of Tampere, Finland and is presently University Lecturer in Political Science at the Department of Political and Economic Studies, University of Helsinki, Finland. He is the author of seven monographs, the most recent being *The Biopolitics of Stalinism* (Edinburgh University Press, 2016). He has also published articles on political philosophy and international relations in *Theory, Culture & Society*, *Political Studies*, *Philosophy and Social Criticism*, *Political Geography*, *International Theory* and other major journals.

Jason E. Smith's writing and research are largely concerned with contemporary art and aesthetics, modern continental philosophy (Spinoza, Hegel, twentieth century) and post-1968 political thought (primarily French and Italian). He has published in *Artforum*, *Critical Inquiry*, *Parrhesia*, *Radical Philosophy*, *South Atlantic Quarterly* and *Theory & Event*, among other places. With Jean-Luc Nancy and Philip Armstrong, he has published *Politique et au-delà* (Galilée, 2010). He recently edited and contributed to a special issue of *Grey Room* devoted to the films of Guy Debord, and is currently working on a monograph on the same subject. He was a Cornell Society for the Humanities Fellow in 2013–14.

Miguel Vatter is Professor of Politics at the University of New South Wales, Australia. His most recent book is *The Republic of the Living: Biopolitics and the Critique of Civil Society* (Fordham University Press, 2014). Together with Vanessa Lemm, he has edited *The Government of Life: Foucault, Biopolitics and Neoliberalism* (Fordham University Press, 2014).

Jessica Whyte is Senior Lecturer in Cultural and Social Analysis at the University of Western Sydney, Australia. She has published widely on theories of sovereignty and biopolitics, critical legal theory, critiques of human rights and contemporary continental philosophy. Her book *Catastrophe and Redemption: The Political Thought of Giorgio Agamben* was published by State University of New York Press in 2013.

Index

Adorno, Theodor, 6, 75
alienation, 82–4, 110n31
Althusser, Louis, 71, 81–2, 84, 90n82
anarchism, 6–7, 49–55, 60, 64
anarchy, 7, 23–5, 51, 54–7, 64, 236
anomie/anomy, 66n25, 181, 240
antagonism, 10, 129, 191, 192–3, 201, 203–4
apparatus, 2, 7, 12, 37, 40, 42, 56, 66n25, 79, 82, 99, 106–7, 114n72, 117, 169, 172, 215–16
Arendt, Hannah, 5, 74, 76
Aristotle, 27, 37, 41, 80, 126, 132, 143–6, 156, 195, 208–9
Arius/Arianism, 24
Augustine, 9, 31, 71–2, 79, 141–2, 148–51, 153–4, 157, 158n3
Auschwitz, 125

Bacon, Francis, 229n9
Badiou, Alain, 5–6, 115–16, 165–9, 171–84
bare life, 64, 75, 80, 122, 131, 166, 173–80, 182, 184, 194, 238–9, 246, 248
Bauer, Bruno, 59
Bauer, Edgar, 59
Benjamin, Walter, 5, 16–20, 23, 29, 38, 53, 64, 69n59, 72, 95, 124–8, 169–70, 182, 197, 199, 226–7, 238, 255
biopolitics, 4, 30, 116–17, 122–4, 126, 165–6, 176–8, 189
    affirmative, 166–7, 176, 178, 180, 251
biopower, 104, 118–19, 121–2, 130–1, 191, 204

bios, 37, 57, 64, 158, 179–80, 182–3, 193, 246–7, 255
bourgeoisie, 110n29

camps, 39, 124–5, 126, 128, 130–1, 153, 173, 175
capitalism, 2–4, 28, 36, 37, 39, 50, 53, 64, 73, 77, 82, 85, 91–8, 101–7, 130, 167, 198, 200–1
    criticism of Agamben re, 2–3, 91–2
    finance, 19, 22, 92, 94, 97
    post-Fordist, 105–6; *see also* post-Fordism
    as religion, 15–25, 95, 255
    spectacular, 7, 92
Church, the, 3, 18, 23–4, 32, 40, 91, 99–100, 105, 107, 132, 134, 153–7, 164n74, 217–18, 220, 238–9, 241, 246–9, 251, 255–6
Church Fathers, 31, 39, 77–8, 98, 141, 152
common, the, 249–50, 254, 256
communism, 5–6, 49–51, 53, 59–60, 115, 165, 184, 203–4
constituent power, 100, 175
corporation, 236, 242–4

Dante, 196–7
Debord, Guy, 5, 20–1, 36–7, 94–5, 97, 100, 108
debt, 16, 20, 256
desubjectivation, 114n72
Digne, Hugh of, 215–16

economic theology, 29–30, 32, 73, 75, 77–8, 101, 132, 141–2, 151–2, 154, 235–6, 247, 255

266

economy, 2–3, 4–6, 23–5, 28–32, 35–7, 40–1, 49–50, 55
Eden, David, 96–7
Engels, Frederich, 53, 83
Esposito, Roberto, 249, 250
eternal life, 56, 143, 156–8, 247
exception, state of, 2–3, 23, 39, 54–7, 64, 67n25, 114n71, 119, 121, 126, 131–2, 175, 179, 181, 191, 194, 210, 217, 236–8, 240, 242, 245
    fictional, 240
    'real', 64, 238, 240

Feuerbach, Ludwig, 73–4, 80–4, 90n82
Fiore, Joachim di, 247, 255
First International, The, 49–50, 65n3
form-of-life, 4, 5, 6, 57–8, 63–5, 102, 165, 167, 176, 179–80, 189–97, 200, 202–5, 207–8, 211, 219, 221, 223, 225–9, 234–6, 238, 246–8
Foucault, Michel, 5, 25, 29, 77, 105, 117–24, 126, 128–31, 176, 191, 201, 209–10, 223–4
Francis of Assisi, Saint, 232n61, 238–9, 244, 248, 255
Franciscans, 5, 38, 40, 57–8, 60, 62–3, 135, 175, 189–90, 212–23, 227, 231, 234–6, 238–48, 251, 254, 260–1n42
Freud, Sigmund, 17

general intellect, 191, 196–7, 199–203, 135
Gierke, Otto von, 249–50
glory, 6, 27–30, 32, 37–9, 42, 55–7, 71, 91, 98–9, 101–2, 106–8, 114, 115, 117, 119, 122, 132, 134–5, 157, 173
Gnosticism, 31, 35, 77, 133
Godwin, William, 51
government, 2–6, 15, 21, 23–4, 28, 30–2, 34, 35, 37, 42, 49–51, 54–7, 64, 66n37, 72–3, 77–80, 91–3, 98–102, 105–8, 114, 122, 131, 140, 152, 235, 247–8
governmental machine, 66, 105
governmentality, 29, 64, 91, 106, 118
guilt, 17–18, 95, 253

Hegel, G. F. W., 46, 60–2, 68n55, 69n58, 69n59, 74, 84
Heidegger, Martin, 1, 4, 27–8, 37–9, 43, 53–4, 75, 120, 123, 126, 197
Hippolytus, 31, 133, 162n55
Hobbes, Thomas, 202
Holloway, John, 97
homo sacer, 39, 55, 64, 95, 126, 173, 177, 214, 219
Hugo, Victor, 228–9

inoperative, 29, 37, 41, 52, 56, 63–4, 98, 126, 169, 216, 220–2, 226, 246
inoperativity, 28–9, 35, 37, 40–2, 51, 56–7, 158, 166, 174, 176, 190, 198, 247

Jesus, 17, 127, 151, 155, 158, 238–9, 244–8, 256

Kafka, Franz, 1, 33–4
kairos, 51, 128, 157–8
Kantorowicz, Ernst, 252, 256
katechōn, 132, 142–3, 153–7, 162n57
Korsch, Karl, 42, 47n67
Kropotkin, Peter, 51, 57

labour, 5, 20, 40–2, 58–9, 74, 76–7, 82–6, 92, 93, 96–8, 101, 102–7, 110n30, 112n52, 112n55, 113n59, 192–3, 198–203, 209, 251–6
    immaterial, 97, 102–5, 107, 112n53, 113n61 255
    liturgical, 93, 108
    living, 199, 201–3
labour power, 36, 84, 93, 103, 110n30, 199–200, 252
liturgy, 3–4, 32, 35–6, 40, 98–9, 105–7, 211, 218–19, 220–1, 238, 255

Maitland, F. W., 248–53, 256, 261n57
Marx, Karl, 5–6, 17, 38, 39, 47n67, 47n69, 49n69, 51, 58–62, 65n3, 68n55, 71–8, 80–6, 90n82, 93–4, 96–7, 101, 110n30, 110n31, 139n36, 192, 198–203, 251

Marxism, 28–9, 36, 42, 47n69, 72, 96, 190, 195, 197, 199, 203
productivist, 42, 47n69
messianism, 69n59, 72, 133, 156, 165–6, 168, 171, 248
Mills, Catherine, 124
Milner, Jean-Claude, 115, 120–1
Monarchianism, 31, 39, 133
monasticism, 4, 60, 93, 105–6, 179, 211–12, 214, 218
multitude, 10, 191, 193, 195, 197, 202–4
muselmann, 39, 125–7, 138n22, 173, 177, 219

Negri, Antonio, 3, 6, 96–7, 103–4, 111n47, 114n72, 190, 197–9, 250, 254
Nietzsche, Frederick, 17, 75, 120, 125
Nixon, Richard, 15, 17, 20

Ockham, William of, 32, 215–16, 235, 239–41, 245
office, 4, 23, 41, 105, 107–8, 174, 212, 217–20, 224, 238, 246, 247, 249
oikonomia, 3, 29–31, 34–5, 39–40, 54, 56–7, 72–4, 77–9, 81–6, 91–2, 98, 101, 106, 129, 131–3, 152–3, 162n55; *see also* economy; government
Olivi, Pierre Jean, 219–21, 235, 245–8
Operaismo (workerism), 190, 197–9, 202–3

Pasolini, Pier Paolo, 23
Paul, Saint, 18–19, 30–1, 49, 51–4, 61, 126, 128, 132–3, 135, 152–3, 157–8, 162n55, 164, 165–9, 171–2, 221–3, 226, 246
Peterson, Erik, 32, 34–5, 99–100, 132, 141–2, 153–5, 163n69, 164n71
Plato, 126, 132, 145–7, 208
Plotinus, 146–7, 149–51, 153, 161n31
political theology, 29–30, 32–5, 77, 132, 141–2, 153–4, 163n69, 235, 239–40, 243
post-Fordism, 102–4
Postone, Moishe, 47n71

post-operaismo (post-workerism), 93, 96–7, 102–3, 105, 107, 111n47, 111n48, 114n72, 191, 197, 203
praxis, 3–4, 24–5, 28–9, 37–8, 42, 50, 52–3, 56, 57, 63–4, 71–2, 74–8, 80, 82, 84, 95, 99, 245, 248, 252
divine, 31, 45n26, 66n25, 71–3, 78–9, 98, 133–4
revolutionary, 50, 53
production, 20, 42, 47, 85, 92, 94, 96, 97, 101, 104, 108, 111–12, 114n73, 199, 203, 254
of bare life, 122, 131, 191–2, 194
capitalist mode of, 12, 85, 92, 94, 96, 103, 104, 105, 114, 192, 200–1, 203–4, 251
commodity, 42, 96–7, 101, 107, 198
immaterial, 93, 97–8, 102–4, 108, 113n61, 200–1, 254
Man's being as, 74, 78
material, 85, 103, 107, 254
metaphysics and, 75
post-Fordist, 96, 102
proleteriat, 49, 86, 199
Proudhon, Pierre-Joseph, 50–1, 53, 58–62, 64, 65n3, 68n55

Revolution, 4, 29, 48n73, 49, 50, 52–4, 58, 60, 63, 116, 175, 209
papal legal, 234–5, 239
revolutionary tradition, 5–7, 12, 175
Rousseau, Jean-Jacques, 3, 101

Savigny, Frederich Carl von, 241–2, 249, 260n11
Schmidt, Christopher, 163n69
Schmitt, Carl, 5, 16, 32, 35–7, 72, 100–1, 111n39, 132, 141–2, 153–5, 210, 235–9, 243
Schumpeter, Joseph, 16, 23
Schürmann, Reiner, 161n34
Smith, Adam, 3, 73, 84, 101–2
socialism, 16–17, 174, 203–4
sovereignty, 3–5, 15, 30, 41–2, 50, 55, 64, 77–9, 91, 99, 101, 107, 118, 121–4, 127–8, 130–1, 136, 171, 175, 179, 194–5, 204, 210–11, 214, 234–7, 239–40, 242–3, 245, 249–51
spectacle, society of the, 3, 20–2, 27–9, 32, 36–7, 41–3, 91–4,

96–8, 100–3, 106–8, 114n73, 127, 201
Spinoza, Baruch, 56, 61–2, 68–9, 256
Stirner, Max, 49, 51–3, 64, 81

Taubes, Jacob, 53
teleology, 124, 126, 138n20
Tertullian, 31, 39–40, 78, 132, 133, 153, 162n55
Tiananmen protests, 167, 174
Tolstoy, Leo, 51, 57
totalitarianism, 105
Tronti, Mario, 190, 197–200

Virno, Paolo, 96, 103, 107, 111n47, 190, 194, 197–8, 200–2

Warburg, Aby, 126, 129
Weber, Max, 16, 72
Weeks, Kathi, 42, 47n69, 48n73
whatever being, 65, 167, 172, 180, 183
Whyte, Jessica, 28, 44n10, 48n73, 69n59, 88n57, 92, 96–7, 110n29, 138n20, 206n14
Wittgenstein Ludwig, 207, 224–5, 232n65

Young Hegelians, 59, 80, 83

Žižek, Slavoj, 4–5
zoē, 148–9, 156, 158, 177–80, 182–3, 193, 246–7, 252